294

Key
Management
Tools

Key Management Tools

50 Time-Saving Techniques to Solve Everyday Business Problems

TOM LAMBERT

FINANCIAL TIMES

PITMAN PUBLISHING

PITMAN PUBLISHING
128 Long Acre, London WC2E 9AN

A Division of Longman Group Limited

First published in Great Britain 1993
Reprinted 1994 (twice)

British Library Cataloguing in Publication Data
A CIP catalogue record for this book can be obtained from the British Library.

ISBN 0 273 60384 1

Typeset by PanTek Arts
Printed and bound in Great Britain by
Biddles Ltd, Guildford and King's Lynn

CONTENTS

ROUTE MAP

This book is designed to be primarily useful as a reference book for the busy and perhaps undertrained professional. That does not mean that it cannot be read from cover to cover if the reader chooses to approach it that way. Arguments are developed with such a reader very much in mind.

The busy manager may, however, prefer to go directly to the chapter which offers most promise of meeting his immediate needs, leaving the rest to a time of greater leisure. This short 'route map' seeks to meet the needs of the manager under time pressure.

Chapter One. Sets the scene by indicating how management models or tools are developed and how they reflect reality in such a way as to organise otherwise chaotic data into logical information.

Chapter Two. Provides a comprehensive basic kit for strategic, tactical and marketing planning and implementation. It offers proven models or tools to enable the manager to:

- Establish a *vision* and *mission* for the company, division or department (14).

- *Analyse* the firm against the realities of the market place and the business environment (14).

- Develop meaningful *objectives* (22).

- Establish *strategic alternatives* and select the best *strategy* (23).

- Develop a comprehensive *tactical plan* (24).

- *Implement* and support implementation (27).

- Identify and avoid *potential problems* (28).

- Develop *contingency plans* (28).

Chapter Three. Deals with the behaviour of people at work and offers:

- *Motivation* assessment and analysis tools (49).

- An *anti-demotivation* toolkit (49).

- Tools for *job performance management* and *performance appraisal* (54).

Chapter Four. Considers team building and presents tools to:

- Handle *conflict* and *competition* (63).

- Use *consensus* effectively (66).

- Analyse simple and complex *relationships* (67).

- Build *winning teams* (68).

- Avoid the dangers inherent in *losing teams* (72).

- Avoid *complacency* and *inflexibility* (72).

- *Win* and go on *winning* (74).

Chapter Five. Looks at Leadership in a volatile business world and provides instruments on how to:

- Develop a *leadership style* which is simultaneously flexible and consistent (80).

- Identify and develop essential *leadership skills* (82).

- Analyse the key features of the *leadership environment* (84).

- Manage *maverick behaviour* (88).

- *Delegate* work effectively (90).

- Evaluate and, if necessary change, the *dominant leadership style* of the business (98).

- Reduce the tendency of the leader always being *'piggy in the middle'* (100).

- Use *power* effectively (103).

Chapter Six. Focuses on Problem Solving and Decision Making and describes tools which enable the manager to:

- Employ *consensus decision making* economically and successfully (106).

- Select the appropriate *problem solving technique* (113).

- Increase *creativity* (115).

- Evaluate and implement *solutions* (116).

- Use *rational techniques* (120).

Chapter Seven. Approaches financial management from the perspective of the non-financial manager and offers tools which:

- Simplify without trivialising the basics of *management accounts* (127).
- Define *financial key words* (129).
- Develop and use the *key ratios* (131).
- Show how the *balance sheet, profit and loss account* and *cash flow forecast* are interrelated and provide simple management tools (135).
- Simplify financial *problem solving* (143).

Chapter Eight. Considers marketing in greater detail with tools and models of:

- Strategic *pricing* (149).
- *Market planning* (152).
- *Competitive analysis* and *benchmarking* (157).
- Company *capability analysis* (157).
- *Product life cycle* as a planning and *product development* tool (158).
- Development and evaluation of *advertising* and *sales promotion* tactics (162).
- *Placement* for promotional material (167).

Chapter Nine. 'Sales Management' provides tools for:

- The analysis of *product* acceptance (184).
- Company *systems* and the *work environment* (185).
- The salesperson's *job satisfaction* (185).
- The perceived quality of *leadership* (186).
- Optimising *sales performance* (187).
- Understanding *buyer behaviour* (188).
- Enabling the buyer to buy and *go on buying* (189).
- Handling *objections, obstacles* and *complaints* (190).
- Selling *ideas* and *concepts* (191).
- Understanding and handling *problem customer behaviour* (192).
- Selling *services* or *high added value* products (193).

Chapter Ten. Develops models of the organisational culture and offers tools to:

- Understand *attitudes to change* (210).
- Define the *culture* and trace it to its roots (212).
- Complete a *cultural audit* (217).
- Create successful *culture change* (223).

Chapter Eleven. Considers training and development as the key to success in the post-smokestack economy and develops tools and models to:

- Identify when *training* is really needed (229).
- Assess *training needs* (233).
- *Design, develop* and *conduct* training (237).
- Ensure the *transfer* and *reinforcement* of learning (240).
- Develop a *learning community* (241).

Each chapter has one or more definitions of excellence in the area under consideration, and each ends with a summary of pitfalls to be avoided.

In all, the book has more than 50 tools and models for immediate application.

INTRODUCTION

Model: *A simplified description of a system to assist analysis, calculations and predictions.*
The Concise Oxford Dictionary

Management: *Trickery, deceit.*
The Concise Oxford Dictionary (part definition)

'I saw great businesses become but the ghost of a name because someone thought that they could continue to be managed just as they had always been managed, and though the management may have been the most excellent in its day, its excellence consisted in its alertness to its day, and not in slavish following of its yesterdays.'
Henry Ford, 1922

OFF-TRACK EXCELLENCE?

When Peters and Waterman wrote their blockbusting international best seller, *In Search of Excellence* in 1982 they identifed 43 organisations which they offered as exemplars of excellence in action. By 1988, however, Richard Pascale showed in his book *Managing at the Edge* that at least 30 of the 43 companies had slipped, most of them drastically, from their position of quality leadership.

More recently one of *In Search of Excellence's* surviving role models, IBM, has announced annual losses of $5 billion, which, following their previous year loss of $2.8 billion is leading some commentators to predict the demise of 'Big Blue' within the decade. Pick up almost any journal and if IBM is mentioned words like 'arrogant', 'lumbering' and phrases such as 'the living dead, a corpse in all but name' abound. Could Peters and Waterman really have got it so very wrong such a short time ago? With sector experts like Bill Gates expressing publicly the view that eight years is the most that the once most profitable corporation in the world has a reasonable chance of surviving, it seems that we may be about to see the time when it is no longer accurate to claim that 'No-one was ever fired for buying IBM'.

What has changed so totally that a world leader with 75 per cent of the sales in its market sector is suddenly presented as being on the verge of going 'belly-up'?

Change and excellence

What has changed is the rate of change. That simple and perhaps apparently vacuous statement lies, in different ways, at the root of Peters' and IBM's miscalculations. IBM chose to believe that they could continue to dominate the market through 'sticking to their knitting' and doing what they knew they could do best. In so doing they had to assume that they could control simultaneously the customer ability to transfer to another supplier of different and technologically-superior products and the competitor ability to make headway in a market which they dominated to an unprecedented degree. They were wrong on both counts. And yet they were, and continue to be in many respects an excellent company committed to quality in all that they do.

Does that mean that Peters and Waterman were even worse gurus than some are beginning to claim? Was their encouragement toward excellence altogether misplaced?

No, Peters and Waterman gave an eager world the right overall message. Excellence is the sole key to lasting success. Sadly, however, either they failed to emphasise sufficiently the critical point for the level of understanding of their readership, or the basic lesson has been wilfully misunderstood.

Major corporations seem to have taken up the erroneous message that excellence is something that you achieve once and for all time. You don't. Excellence, like Total Quality and, I would argue, like marketing, is an ever-moving feast. You may be at the top of the league today, but next year, next month or even next week you will find, if you stop to take breath, that all you have gained is lost because the customer definition of excellence has changed and the high ground to which you aspired is drifting beyond your reach in an increasingly volatile world. The accelerating rate of change has a new and frightening capacity to catch the very best and most prepared of us wrong-footed. Social change vies with technological change in an apparent effort to establish which can change the quicker. Today's excellence is tomorrow's mediocrity and in a surprisingly short time what was state of the art becomes no longer acceptable.

Ironically the troubles at IBM are partly caused by the sheer quality of their past operations. Big Blue was the ideal corporation in a world to which it was totally suited in the years leading up to Peters and Waterman's study and that is their problem. As Heller says: 'Excellence, along with procedures, systems and attitudes are set in granite by past success'.

The business world, like the biological world, is subject to the laws of micro-evolution and the survival of the fittest. In the biological world it has been demonstrated again and again that it is the organism which is most perfectly suited to its environment which is at risk in a changing world. The plant or animal which fits its niche to perfection is under no pressure to change, but if the environment changes, even in a minor way, it is at risk. The business environment has not been changing in a minor way, it is subject to a massive and accelerating change. Those who fail to change with it are doomed as certainly as were the dinosaurs when the smaller, faster, warm blooded protomammals began to compete in a cooling climate.

IBM, and others like them, made complacent by their success are now emerging from a dinosaur stage. Whether they are emerging in time, only time itself will tell. Meanwhile their plight causes deep concern to their employees and customers and mild embarassment to the gurus. Henry Ford recognised the tendency towards complacency and recorded its effect on previously successful businesses in the early twenties. How easy it really is to see clearly the mote in another's eye. How difficult to be aware of the beam in one's own.

A second factor which bedevils the search for excellence is a form of organisational myopia which leads to a failure to see that any organisation is an holistic system in which excellence limited to specialised high profile operations, is not enough. Excellence must permeate the whole system or, at best, the competitive edge which must be sought after as passionately as any quest for the Holy Grail will not be found. With genuinely global competition customers have an almost unlimited range of potential suppliers ready and able to satisfy their fast-growing and infinitely variable demands. Furthermore the search for excellence limited to one part of the organisation can create strains which will unbalance the system and lead to major, possibly fatal, problems.

Information-based excellence

Our unstoppable and unequal progress from what Toffler calls a 'smoke-stack economy', willy, nilly, into a world increasingly dependent on information creates and exacerbates the third problem.

Now and in the future the rapidly-changing definition of what is excellence will depend on the timely and accurate application of an ever-increasing base of knowledge. The manager will have to be flexible and quick on his feet to maintain consistently high standards of excellence, as he must, throughout the organisation. But information is a two-edged weapon. We can create a sound competitive edge through the judicious use of new technology and the vast influx of knowledge which it facilitates. Or we can drown in a sea of irrelevant information.

We need a sound framework in which to reject what is extraneous, analyse what is useful and implement timely knowledge-driven plans. Lacking this framework we will be in the position of the director of an automotive dealership who, almost thirty years ago now, found that the advent of computerised stock control provided him with enough reports and information each month to fill his happy days with analysis and interest till the arrival of the following month's mountain of paper. The seductive element of the easy acquisition of facts is not to be underestimated as a prime motivator of busy inaction.

The head count factor

The fourth problem relates to down-sizing the organisation at the first signs of a downturn in trade. What American gurus are beginning to call 'dumb-sizing'. The panic driven 'Me too! Me too!' Gadarene swine approach to cutting staffing levels to the bone. This misplaced concept has created a knowledge and skill shortage in many corporations and has put management's eyes on too many balls at the same time to admit of the luxury of the innovative pursuit of excellence. A study by the American Management Association in 1992 indicated that in more than 75 per cent of the 500 firms which had cut jobs since 1987 morale had 'collapsed' through a combination of stress, frustration, falling creativity and a related undermining of corporate loyalty. Some companies nominated in *In Search of Excellence* have chosen to be either in the forefront of headcount reductions, or have swung happily onto the redundancy bandwagon shouting 'Me too!'

Excellence does not arise from process although effective process is important. Excellence is, in the final analysis, an optional extra which is dependent on the way in which people desire to work. It is the gift of loyal employees who strive far beyond mere necessity to ensure a continuous and economic raising of standards. Excellence can neither be imposed from above nor supervised or inspected into the system.

Yet, in the West, loyalty is being systematically and wilfully destroyed. The largest private employer in the United States today is Manpower Inc. with 560,000 workers. Manpower Inc. was created to supply the ever-growing demand of some of the once excellent corporations for 'disposable workers', workers without pensions, security, health care or other benefits, who are brought in only when required. Workers who receive no loyalty and presumably, since they must be available to a number of competing firms to survive, give none.

Hardly a recipe for the committed pursuit of excellence. Yet pursue it we all must: Peters is right in this. Proof of excellence in everything that a company does is becoming the only sufficient and necessary prerequisite to trade in a growing number of sectors. Globally excellence remains the key determinant of success. It will be essential in all segments of all sophisticated markets before long, but it must be understood that yesterday's concept of excellence will no longer do. Excellence today must reflect the needs and wants of today's market. Tomorrow things will be different. And you can bet your survival on the assumption that things will need to be better.

Training

Finally there is the problem of training. It has become a favourite theme that there is insufficient training of management and employees outside the Pacific Rim. Politicians, when they have nothing original to contribute to the solution of the cyclical and it seems permanent problems of an economy, cling to the training theme as if the availability of additional training would alone solve all economic woes. As usual they are grossly over-simplifying a complex problem. IBM and the others in a similar state have never been short on training.

Before more training is needed, better training must be available. Research shows that, regardless of the training methods which are used, from 'chalk and talk' through to 'experiential participative skill building', (God help us), the transfer of knowledge and skill to the workplace varies between a miserable five to an almost equally miserable thirteen per cent. With results such as these is it any wonder that the training budget is first under the knife when markets show signs of disease? If managers do not believe in the efficacy of training it is with good reason. One major corporation in Britain spent millions of pounds and 40,000 man-days on 'customer care training'. The only visible results of their investment were a fall of almost 50 per cent in their penetration of a drastically reduced market and a high level of frustration on the part of employees who had been hyped up to want to give a higher standard of customer service, but had not been told (among the welter of information on Transactional Analysis and other unproven esoteric areas of psychology) what they should actually do to achieve the desirable goal of delighted customers. People found the courses interesting. They evaluated the quality of the presentations highly. They even left the conference centres fired up for action. If only someone had spent a little time telling them what was expected of them the results might have been dramatic. As it was the result was frustration and a growing desire by management and employee alike to waste no further time on training.

Meanwhile qualitative market research among the company's customers showed that there were even some who longed for the warranty on the products which they had bought to run out. This rather odd desire rose from their wish to be free to take their purchases for repair and maintenance to others rather than the franchised distribution network. It was the employees of these same distributors who had 'enjoyed' the customer care seminars.

When trainers are sufficiently professional and training is designed to achieve predetermined, measurable and worthwhile goals, more training, much more, will be needed, valued and actively sought. Until then, who can blame managers who believe that they have other priorities to which they must direct their small resources of people and cash. Training must be designed to ensure the transfer of appropriate, consistent, observable and desirable behaviours to the workplace. Those behaviours must be known to have a significant effect on the company's ability to achieve its business plan. Training, in short, must be prepared to stand up and be measured. The technology to ensure transfer has been designed, tested and proven: only trainers and the managers whom they claim to serve seem to be unaware of it.

Attaining and maintaining excellence

So there we have it. Gobal pressures increasingly dictate that a need for integrated excellence throughout the organisation is critical to building and keeping a competitive edge. And global pressures are inescapable.

Excellence is, however, an everchanging, ultimately market-driven phenomenon and like the market it changes as new needs and expectations emerge. The hard-pressed manager, under-resourced, understaffed, and either untrained or perhaps more dangerous, badly trained, must find a way, not only to achieve excellence, but to maintain it in an increasingly volatile world. A challenge indeed, but a challenge which we have no other choice but to accept and master. Survival, individual, corporate and, in hard-pressed economies, national, is at stake.

Were Peters and Waterman unaware of all this? Certainly not, they knew it and knew it as well as anyone. Consider if you will the evidence of their colleague and collaborator Richard Foster. In his best seller, *Innovation – The Attacker's Advantage* Foster makes the situation totally clear;

> *'... most companies achieve what Bob Waterman and Tom Peters have defined as excellent financial performance in only one year out of twenty, and then immediately drop back into the great middle ground of average financial performance. Even the best companies, by anyone's definition of excellence, retain their superior competitive performance for only three to four years.'*

They knew alright. More than that they believed that backsliding was virtually inevitable, unless management made ever evolving and improving excellence a matter of daily priority for thought and action. In the new world, which has changed a great deal since 1982, that backsliding could prove fatal even for the biggest and apparently the best. Management can and will assume the task of the everlasting pursuit of excellence, they need the tools to enable them to 'finish the job' which never ends.

Some are approaching this challenge with energy and imagination. The global shift from emphasis on resource to emphasis on the market place is being felt everywhere. It is leading to an increase in the value of information which is logarithmic. Primary resource producers and smokestack economies will retain a role, but it will be the role, ironically of greatest investment and smallest return. Those who are rich in information will find costs reducing dramatically while the value of their product soars.

Australia, as a key aspect of national policy, has recognised this situation. Freed of any need to run down obselete smokestack industries and still secure in the role of major primary producer to the Pacific Rim, Australia has the specific goal of becoming the global centre for information in an information age.

A new city with the functional, but unmusical name of MFP (Multi Function Polis) is being created near Adelaide. A new city which is planned from the start to offer the quality of life and the resources and opportunities to attract and keep the pick of the world's brainpower.

With unique advantages of a young, energetic and small population, immense space, no limiting past record in global competition, a geographic location on the edge of the Pacific Rim, the English language and abundant primary resources capable of early funding of the project, it is difficult to see how Australia can fail.

It is equally difficult to see how Britain can avoid becoming, drastically quickly, a second class player in spite of our first class minds and a proud history. Government and business have conspired to minimise investment and maximise the quick profit for the past 50 years. Some authors, particularly Alistair Mant, would argue that the rot can be traced back for 160 years. As the first genuine signs of national and global economic recovery emerge, there is no sign of any change. Our only hope lies in our people. This book is a small, a very small, attempt to empower them by informing and empowering an enlightened management.

HOW THIS BOOK WILL HELP

This book then is designed to help the hard-pressed manager to achieve and go on achieving excellence with minimal resources in a rapidly changing world. Because the complexities and pressures which are faced routinely by any manager today and for the foreseeable future require wide-ranging and deep knowledge which go far beyond the scope of any specialism, it aims to provide a basis for that knowledge.

It is not, however, an academic book. It is a hard-nosed volume of practical 'how to' tools and job instructions which will enable the manager to achieve the essential tasks in the shortest possible time with the least effort and at the lowest cost. The tools which are offered have been proven by experience, sometimes long experience. If old favourites occasionally appear here in a new guise, they have been redesigned to make their use more simple and more certain regardless of the prior experience or education of the user.

Each chapter is devoted to a key result area of the business. The chapters are designed to be looked at in sequence or to stand alone. From time to time material in one chapter will be annotated to direct your attention to related material elsewhere. That apart, the reader is free to approach the book in any sequence which personal interest and needs of the moment dictate. Each major area has a short introduction which emphasises the importance of the contribution which the operation makes to the firm's ability to meet the primary objectives of a business:

- to grow, in terms of size, profits or quality;

- To perpetuate itself;

- To create and retain a customer (Revson's phrase).

Excellence is defined for the function and sometimes for key results areas within that function. This may seem to be a contradictory and pointless task given the volatile nature of what is perceived as excellence today and the even greater state of flux which is promised for tomorrow. My reason, however is simple.

It has been my experience over the last thirty years that if I ask the average executive to undertake a task from the ground up, so to speak, I often create a situation which is unnecessarily time-consuming and difficult. If, on the other hand, I present my best informed stab at what is required as a foundation and ask the manager to build on it, improve it, and make it his own by rethinking it until it is specific to his operation and the environment in which he works, he will develop a sound and detailed practical outcome. This way a definition of 'excellence' as it needs to be understood today in his organisation emerges. Only managers at the coal face understand what they are up against in sufficient, timely detail. The needs and expectations of customers are volatile driven by a specific and constrained competitive environment.

So in their different ways are the changing needs and expectations of employees, shareholders and the community.

Following a brief indication of what I mean, in general terms, as I consider the basis of excellence in the business, I compare it with both mediocrity and potential disaster. Then I suggest some carefully selected tools to help the manager to achieve practical excellence and offer guidelines for their use. These tools are the guts of the book.

I hope to provide with them a secure framework in which those who choose, when problems or opportunities arise, not to bring in external help, may do the job themselves, and grow a little in the process.

Finally, each chapter finishes with brief, bullet point indicators of some of the pitfalls which can be met and ought to be avoided.

Intelligent rather than intellectual

I make two assumptions about my readers.

Many years ago the Nobel Laureate physicist, Leo Szilard was visiting the laboratories of Crick and Watson, the first scientists to successfully map the structure of DNA. Watson, a physicist himself, was concerned that they should pitch their explanation of their work in biochemistry at the right level for a distinguished scientist from another discipline who might, in spite of being a world leader in his own field, know little or nothing of biology.

Rather than risk a patronising oversimplification, or a potentially unintelligible advanced dissertation he put the dilemma to Szilard. The great man's advice has become for me a classic of how to proceed when you are less than sure of your listener's *a priori* knowledge.

'Assume total ignorance and unlimited intelligence.'

Those are the twin traits which I am happy to assume for my readers.

Total ignorance of at least some of the tools offered here. Were it not so there would be little point in your investing in this book. Further, since most of the tools, though based on well-validated research and successful application over many years have not previously appeared in the form in which they are offered here, detailed knowledge of them is unlikely.

So, far from patronising, I assume total ignorance. This places a duty on me to try to describe the purpose and application of the tools clearly from first principles.

I also, based on many years spent one way or another in training and educating business people, assume unlimited intelligence. This means that if I explain, fully, concisely and in English, my readers will be able to adapt the appropriate model to their own needs and will use each of them effectively.

If they are unable, after considering the models and reading the text, to use what they find, the fault is mine.

Bear with me if you will while I put to you the basic philosophy which underpins all of my professional work, including my writing. I believe that it is important that I always remember that I am communicating to a business audience. Such an audience is seeking practical ways of achieving objectives amongst which the most important are that the business shall be there tomorrow and for all the tomorrows yet to come, or to use Drucker's phrase 'the business should seek to perpetuate itself.' And the business will seek to grow. Not necessarily in size, but if not in size then in excellence, or better yet, in excellence, size and profit combined. In my experience those objectives are most readily achieved where everything which is done:

1. Makes a significant contribution to the Business Plan;

2. Will pay for itself in a reasonable and predetermined time;

3. Can be explained in simple language to all those who will be expected to make it work.

That reinforces for me my two assumptions and dictates the shape of this book. My role is twofold. I am to provide managers, trained or not with proven tools and 'recipes' for immediate and easy use. And they must be concise, yet in sufficient detail to enable both direct application by the reader and clear communication to others who have a contribution to make to a successful outcome.

1 MODELS OF GOOD PRACTICE

'While philosophy and abstract vision are important executive strengths, the actions which executives take to realise these visions, are critical.'
Tom Peters

Models are important in modern business. They will become increasingly important with the passage of time.

Technology is providing business with the opportunity to enjoy and exploit a treasury of data greater than any would have believed possible only ten years ago. Computers and the systems which support them continue to develop at an accelerating rate. It is conceivable, indeed it is likely, that the sheer availability of data will become such that organisations may drown in it.

There has been a technological revolution. According to most commentators it has come just in time to avert a crisis in a post-industrial society. For that revolution to bear its promised fruit the data which it provides must be readily and comfortably used.

As Drucker has made abundantly clear, the challenge is to turn data into information. Whereas **data** is characterised by being an accumulation of facts and figures without regard for their relevance or application, **information** is data which is selected, refined and relevant to the situation in hand. As Alistair Mant has pointed out, the manager should constantly look for opportunities to ask and answer the question; 'What's this for?'

The need for ternary thinking of that kind becomes ever more urgent with the constant acceleration of both the range and the availability of data. In Drucker's words; information enables the organisation to 'engage in analysis and diagnosis'. Models will play an increasingly important role in providing a framework to enable the manager to transmute data into information.

In short, models provide the tool which enables the busy professional to create usefulness.

A MODEL MODEL

One of the key minds to address the usefulness of models is Professor Charles Handy. Imaginative models have consistently illuminated his thinking on the organisation and its evolving shape. From spider's web to clover leaf, Handy has provided simple but rich models to help to clarify our understanding.

By way of illustration of how a model can help to stretch and consolidate our thinking I would like to steal shamelessly from Handy, using models of my own devising which as closely as possible reflect the style and content of his, but which, in their modest and limited way, are original to this work.

Handy has identified four basic types of organisational structure. The **entrepreneurial autocracy** which he likens to a spider's web with all lines of communication passing directly or indirectly to the entrepreneur autocrat who, sitting spider-like at the centre, controls every organisational activity.

The **bureaucracy** is characterised by Handy as a Greek temple with the top management team sitting, as it were, in the pediment and the line functions filling each of the pillars. The easiest form for communication is directly up or down the pillars with the result that the senior management are the only people who have easy lateral communication to any individual. Because all information tends to pass only up and down the heirarchy any position holder in any pillar can act as a barrier to further communication. Thus he who believes that 'power flows to he who knows' is tempted to act as the last call of information in either direction to build a knowledge power base. The weakness of the bureaucracy thus lies both in its inherent inflexibility and in its inbuilt temptation to restrict communication.

The **matrix** organisation Handy perceives as a net. Communications are facilitated, as required in all directions without any form of centralised control.

The clover leaf model

Finally, the organisational structure to which the balance of competitive advantage will swing during the early development of an information-based society is seen as a **clover leaf**. One of the three leaves houses, in Handy's scheme of things, the core workers, the essential holders of corporate information and wisdom. The second is the external supplier of services used to ensure that the basic and repetitive functions of the organisation are efficiently completed, when required, at minimal cost. The third leaf represents the flexible labour force, permanent outworkers who will owe loyalty to no single organisation, but will be available, when required to ensure that the necessary nonrepetitive functions are completed on a timely and economic basis. This is coming to be known in America as the 'disposable workforce'.

Do not harbour doubts as to whether the clover leaf organisation is a realistic possibility. It is already happening. Janice Castro in an article in *Time Magazine*, 19 April 1993, discusses the role and plight of disposable workers in industrial giants like General Motors and IBM. As I mention in the Introduction to this book, Manpower Inc., the company which provides the 'New Temps' as they are required, has more than half a million workers currently on its books and is growing fast. In a world in which global competitiveness is seen by most commentators to be the key determinant of corporate success how long do you think that it will take for the idea of 'New Temping' to cross the Atlantic and take root here?

Similarly an ACAS report published five years ago indicated that 40 per cent of companies surveyed already contracted out some services while a further 18 per cent had specific plans to do so.

This clover leaf model is one which has the greatest potential relevance, and carries the greatest threat as well as promise, so I wish to take it a little further. In fact I feel lucky, so let us consider **the four leaf clover model.**

Like Handy, I foresee the development of permanent, costly knowledge workers crucial to the ongoing success of the organisation as the first leaf. The design of an education system aimed, whatever governments may say to the contrary, at perpetuating class differences combined with the richness of newly-available information will ensure that there will not be enough of these people to go round. They will be rare, precious (probably in both senses of the word), expensive and highly mobile. They will make high demands on the organisation and will be difficult to retain. It is their combination of scarcity and mobility which necessitates the denizens of my second leaf.

During 1992 at the depth of the recession, the growth of business for small consultancy practices was estimated as being in the order of 30 per cent. With skills in short supply and activity and confidence increasing that business will grow. Expertise will be bought in as required by a growing range of organisations. The good consultant will be a bird of passage, but his passage will be characterised by temporary and total loyalty to his client. That, in my view, makes this transient a vital part of the business. A key role of the consultant will be to leave the valued core workers more knowledgeable, more autonomous and ironically, more potentially mobile than before. The delicate balance between contribution and threat will be such that the consultant must be part of, and seek to help develop, the core team for as long as they are working for the client. So the second leaf of my clover is the peripatetic expert, the increasingly professional consultant.

The third leaf will be filled by a growing army of temporary or part–timers who minimise costs and commitment by the variables of their shifting employment. As fixed costs escalate the temptation to employ workers on an 'as needed' basis will become all but irresistible. This is why I am confident that the tendency already noticeable in large organisations to employ people on a disposable basis will spread rapidly.

Thus the fourth leaf. The routine operations of administration and maintenance for example will always carry a heavy element of fixed cost while they are internal to the business. To create around them an element of variable cost is, however, simple. Many organisations will elect to outsource these services. Those who today are employees will become increasingly suppliers of services and subcontractors. Almost all clerical functions, along with their supervision could go down this route. As today, their output may be undervalued, but it will continue to be vital to the well-being of the firm. It will be bought in when required rather than offering nine to five, Monday to Friday employment. Those 'service' activities, such as Personnel or, more fashionably, Human Resource Management who tend to deny any need to measure their contribution to the bottom line, or to quantify added value from their contribution, are ripe for outsourcing. These people are different from new temps in that they are employees of external companies. Their employment is relatively secure, but their loyalty is to those who pay their wages.

Finally my model will not stand in splendid isolation but will grow in feminine characteristics. Men tend to communicate in order to establish relative status and pecking orders and in the organisation of the very near future pecking orders will have very little place. What will be important will be the development of lasting relationships and that, as psychologists are increasingly pointing out, is what woman communicate for. If people have no concrete reason to be loyal to the organisation, only enhanced personal relationships will drive and sustain their commitment.

And so my model is complete. Now I could add that for the best use of essential skills some of the core workers will telecommute or I could expand on the growing role of the intrapreneur, but that would add little of substance. The value of a model lies in part in that it enables me to express some of the most complex and important ideas in modern management in a few paragraphs, while it leaves the reader free to add more detail specific to their thoughts and experience without invalidating the basic shape.

WHY MODEL?

The value of any model then, lies in its ability to facilitate the analysis of complex data, illustrate difficult or even obscure ideas and remain sufficiently flexible to enable the astute manager to make accurate predictions about a real and changing world.

Few of the models in this book will have the somewhat romantic overtones of my shameless theft from Charles Handy. Most will be simple, pragmatic and of immediate use by the most avid of non-academics.

This use of models has importance and relevance globally, but in a country like the United Kingdom where the training of managers has been sorely neglected, and as I shall argue in Chapter 12 sadly inept, they are crucial to the speedy and economic development of the individual decision maker. But their use goes much deeper.

The best models are the key to planned and responsible organisational development, and as such they have a major role to play in the pursuit of the ever-changing goal of total excellence throughout the business. And, as I have argued in the Introduction to this book, consistent and relevant improvement of processes and performance will continue to be the the only road to global competitiveness and corporate survival.

DEFINITION OF A MODEL

I come from a background and an age in which it was regarded as essential to define your terms. With models, their diversity is such that this becomes difficult if not meaningless. What I believe can and should be defined however is not so much what a model is, but what it is for.

A good model will:

1. Enable the manager to identify the full range of critical data relating directly to the situation under consideration;

2. Facilitate the rejection of data which has no direct and immediate bearing or use;

3. Provide a framework in which the resulting, often complex, information can be analysed;

4. Supply a proven process in which information can be applied and management decisions made.

There has been a tendency throughout the Western World for the last twenty years to look at what Japan has done and is doing to achieve and sustain commercial supremacy, and to seek ways to mimic **Japanese processes**. It is fondly hoped, through imitative processes, to enjoy similar achievements. Not surprisingly, an attempt to copy, often half-heartedly as well as belatedly, what your competition has been doing flexibly and consistently with total commitment for forty years seldom succeeds in creating a competitive edge.

Competitive benchmarking, in the sense of being fully aware of what the best of your competition is doing is essential to survival. Benchmarking, however, in the often used sense of enabling yet another round of 'me too-ism' is unlikely to lead to any change in the balance of competitive advantage. And it is a major change in that balance which is required if troubled corporations in the West are to do more than survive. The need is to prosper. That, I continue to be convinced, can only be achieved in the face of growing global competition through constant attention to excellence. The **pursuit of excellence** is mediated through the flexible and thoughtful application of a constant, relevant and accurate stream of information. The models in this book are designed and selected to help to keep that information stream within its banks.

Companies, like people, are different. Above all perhaps, as Professor John Kay makes clear in his recent and exciting book, *Foundations of Corporate Success,* there is no single strategy. There is no snake oil panacea. Each organisation must define and establish the standards of excellence which are applicable at this time, in their company and sector, operating in their environment and responding to the needs, current and predicted, of their customers. The prescription for a prosperous future is not the same for ICI, IBM and Marks and Spencer. It is not the same for General Motors and the Bedford branch of Prontoprint. Every business, large, small or medium, service or manufacturing, needs to take one clear message to heart. You will design your own future success not by copying others, but by analysing, creating and identifying appropriate standards of excellence for your company, operating in its proper markets, right now. Having done that, the need is to constantly and forever proactively seek new standards of excellence in a rapidly changing world. There is no other way than to:

1. Identify and endorse existing standards of excellence;

2. Seek new standards of excellence to achieve as changing circumstances dictate.

The use of management models reduces that essential task to one of manageable proportions.

LEARNING FROM OTHERS

An important role of a management model is in taking the theories of one or more gurus and adapting their thinking to the specific and unique needs of the firm.

There has been in recent years a misguided mindset which automatically rejects anything which is perceived as 'theoretical'. Such is the power of this restraint on thought, adaptation and effective adoption that many, myself included, have taken to disguising theory by refering instead to 'concepts'. Both the rejection of theory and the attempt to circumvent that rejection are just plain dumb. Without a theory we have nothing.

The most prosaic and practical of products starts as an idea in some mind. And that is what theories are, but they are much more than that. A theory, by the time it is in the public domain, has been tested and validated at least in a specific situation. It can be effectively applied in the real world as a practical tool once the situation and the applicability of the theory are fully understood.

A good model, if intelligently applied, can and will clarify and apply the often rarified thinking of the academic to the intensely practical world of operations. It will also enable the combination and development of ideas and reduce the danger of the informed manager being seen as one whose only consistency is the passion with which he pursues any current flavour of the month.

Consider for a moment the theories which have illuminated the last thirty years of management thinking. The following list is by no means exhaustive, but it will give an idea of the range that has emerged from the hallowed halls of academia and the word processors of the gurus of all nationalities.

1960 - 1970

Decision Trees

Managerial Grid

Motivators and Hygienes

Theory X and Theory Y

Brainstorming

T-group Training

TQM (Total Quality Management)

Management by Exception

SOFT Analysis

SWOT Analysis

1970 - 1980

Management by Objectives

Theory Z

Conglomeration

Quality Circles

Zero Base Budgeting

Strategic Business Units

Job Engineering

Synergy

Androgeny

Management by Consensus

1980 - 1990

Diversification

Acquisition Trail

Experience Curve

Value Chain

Decentralisation

Wellness

Empowerment

Pursuit of Excellence

JIT (Just-in-time)

Restructuring

Portfolio Management

Matrix Management

Kanban

Kaizen

Intrapreneuring

One Minute Management

Transformational Management

Management by Just Walking About

Superleadership

TQM (again)

I could go on certainly *ad tedium* if not *ad infinitum*. As business journalist John Byrne has been quoted as saying:

> *'Business fads have always been with us. What's different – and alarming – today is the sudden rise and fall of so many conflicting fads and how they influence the modern manager.'*

Yet surely many of these so-called 'fads' still have relevance today. They are based on the deep and careful thinking and often, though not always, the carefully designed and validated research of some of the best minds ever to address the needs of business. Theories emerge, as does so much in a rapidly changing world, at an ever-increasing rate. Are we to throw away the old every time someone produces a bright and shiny new example for us to cleave to?

I suggest that to do so would be fraught with more than one danger. At the very least such a policy might tend to the throwing out of some potentially high flying babies with the barely soiled bath water. At worst the taking up and dropping of management theories by over-eager and credulous managers has led, in numerous organisations to what I have come to think of as the 'bus queue syndrome'. This is the growing belief from within the organisation that there is little or no need to expend effort on trying to exploit today's theory to the full for the compelling reason that there will be another one along tomorrow.

This failure to make ideas work creates at the same time a sense of organisational paralysis in which tomorrow and its promise, like Godot, never come, and develops a self-fulfilling prophecy that the new approach won't work. Failure drives management to drop the concept and embrace another at the dawn of the promised new era, only to be disappointed again and again.

Models which can bring together the key and relevant ideas from different theories can be the only practical way to ensure that the organisation moves forward on the basis of best relevant practice in a never ending progress of excellence.

And such opportunities are coming. It has become too easy in a period of savage recession and apparent impotence to be cynical. The green shoots of recovery have become, to some, 'The Darling Buds of Maybe' and optimism has begun to look like the last refuge of the liar and the incompetent. However, Dr. Carl H. Hahn, Chairman of Volkswagen has written:

> *'Dramatic changes are taking place in Europe – representing a dream of my generation – ... that are being echoed all over the globe... We are at the precipice of a new age, not just of international business, but of global prosperity. Our responsibilities are as unlimited as our opportunities.'*

Can you afford to believe that he is wrong? Models which facilitate the transformation of competent theory to effective action will help the manager to shoulder the responsibilities and grasp the opportunities that optimists are now seeing.

THE COMMON LANGUAGE OF MODELS

Models create a common language or ground which can have far-reaching effects through the organisation. As long as management and their teams understand the dangers of complacency and are committed to a concept of life-long learning, models can play a significant part in the growth of individuals in a learning community and, through the development of individuals, the growth of the firm.

There are significant dangers in the unbridled growth of a style of thinking restricted only by 'the way things are done around here', but these dangers are avoidable as will be explained in some detail in Chapter 4.

The experience gained from the selection and application of various management models and tools can be distilled into an eightfold path to enlightenment:

1. Models must reflect, as nearly as possible what actually happens in the workplace.

2. The model should provide a framework for managerial activity, not a straightjacket.

3. A model, and the theories which underpin it must be explainable in simple language to those who need to use them.

4. The model used must be consistent with the culture of the organisation.

5. The same, or similar models should be used throughout the organisation to bolster the concept of a common language.

6. Models should be recognised for what they are; an approximation to the real world which is sufficiently comprehensive to act as a practical checklist so that nothing critical is overlooked. They are not, however that real world, and they should be used in conjunction with a deep knowledge of how the real world works and how it is changing.

7. Models should be widely used in company training activities and training should be designed to ensure the application of learning beyond the conference room.

8. Models are not an alternative to well-designed and well-conducted training. They are an essential support to it.

2 STRATEGIC AND OPERATIONAL PLANNING

Any organisation of any size has a need to understand fully where it is now and where it chooses to go in the future. It must have the clearest possible understanding of:

- its purposes,
- its markets,
- its structure
- its culture,
- its policies,
- its philosophical guidelines on which key decisions depend,
- its needs in terms of human and physical resources,
- its total development requirements.

It must have, in short, a **long term strategy**.

This is true not only of the organisation as a whole, but of its constituent parts right down to departments and project teams. That is why there is a need to recognise that **strategic planning** is not and cannot be the sole province of the highly paid and highly qualified specialist sitting in an ivory or (save the elephant), plastic tower in a major international conglomerate. It is a primary responsibility of senior management in organisations of all sizes and types. It is the essential tool in building, simultaneously, commitment and competence of the total work team. As such it is the fundamental pre-requisite for any grouping of people brought together to own and achieve organisational goals.

Because planning must be universal, it must be simple: a simple approach which is applied successfully at every level in the organisation to produce long and short term plans for organisations, divisions, departments and project teams is based on the ideas of Beckhardt. To have a single tool which meets all requirements, not by force-fitting, but by design is a rare luxury.

THE MODEL FOR STRATEGIC PLANNING

The key concept of the model is that it takes the team from where they are today to any ideal future they care to design. It moves thinking from the vague to the concrete, from creativity and speculation to precision and exactitude and it does this one simple step at a time. The model incorporates other models and techniques and as modified, it facilitates a clear focus on the essentials which will play a key role in achieving the future design, culture and achievements of the organisation.

Looking at the model on paper (Fig. 2.1) it moves from the present which is depicted as the 'here and now' on the bottom left through a step-by-step achievement of a tactical plan to the ideal future incorporated into the vision of the top management team which is symbolised at the upper right of the page.

However, to ensure the relevance of the analysis of the current situation and to avoid the emergence of irrelevant 'war stories' and 'hidden agendas' in group applications the process begins with the development of the desired future. A shared view of where the organisation is going provides a sound basis for focusing thought on how to get there and limits consideration of the present state to those factors which are relevant to the desired outcome. Thus the present situation is analysed strictly as it pertains to the organisation's ability to reach the required future state using a more effective variant of **SWOT analysis (COST analysis)**.

So that, in terms of movement across the paper, the planning process in practice sweeps from top right to bottom left in order that the desired and actual situation are comprehensively and relevantly explored before turning attention to the central, planning part of the model. With a clear consensus of where the organisation is, and where it is going, it is relatively straightforward to produce strategic and practical plans for committed and effective implementation.

The **Company Mission Statement** can then be written, or revised to ensure consistency with the ideal future state of the organisation. The Mission will be meaningful in terms both of the ideal future and the real world of the present. It will avoid meaningless, but high sounding phrases and express a meaningful challenge to all employees. From the interplay of the Mission Statement the COST analysis objectives are developed and the various strategic alternatives relevant to the achievement of those objectives are identified. With the most promising strategy agreed, the **tactical plan** which moves the organisation from where it is today, step by step, function by function, to where it chooses to be, is developed and implemented.

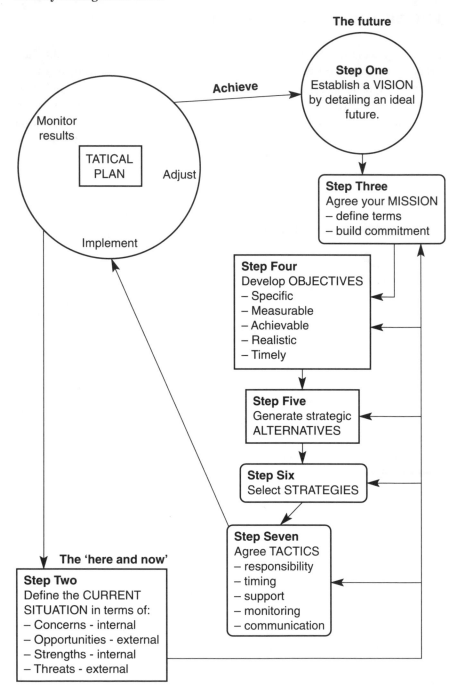

Figure 2.1 Model for strategic planning

USE OF THE MODEL FOR STRATEGIC PLANNING

Each team typically completes the planning process within the time constraints of a two or three day workshop. Individuals, without the need to manage group dynamics can obviously apply the tools with even more economical use of time. (But may, of course, devote considerably more time selling their vision to those who will eventually make it work.) Detailed step-by-step instructions and additional planning tools follow this introduction after an outline of **Excellence in Strategic Planning** which will enable the executive to assess precisely where the organisation stands today.

Strategic and operational planning

EXCELLENT We have a detailed plan which is based on a rigorous logical appreciation of the current and foreseeable business environment. Our strategic plan has a timeframe appropriate to our business of between five and fifteen years and our tactical operational plans roll forward one year at a time. The plan(s) are written and have been communicated to all members of the organisation in an appropriate form. Each plan has the wide and enthusiastic support of all who are expected to make it work. Plans are flexible in that they are reviewed continuously in the light of actual business experience and are revised in good time by the top team with revisions fully and quickly communicated to all. The strategic plan drives both the effectiveness and the development of the organisation. All of our plans are fully integrated, and each is driven by a shared set of values. These include:

- Our total and ongoing commitment to total quality;

- Respect for the individual;

- Our active commitment to lifelong learning for all.

AVERAGE A strategic plan exists in outline and in the minds of senior management. It is reviewed informally from time to time as market or other conditions dictate. It is based less on a rigorous evaluation of the business realities than on the best judgement of those involved at the time. In general terms it has been communicated down through the organisation, but little attempt has been made to evaluate the level of commitment. Operational results and business operations are reviewed through monthly target review meetings.

UNACCEPTABLE The organisation evolves opportunistically or as a result of tradition and past experience. No formal plan is in place, and the need for such a plan is not recognised.

Step one: the vision

There is a Japanese proverb which says, 'If one aims at a tree and falls short, one may only hit the ground. If one aims at the sky one may hit a tree.'

The purpose of this first step in the model is to reach for an ideal future and create a strong sense of vision for the organisation. This is different from the Company Mission in that it is an attempt to establish the ideal future rather than provide a challenging but strict guide for management decision making. Its primary role is to establish a dream to which all employees will subscribe and to the attainment of which they will enthusiastically direct their efforts. Reality will later be re-instated, but to ensure challenge and a sense of commitment to a highly desirable outcome let minds be as creative and idealistic at this stage as possible. Seek to create a passion for excellent outcomes.

The answers to the following questions should be sought, assuming an ideal world:

- What will the organisation be like in 5–15 years' time?
- What will be the major products and services?
- Who will be employed?
- What will be their qualifications or educational attainments?
- What will be their key attitudes and behaviours?
- What will be the shared values of the organisation?
- What will be the culture of the organisation?
- What will it feel like to be a member?
- How will those involved talk about or present the organisation to outsiders?
- How will the organisation be perceived by:
  - its members and employees?
  - its customers/clients?
  - its community?

Step two: the 'here and now'

In a workshop setting copy the following forms (Figs. 2.2 to 2.5) onto 'flip pads' and adhere strictly to the sequence given here in order to perform the COST analysis: company concerns, opportunities, strengths and threats.

Company concerns

Identify and record on the chart depicted in Fig.2.2 those weaknesses which adversely effect the organisation's ability to consistently satisfy its customers at minimum cost. Ensure that those recorded are not exceptional one-off occurrences which happen to be in people's minds only because they were recent or caused maximum confusion at some time past. Ensure that *causes* of problems, actual or potential, are recorded rather than *symptoms*. A detailed analysis of the cause will not only facilitate the planning of a mitigating or eradicating strategy, but will also specify the likelihood of reccurance.

Prioritise the need to take action as indicated and where possible and appropriate sketch in solutions to important problems under the heading ACTION.

Opportunity analysis

Record on chart Fig 2.3 all opportunities to build revenues, profits and resources.

Take an entrepreneurial rather than managerial approach to assure that none are excluded as being impractical. Brainstorm initially without concern for practicality considering as wide a market place as possible and when the list is exhaustive screen for immediate exploitation by considering:

1. Do we have, or can we acquire the necessary resources and people to exploit the opportunity effectively?

2. Is the exploitation of this opportunity likely to provide an adequate return on our investment of time, materials and resources?

3. Would exploitation of this opportunity divert key resources or people from other more important activities in the light of the current business plan or priorities?

Company strengths

Identify *all* strengths, no matter how apparently trivial or common to other organisations using the chart in Fig. 2.4. Again, use a brainstorming approach to ensure that all internal resources are recorded without evaluation before considering whether any specific strength contributes to the organisation's ability to exploit its market or effectiveness opportunities.

COMPANY CONCERNS

DESCRIPTION OF WEAKNESS (and evidence that it occurs periodically)	PRIORITY			ACTION
	S	U	G	

To prioritise, score 0 (low) to 5 (high) in categories S, U & G:
Seriousness = effect on ability to give customer service
Urgency = degree to which weakness affects ability to meet needs of current Business Plan
Growth = tendency of problem to worsen if not addressed

Figure 2.2 Analysing company weaknesses as part of a COST analysis

OPPURTUNITY ANALYSIS

DESCRIPTION OF OPPORTUNITIES	Qualified to Exploit?		Exploit?		
	Yes	No	Now	Future	No

Figure 2.3 *Analysing opportunities of revenue, profit and resources as part of a COST analysis*

COMPANY STRENGTHS					
DESCRIPTION OF STRENGTH	Marketable?		Possible USP?		ACTION
	Yes	No	Yes	No	

Figure 2.4 Assessment of exploitable strengths as part of a COST analysis to determine unique sales propositions (USP's)

Filter strengths to identify those which are, or can be promoted as unique to the organisation, alongside those which are necessary to remain competitive. Where an opportunity is recognised to use an existing strength in a new way and enjoy a business benefit, outline the use in the ACTION column.

Threat analysis

From the present business environment establish and record (Fig. 2.5) what threats could cause problems for the attainment of any planned goals, e.g.

- The growing market strength of a competitor;

- A worsening economic situation;

- A suspected rise in input costs or taxation;

- Proposed legislation with which it will be expensive or difficult to comply.

Identify those (few) which are to some degree within your organisation's control and which can be avoided and develop an outline avoidance plan. Do not become overly concerned with detail: this plan will be incorporated with an overall problem avoidance and solution plan as the final step of the planning process.

Similarly mark those which are unavoidable and outline a contingency plan which will mitigate the losses if the forecast problem arises.

Step three: defining your mission

When you have completed the COST analysis, what Beckhardt calls the 'here and now', consider your future in challenging detail. Continue to take the approach that nothing, with appropriate planning and commitment, is impossible and answer for yourself the question,'*If I knew that I could not fail, what would I attempt?*'

Answer the question for your organisation as specifically as possible. The Mission should be specific enough to ensure that:

- Management, employee, supplier and customer commitment is assured;

- Management and employees have a firm guide for unsupervised decision making;

- The organisation is challenged to develop excellence and make exemplary use of resources.

THREAT ANALYSIS

WHAT COULD GO WRONG?	AVOIDANCE PLAN	CONTINGENCY PLAN

Figure 2.5 Record of possible business threats as part of a COST analysis

As you look at the organisation both now and in 5 to 15 years' time record the answers to the following questions.

1. Precisely what business are you in? Avoid an over-narrow interpretation of what the business is. Concentrate attention on the customer/client needs that you seek to satisfy rather than a listing of products, e.g. an automobile manufacturer may define his business as 'the transportation of people and goods and for sport and recreation' rather than 'building/selling cars'. This enables the organisation to exploit changing technology without the danger of what Levitt calls 'marketing myopia' – blindness to closely related market opportunities.

2. Where will you be in five years' time? Who will be your clients/customers? What will be your revenues and profits? What will you be doing or making? Where will you be doing it? Will you seek to build commercial partnerships? With whom, if anyone?

3. What will set you apart from the herd, now and in the future? Why specifically should people choose to trade with you rather than with your competition? What are your brand values? What do your values offer to your potential customers that your competition do not? What are the sources of your unique selling propositions?

4. What are the key values and principles which will drive your business and guide management decision making? What motivation will carry you beyond the truism stated by Martin Luther King: *'A man who has nothing that he would die for has little to live for?'*

5. How does this organisation perceive and treat: its employees? its suppliers? its distributors? the community within which it is a neighbour? the environment? Try to avoid being carried away by the emotive issue of the environment. You are developing a business rather than a social plan. That is not to say that there are not a whole range of compelling reasons why a business enterprise should not pursue a positive and proactive environmental policy. There are many cogent business arguments for caring. These, rather than sentiment should drive the business plan.

6. How will you know when you get where you want to be? What will be the specific behaviours of others toward the organisation which will tell you not only that you have made it, but also the you ought to start to redefine your Mission for a challenging future. Dinosaurs are impressive, but their death, when it comes, comes quickly.

Avoid ambiguity

To ensure understanding by all those who must make the Mission a day by day reality; define all potentially ambiguous terms. For example, if you have described your organisation as being 'the biggest and best' you may consider it wise to define 'biggest' and 'best', e.g.

Biggest in: Sales volume?
Revenues?
Profits?
Range of products/services offered?
Numbers employed?

Best in: Customer service?
Customer satisfaction?
Product quality?
Profitability?
Cost control?
Prospecting new business?
Training and development?
Research and development?
Employee satisfaction?

Step four: objectives

Write a full range of SMART objectives:

Specific. They express exactly what you intend to achieve.

Measurable. Put figures to things whenever you can, not just profits and revenues, but numbers of clients or customers, standards of quality. Don't forget that 'All' or '100%' is a figure appropriate to some but not all objectives.

Achievable. Aim high, but don't saddle yourself with failure by going for the impossible dream. Identify the very best that you think that you can do and then stretch yourself just enough to make the extra effort fun.

Realistic. Test your objectives against your resources. The Mission is intended to bring out your dream. This should ensure progress toward the attainment of your dream by moving in the right direction with what you have right now. Tomorrow you will get the other resources you need.

Time. Make it clear to yourself when you intend to achieve your key results, including critical sub-objectives *en route.*

Always check then to ensure that objectives are specific, measurable, achievable, realistic and time constrained. Unless you do, the tendency to write a mixture of vague wishes and statements is almost impossible to avoid.

Step five: identify strategic alternatives

Brainstorm as many strategic alternatives as possible. Take no account at this stage of their feasibility or desirability. There are many potential paths to your final goal. Look for options not objectives. Establish the range of possible strategies which are available to the organisation and when the flow of ideas is exhausted filter them by assessing:

- Which alternatives make best use of resources?
- Which maximise the differential between potential reward and risk?
- Which relate most appropriately to your assessment of opportunities, now and in the longer term?
- Which are most appropriate to your best forecast of the needs of your market?
- Which are most consistent with your desired future?

Step six: strategy

Write a strategy statement clarifying your chosen approach and screen for ambiguities or areas of potential vagueness. Where necessary define your terms so that all will be able to understand and commit to the Strategic Plan.

A strategy statement will typically include:

- An outline of markets, sectors, products and services;
- The trading and pricing policy;
- Key factors of the promotional strategy;
- The intended organisational image and culture.

All will, of course be consistent with and supportive of the desired future and will be feasible in the timeframe and relevant to the COST analysis.

At strategic or board level the plan needs to include, at least, the following:

1. **The Physical Resource Plan.** Acquisition and control of essential physical resources – plant, equipment, premises and systems relevant to known and forecast needs.

2. **The Financial Resource Plan.** Acquisition and control of adequate financial resources from internal and external sources to ensure availability of financial resource and achievement of objectives.

3. **The Marketing Plan.** Identification of current and potential markets, key sectors and customers along with the critical strategic steps toward meeting the established and emergent needs of the market place and also organisational image and environmental needs and community policy.

4. **Human Resource Plan.** Establishment of the key criteria driving the culture, values, norms and organisational and personal development of the business or organisation.

5. **The Quality/Excellence Plan.** The critical competitive edge ensured by a total commitment to excellence in every aspect of operations within and beyond the firm is sufficiently well-established to indicate that the Strategic Plan should provide a clear framework for how excellence is to be achieved and maintained in the organisation and its suppliers and distributors. The strategy should make clear the top team's absolute and proactive commitment to excellence.

Step seven: the tactical plan

Imagine if you would the organisational strategy in the form of a large sheet of paper. Imagine further that the sheet can be effectively torn into strips in such a way that relevant pieces could be given to each operational area and that each operation simply makes its appropriate contribution by achieving the goals which it is allocated, resulting in the full attainment of every organisational objective as the torn pieces are reassembled.

THE RAISE MODEL

A model which facilitates this situation uses the RAISE acronym. Departmental/divisional goals are defined in terms of the organisational goals to which they make a significant and worthwhile contribution using Figs. 2.6 and 2.7.

The acronym RAISE covers:

Responsibility. A line manager or director is personally responsible for achievement of the objective within the specified timeframe. On the RAISE planning form the designated individual should ideally write her signature in the column provided. The application of a signature rather than the entry of a name emphasises ownership of the project and personal responsibility for the outcome.

RAISE PLANNING FORM

Organisational Objective _____

Departmental Objective _____

Commence (date)	Complete (date)	Responsibility accepted (signature)	Authorised by: (signature)	To be informed (by name and department)	Support committed signature(s)
Execution: notes and comments					

Figure 2.6 Planning form for RAISE: Responsibility, Authorised, Informed, Support, Execution

RAISE SUPPORT REQUEST FORM

Departmental objective

Responsible department

Responsible executive requesting support

Nature of support/information required	Required by: (date)	Recieved by: (date)

Figure 2.7 Additional RAISE planning form for requesting extra support

Authority. If the application of organisational resources toward the achievement of the objective requires authorisation at a higher organisational level the signature of the authorising executive/director should appear in this column. A signature in the column indicates:

1. The signatory confirms the *significance* of the goal;

2. The signatory commits his *support* to the manager responsible for achieving the goal should this prove necessary;

3. Authority to take all necessary action in pursuit of the goal is *delegated* to the responsible manager.

Informed. Any changes which result from the pursuit of a new goal are liable to affect the work of other departments and individuals who are not directly involved. This column permits the manager or employee responsible for the attainment of the objective to ensure that disturbance is minimised by proactive communication.

Support. Should the objective to be achieved be one where success is dependent on the provision of data or other support by other individuals or departments this column enables the provider of support to commit to timely provision, again by signature. The additional support request form (Fig. 2.7) may be used for this purpose.

Execution. This column enables the person responsible for action to note any ideas relevant to getting the job done which may expand the entries in other columns. For example, as the activity matures it may become clear that there is a necessity to inform a wider range of co-workers of emergent or imminent changes.

Note: When used in a planning workshop *all* signatures should be negotiated and appended before the group disperses.

POTENTIAL PROBLEM IDENTIFICATION

Two different types of problem can scuttle a plan and because they are different they must be handled in a different way.

Analyse all of the potential problems which could arise in implementing the plan. Separate the *avoidable* from the *unavoidable*.

1. Avoidance planning

Having identified the avoidable potential problems, build into the plan specific steps to be taken to ensure that they do not arise, using Fig. 2.8 to assess the threats and to analyse the risks inherent in the plans.

2. Contingency planning

Establish the first indicators that are likely to suggest that an unavoidable problem is emerging or about to emerge.

Consider at what stage in the implementation of the plan it is most likely to emerge and who will be most quickly aware of the problem.

Outline a contingency strategy which can be speedily put into effect if the problem arises and which will resolve it or mitigate the losses. Allocate, if practical, responsibility for timely implementation of the contingency plan.

COMMUNICATION STRATEGY

Experience in conducting many hundreds of Organisational Development Workshops and Top Team Business Planning Sessions confirms the obvious. Planned communication is the essential prerequisite to effective and committed implementation of a strategy and problem avoidance.

Where the organisational top team have, perhaps untypically, removed themselves to an off-site location to develop the plan, strong interest in, and concern about what has been happening, is natural in those left 'minding the store'. Gossip and rumour, often unconstructive, is a strong possibility.

It is therefore almost mandatory that communication of the outcome should be speedy, consistent and complete.

The following guidelines have been forged and tested by experience and have been found useful:

1. The communication strategy should be designed and agreed by all as part of the planning process.

2. Briefings of *all* those affected should take place at the earliest possible opportunity before rumour has had time to surface, e.g. it is always helpful if planning workshops are held during weekends with the briefing sessions completed early on Monday morning. (This has the added psychological advantage of introducing something new at the start of a week.)

3. Either a single briefing to all concerned, or simultaneous briefings should be held to avoid any watering down or distortion of the messsage as a result of peers reporting back after each session.

POTENTIAL PROBLEM WORKSHEET

What could go wrong? – assess threats – analyse risks inherent in plan(s)	What preventive action(s) will remove risk?	What contigency action(s) will minimise losses? List first indicators of possible problems	Triggers to implement plan

Figure 2.8 Control form for risk avoidance

4. Where a number of briefings are unavoidable, it has been found useful to script these to ensure consistency.

5. A video, audio or simple written message to all from the Chief Executive, emphasising key points is often helpful.

The above may seem like a great deal of effort, but this must be evaluated against the fact that the long-term strategic plan will drive the organisation for anything between five and fifteen years. Time invested in getting it right first time will pay abundant dividends.

Note: although, because of the relative complexity, it has been necessary to emphasise the use of planning tools in a group setting, all of the tools and models suggested are equally suitable for individual managerial use.

POTENTIAL PITFALLS OF STRATEGIC PLANNING

Corporate planning as envisaged in Fig. 2.9 often fails when:

- The Chief Executive dominates the decision making process.
- The culture, leadership style, products and services of the organisation are perceived as being unchangeable.
- Change is introduced for the sake of novelty rather than in response to a new vision or internal or external forces.
- Time cannot be found to fully develop strategies and develop a comprehensive written plan.
- Hidden agendas and company politics are allowed to motivate contributions.
- The people involved are not committed to ensure that the organisation does measurably better as a result of planning than it has ever done before.
- The plan is not communicated to all those whose efforts and commitment will be needed to make it work quickly and in simple concrete language.
- Reasonable aspirations of employees, management, shareholders and other stakeholders are ignored.
- The establishment of objectives is rushed and goals are vague.
- The company is so close to going 'belly up' that long term planning is irrelevant to survival.

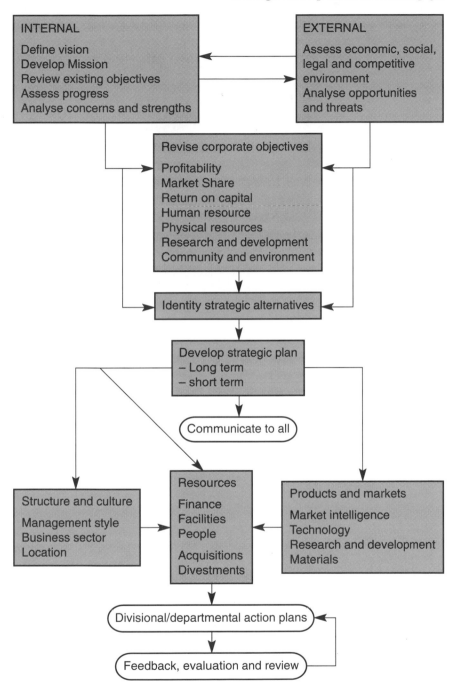

Figure 2.9 Top team coporate planning; strategic: shaded boxes; tactical:
clear boxes

- The Chief Executive does not believe in the planning process and senior management are not committed.

- The top management team do not proactively and daily demonstrate their commitment through their consistent behaviour. To use an Americanism which puts it succinctly, 'management must walk like they talk' for strategic planning to succeed.

3 BUSINESS IS ABOUT PEOPLE

It is a fairly obvious, but nonetheless frequently ignored fact that all results in business depend ultimately on people. Take for example General Motors Saturn Plant and its early problems. Given a greenfield site with state-of-the-art processes and the best facilities that intelligent investment could provide, results ranged from disappointing to near disastrous. Roger Smith, not normally credited with being oversensitive to people's needs, made it clear that the problem was that the development and empowerment of people was given insufficient attention amid the euphoria of having the best of everything available at the flick of a switch.

It is an irony that company after company publishes in Mission statements and elsewhere the worn out phrase that 'people are our greatest resource'. What is the reality?

HOW NOT TO TREAT PEOPLE

Along comes a recession and companies indulge in a headlong rush to reduce headcount. In the name of fairness they take this unnecessary step on the basis of some bureaucratic rule book which ensures that not only do they cut the manpower resource to the bone, they often cut away the sweetest meat. Those who leave, particularly if leaving is voluntary, are often the most skilled and consequently the most mobile. Where the separation is involuntary, management use it as an opportunity to remove threat to their position and time-honoured complacency. Ways are often manufactured to remove the imaginative, the creative and those who are committed to the ongoing well-being of the company rather than to the continuance of the *status quo*. Those who remain are frequently mismanaged in a way that is designed to damage relationships for years to come.

Of course, it would be a wild exageration to claim that what is outlined above is true for every firm. There are some, are there not, where people are treated with dignity and respect? But in too many organisations that treatment is based on ideology and self-delusion rather than understanding. People are only treated better because it is assumed that those who are treated better perform better.

If good treatment alone is a necessary precursor for high levels of performance then the pyramids and the Burma railroad would never have been built. And what is interpreted as 'treated better' is usually identified from the wrong viewpoint. The manager tends to 'do unto others as he would be done to' – great – except that people seldom want to be done to in the way that others assume that they do.

Building confidence

There is a need to build autonomy, self-reliance, self-discipline and confidence in one's position in the workforce at every level. The growth in the importance of knowledge workers, intrapreneurs, telecommuters and out-workers will increasingly dictate that, but the key word is 'build'. Self-confidence cannot be imposed through a system or an ideology. It grows as a result of an expanding personal experience of success through a track record in which the level of risk is slowly and gradually increased.

Excellence in recruitment

The recruitment policy needs to be based on a clear and timely recognition of the manpower needs of the company as expressed in the strategic plan. Every step has to be taken to ensure that the best and most able people are recruited and retained. There is a need to employ highly professional skills in specifying the people, advertising the vacancy and assessing the respondents. The company which plans to prosper in an environment in which high quality skills are both essential and rare will have a proactive and forward looking recruitment policy. A truly professional personnel operation, whatever its current fancy title, will have a major contribution to make to the profits of the company. Recruitment must be in professional and specialist hands, within or outside the organisation.

So what does that leave for the busy line manager to do?

THE ROLE OF PEOPLE MANAGAEMENT

In simple terms the manager's job is to keep people and to use them. To retain them without excessive and unnecessary cost and to use the best of their ever-developing capacities.

There is an urgent need for the manager to develop a deep and accurate understanding of **motivation**. And there is an equally urgent requirement to use performance management techniques which are related to the needs of the organisation, which are anti-bureaucratic, self-sustaining, focused on growth and the job to be done and capable of building commitment across a wide spectrum of personalities and individual needs.

As Harold Leavitt pointed out when I was a psychology student more than thirty years ago, the difficulty with people arises because they are, at the same time, alike and different. People do different things for the same reason while they are doing the same things for different reasons. Some of the aspects of **behaviour** which are alike for all of us are:

- Behaviour is **caused**, it does not arise out of a vacuum;
- Behaviour is **motivated**;
- Behaviour is **aimed** at the achievement of some explicit or implied goal.

But this is where the sameness ends.

Consider, if you will, the rather common behaviour of going to work, or of staying at home and writing a book. Do you work:

- For the money and the things which money buys: food, shelter, luxuries or leisure?
- For the status and recognition which come with the label which says 'important job holder'?
- For the companionship which comes from being part of a group?
- For the satisfaction that comes from achieving your ambitions and personal goals?
- Because you have grown up under the effect of the Protestant work ethic which tells you that it's beneficial to work, necessary or not?
- To build your knowledge and understanding?
- To increase your power, economic or personal?
- To create security for yourself and for those that you love?
- To create something of beauty and worth?
- For that feeling of pleasure which only comes from the execution or the completion of a job well done?

The list is far from exhaustive, but it offers an indication of the wide range of reasons which people might have for going into work each day. Motivation theories, when related to management, address themselves to what causes us to perform and in the post-industrial society each of us must perform to the limits of our ability. Only through the task-focused excellence of each individual can a vital competitive edge be maintained. As Herzberg said, 'Motivation springs, not from how you treat people, but how you use them'.

In the information age how you use people must be intelligently blended with how they choose to employ themselves. That dictates a more thorough understanding of what motivates.

Motivation with maturity

Maslow's theory, and it is at best that, links motivation with maturity. He argues that we mature as individuals as each lower need is satisfied and we move toward a higher need. In general he sees man as being infinitely perfectable, moving from the physical needs, step by step to the spiritual, always capable of growth, but never reaching a destination. But that upward movement is not an unbroken progress. Maslow recognises that the physical needs which protect the integrity and survival both of the individual and of the species are the strongest, and if they are threatened or denied our whole attention reverts immediately to the satisfaction of lower needs.

The highest needs may fail to enter our consciousness, but it is the higher needs which drive the highest levels of achievement which is why macho management, taking stupid advantage of temporary insecurity to inflict unreasonable controls will fail in the long term. Research shows that when hitherto weak managers start to beat their puny chests and scream 'We are the masters now!' the effect on performance is catastrophic. This is not to argue that disciplines should not be in place at all times. The secret however is to move from imposed, externalised disciplines to self-discipline and personal responsibility and commitment in the shortest possible time. And once self-discipline is the norm, nothing must be done which dilutes its potent power to create ever higher levels of personal performance.

Maslow's conception is nothing more than an hypothesis, there is little experimental evidence to support it. In strict scientific terms it is doubtful whether it justifies the word 'theory' to describe it. So why has it survived and been useful for so long?

First, and most importantly to this book, it is an excellent model. As a model it enables you or me to make predictions about how individuals will behave in a given situation, and those predictions, if well founded are accurate. To that degree it is part way to earning the accolade of being recognised as a theory.

Second, it fits in with the facts as we believe that we know them.

The two most important theories in the biological sciences are Darwin's Theory of Evolution and Cannon's Theory of Homeostasis. Darwin's theory is well known, but less understood. In grossly oversimplified terms it states that changes to any organism which confer survival advantage are likely, over time, to spread through breeding populations. Homeostasis suggests that there exist base states of greatest comfort to which any living system seeks to return through a loop of feedback and action. Thus if we are too hot we perspire, too cold and we shiver. Each response is designed to return us to our state of greatest comfort and efficiency.

Maslow's theory is based firmly on both of the above. Maslow sees motivation somewhat as an itch that just has to be scratched. The drive is a disequilibrium which causes us to act to satisfy the need. But the key point which makes Maslow's approach different is that we no longer return when the need is satisfied to a state of comfortable apathy, we are conditioned to experience instead a new and higher itch that in turn has to be scratched. Thus a satisfied need no longer motivates, but is replaced in turn by ever higher needs, each of which takes us on an never-ending journey toward maturity and personal excellence. Indeed, Maslow goes a stage further. He suggests, and observation of healthy human behaviour confirms, that a lower need does not have to be satisfied fully before a higher need emerges and demands our attention. It is as if the reduction of an itch in one place is enough to start up a demand for a scratch elsewhere.

The basic needs in Maslow's heirarchy are:

- Physiological individual and species survival needs – food, shelter, sex, etc;

- Security needs – protection of what we have gained.

These needs relate directly to the 'R' Complex, the reptilian part of the human brain. The limbic system is in control of our emotions and corresponds generally with Maslow's concepts of:

- Belonging – building satisfying relationships with others;

- Status or ego satisfaction – a strong sense of self-worth.

Finally the cortex, a folded metre square tablecloth of thin grey-pink jelly which is the almost uniquely human part of the brain controls our thoughts, language and sense of beauty, equating to Maslow's:

- Self actualisation – aesthetic, cognitive, spiritual and autonomous growth.

So Maslow's concepts, scientifically unproven, serve as a useful model. In case you find the idea of something which is not necessarily true being nonetheless useful consider Newton's theory of gravitation. Einstein showed in 1906 that Newton's theory was at best incomplete, at worst wrong. It has since continued to be the best model on which to base the exploration of the solar system and beyond. Maslow's concept lies at the foundation of all ideas about motivation for the same reason. It may be incomplete, it may prove at some time in the future to be wrong in some of its ideas. In the meanwhile it is simple, it has credibility and it works. It will repay consideration by tomorrow's manager just as it does today's.

Job enrichment

Motivation needs to be understood because it is a simple rule of life that all behaviour is motivated. If people are not motivated in one direction, they will certainly be motivated in another. The problem for the manager is that we are not motivated directly by others. We motivate ourselves. Motivation strategy is not, therefore, a matter of manipulation, it is more the planned and conscious development of a positive climate in which the natural process of motivation will be directed at personal and organisational goals which are one. The work of Hackman and Oldham has been developed with the aim of building that positive climate. It is on the back of their work that the job enrichment model is built.

In the ultimate analysis a practical understanding of motivation is an understanding of the recipients' perception of the rewards and sanctions which are inherent in the system. The emphasis needs to be on rewards rather than sanctions for the simple practical reason that whereas punishment may extinguish an undesired behaviour, only reward can reinforce a desired behaviour to take its place. I can stop a person smoking by chemically or hypnotically inducing a foul taste in the mouth, but I will have no control over how they seek oral and chemical gratification thereafter. Only through the judicious application of rewards can I hope to direct the previously unhealthy and antisocial behaviour into more constructive channels. And for a successful outcome it must be the ex-smoker, not I, who values the rewards.

Through punishment an undesirable behaviour may be extinguished. Only through rewards can a desired behaviour be reinforced.

JOB PERFORMANCE MANAGEMENT

W. Edwards Deming the father of Total Quality Management was addressing a full conference centre. Most of the audience were personnel directors, or as most now seem to prefer, human resource directors of major conglomerates.

Dr Deming speaks slowly and quietly, but somehow he manages to invest his speech with passion. On this occasion he had been passionate about the annual appraisal and the job performance management systems which support the appraisal process. At first what he had to say was listened to with quiet respect, but as his audience grew in the knowledge that the guru was attacking one of their most cherished sacred cows there was disbelief followed by discomfort, and for some a growing sense of rage. A gentleman close to me was turning more and more red in the face as Deming explained why the appraisal system tended to encourage mediocrity and worse in an organisation. Finally my neighbour could take it no more. He rose, and semi-articulate in his rage, blurted out, after several false starts and loud gurgles: 'What am I supposed to replace annual appraisal with?'

Deming gazed into the semi-darkness which surrounded his audience, he stroked his chin and gave every appearance of careful consideration before speaking more slowly than ever.

'May I be absolutely sure that I have understood what you are asking? You would like to know...' He paused for what seemed an eternity, 'You would like to know what else you may humiliate people with?'

At that moment I knew that I would be a Deming fan for life. Job performance management serves no purpose unless it enhances incrementally and finally leads to optimal performance. It is too often used, in John Cleese's words, as: 'The time when the company tells you what it thinks of you.'

It becomes an opportunity to tick a few boxes and emphasise status divisions. A chance to satisfy the bureaucrat which hides in most of us and destroy any sense of belonging to a team. At best it is condescension, at worst condemnation. And we are led to believe that we are better managers if we do it more than once a year!

Robert Mager considered the problem some time ago and it is on his ideas that I am building in this chapter. General Motors, following Mager's advice, took as an article of faith that every employee had three inalienable rights:

- To know what was expected of him;

- To receive timely, objective and accurate feedback on his performance;

- To perform in an environment free of unnecessary task interference.

If the employee is entitled to know what is expected and to receive feedback on his performance, surely that implies some form of the job performance appraisal interview? My red-faced neighbour had it right and Deming was wrong? Not exactly.

Suppose for a moment that there was a performance management system which:

- Is based firmly on the needs of the job and is designed to recognise and reward ever-higher standards of performance;

- Is not dependent on outsiders for accurate and timely feedback;

- Encourages and develops a partnership between supervisor and supervised throughout the organisation;

- Provides the motivation for ever-improving personal achievement and acceptance of responsibility;

- Accelerates the empowerment of all those involved;

- Is seen as entirely equitable;

- Minimises paperwork;

- Appeals to management, employees and unions;

- Provides clear, concise and visible standards of performance without stifling creativity;

- Helps to ensure that the truly important things are done first;

- Welds strong teams by emphasising goals not roles.

Could such a system satisfy my red-necked friend, Dr Deming and you, the person at the sharp end? If so read on, the other models in this chapter enable you to develop such a system.

Bottom-up appraisal

While we are generally thinking about job performance management, consider this. British Airways, BP and others have introduced appraisal systems which work, as it were, in reverse. Systems in which subordinates rate their supervision. Where the Personnel Department is looking for an appraisal system which is reliable and can make a real contribution to performance overall this could be a useful approach. As Adrian Furnham pointed out in a recent *Financial Times* article, upwards appraisal has a number of advantages.

Subordinates often know the boss better than the boss knows them. Bosses are, in general simply more visible, and their strengths and weaknesses can be seen to affect the performance of the whole team which justifies bringing the boss's real contribution under a magnifying glass.

Since a boss is likely to have a number of subordinates appraisal tends to be both more accurate and more statistically reliable. The extremes of sycophancy and hidden agendas tend to be smoothed out by involving larger numbers of appraisers leaving a realistic appraisal from those who are most concerned.

Thirdly information usually flows more readily down an organisation. Like water, it is difficult to get it to flow uphill without some form of pump priming. Bottom-up appraisal, however, if taken seriously, primes the pump and leads to a better flow of information upwards on all matters.

And, because it is more unusual, upward appraisal tends to make a greater impact. It makes an impact on those that receive it due to its novelty, and it provides those that give it with evidence that their ideas are respected and thought worthy of consideration. With the growth in power and influence of the knowledge worker of the very near future and the reliance by the company on an unfettered information flow in all directions appraising the boss could become the first step in building world-beating teams.

The costs and difficulties, practical, emotional and economic in introducing a system of upward appraisal are not insignificant. A lack of frankness and fear of reprisals, a sense of threat both to the individual manager and to the organisational structure and, at the simplest level more forms to process are among the immediate costs. But the benefits could be considerable. Upward appraisal will depend for its success, as so many things do in organisations, on a philosophy and practice of avoiding **blame-fixing** and a total commitment to constructive **problem solving**. That is an easy thing to suggest, but a tough one to realise. It depends on a rich combination of self-respect and respect for others throughout the organisation. That is why Mager's ideas are critical to those organisations which seek to grow and prosper in a post-industrial age.

Meanwhile Furnham suggests a gentle way in for those who like the idea of upward appraisal and wish to prepare themselves mentally for the ordeal. When sinking their gin and tonics in future, forward-looking management might prepare their minds by ceasing to say 'down the hatch' and try 'bottoms up' instead!

Manpower planning and recruitment

EXCELLENT Anticipated manpower requirements are firmly based on the Business Plan. A rolling programme of recruitment, induction and training ensures that a high quality, qualified and committed workforce is always available when required. Forward planning is against corporate and departmental goals with extended time horizons of between five and ten years. Clear and complete statements of demanding entry qualifications enable human resource planning professionals to specify in detail and in good time the people who are needed for the continued growth of the enterprise. A changing business environment is reassessed at least twice a year to confirm or change priorities and manpower planning is carried out on a regular scheduled basis. The quality and relevance of the manpower planning operation is confirmed in performance against quantified standards and the consistent achievement of corporate and departmental objectives.

AVERAGE Historical growth trends rather than challenging goals drive the recruitment plan and standards of entry are based on the Personnel Department's assessment of the availability and cost of labour. Entry qualifications are pragmatic rather than challenging. The resulting recruitment activities lead to the hiring of a 'mixed bag' of people with excellence in some being balanced by continued performance at below desired standards by others. Recruitment, however, remains a planned process and is capable of relatively swift and economic improvement.

UNACCEPTABLE Vacancies are filled as they occur. Qualifications for entry are either general and undemanding or are ignored in the face of the perceived realities of the available labour pool. Salaries and wages are at a level which attracts only the least able. The belief permeates the recruitment function that the company can save its way into a profit and that low output can be balanced by low output costs. Recruitment efforts aimed at anticipating and meeting future needs do not exist.

Performance management

EXCELLENT A motivating and self-administered system is fully operational. It is understood and accepted by all members of the work team, each member of which knows in quantified terms what is expected of him and receives timely, accurate and objective feedback on performance. All employees contribute to the development of the performance criteria for their positions and these criteria are based on the established Job Purpose rather than personal attributes of the job holder.

AVERAGE A management designed and assessed system is fully operational. The system uses quantifiable outcomes whenever practical, but allowances are made for individual differences in ability. By and large the system is accepted by employees as fair and reasonable. Feedback is either irregular or at widely spaced intervals, but it is as objective and accurate as time and changing work pressures allow.

UNACCEPTABLE No formal performance management system exists and management tend to the view that if employees were told what was expected of them they would perform only to the minimum acceptable standards. It is assumed that the combination of ignorance about acceptable standards of performance and tight management controls will lead to high performance by the majority of the workforce. Laggards will experience coercion, sanctions and threats to bring about an improvement.

Performance appraisal

EXCELLENT Job Performance Appraisal is seen as a shared responsibility of the individual and supervisor. Feedback on performance is timely, accurate, complete and related to identifiable behaviours, not assumed personality traits. The process of appraisal is recognised by both participants as an opportunity for mutual problem solving rather than blame-fixing and it reflects the quality of the supervisor's supportive, enabling and developmental behaviour as much as it does the attainments or shortcomings of the employee. In general the formal appraisal interviews carry no surprises, reinforce the employee's assessment of their own performance and point the way for further professional growth for both supervisor and subordinate. Notwithstanding the frequency of feedback, formal appraisal interviews are conducted and recorded at least twice each year with both participants having adequate time in which to prepare for an optimal outcome. All notes made during or subsequent to the interview are freely available to both participants.

AVERAGE Formal appraisal is carried out on a scheduled basis using standard forms. Because the discussion concentrates on the individual's perceived triumphs and shortcomings it tends to be superficial. Managers are trained to appraise and coach, but because the interview is not designed to be a genuine two-way communication process there is little consistency in the organisation with some managers perceived as being unduly harsh, while others are seen as being an 'easy touch'.

UNACCEPTABLE Either there is no formal appraisal system, or it is so much a matter of 'going through the motions once a year' that it contributes little or nothing to either individual growth or organisational development. The participants and the organisation have no investment in the outcome, other than possible 'hidden agendas' and the appraisal is, for the most part, either superficial, subjective or both.

Motivation

EXCELLENT All employees and management recognise valued tangible and intangible rewards which are directly related to achievement of worthwhile organisational goals. There is a direct relationship between the effort needed for accomplishment and the level of reward. Open two-way communication ensures that all involved see that accessibility to the reward system is equitable and does not reflect a formal or informal status heirarchy. Self-development is encouraged and rewarded at every level. Effective job enrichment strategies are routinely employed.

AVERAGE Some attempt at job enrichment strategies is attempted from time to time, but these are based more on fad and fashion than on proven methodologies. If they fail to motivate, however, they have the desirable effect of amusing those who are involved and bringing some variety to the working day. Management training highlights the ideas of gurus including Maslow and Herzberg and much exhortation to 'get motivated' is implicit or explicit in management communication and in organisational workshops.

UNACCEPTABLE The management team believe in Mager's words that employees 'really oughta wanna!' and those who, for whatever reason, do not should 'get the hell out and make space for some who will'.

Values

EXCELLENT The organisation has a clear vision and the values inherent to that vision have been defined and communicated to all. Individual values are respected throughout the organisation and conflict between sincerely held views is seen as an opportunity to reach a higher ethical standard through synthesis. Where the organisation claims to adhere to a concept of stakeholders the values of management, employees, distributors, suppliers, customers and community are perceived to be of equal status.

AVERAGE The organisation makes a sincere attempt to respect the values of all, but the values which are implied in the company Mission, although circulated to all employees are interpreted inconsistently through a failure of top management to define what they perceive as 'obvious'. A genuine, though inconsistent attempt is made to respect customer values and to be a good neighbour in the community which the company serves.

UNACCEPTABLE No values are expressed by the organisation and all activities are driven by the pressing needs of the moment. Individual employees feel that the wisest course is to keep their cherished values and beliefs to themselves as any expression of what they believe to be important may risk sanctions. Even worse, the organisation is run on totally bureaucratic lines with the only justification for action today being the rule-book or the precedent, successful or not, of yesterday.

A MODEL OF MOTIVATION

Many readers will be familiar with Maslow's hierarchy of needs model drawn in the form of a triangle or pyramid. My understanding of Maslow is not best addressed through the standard model, however. I align myself firmly with Drucker and others who have expressed the view that:

'We can argue until the seas boil as to whether or not we are able to motivate others. What we understand only too well is that we have the power to de-motivate without any excess of effort. It is this ability to de-motivate that we should initially address and correct.'

With that thought in mind I have developed Fig. 3.1. The model shows, in line with Maslow's thought that each individual matures as his existent needs and drives are focused more on higher needs. It also shows that where higher and lower needs are in competition, the lower need strength is greater. Thus if I am an artist who is starving in my attic studio I will be more inclined to write begging letters than to paint. The need to survive being, for the present at least, far stronger than my drive toward immortality. If I were merely somewhat hungry the outcome might be different. Where the model diverges somewhat from those which are normally related to Maslow is in the movement from self-absorption to self-worth, passing through a stage during which self-confidence is limited and dependence on others for expressions of approval is high.

Most importantly, however, this model addresses the problem of demotivation by indicating the results of denial. Changes in employment policies and the exploitation of 'disposable workers' have already begun to show signs of demotivation and demoralisation of the workforce.

This model shows how such results are, in the short term at least, inevitable. If previously valued workers are made redundant and delayering removes simultaneously previously valued positions and career paths the

Need	Definition	Results of Denial
INTERNAL FRAMES OF REFERENCE – NEED TO CONTRIBUTE FOR SELF		
SELF-ACTUALISATION	The need to continuously develop in ways which are personally important to the individual.	Feelings of futility, alienation, bitterness, wasted chances, being in a rut, hopelessness.
	To feel that one is fully using personal resources to become all that one is capable of becoming.	Possibly depression or anxiety neurosis
COGNITIVE AUTONOMY	The need to be proactively understanding and acting on the environment.	Frustration, a sense of being exploited. Resentment at not finding or being given opportunities.
	Taking personal responsibility. Not being coerced or manipulated. In control of one's life and work.	Chronic and growing anxiety, despair
AESTHETIC AUTONOMY	The need to create and have psychological ownership of something of beauty and uniqueness.	Withdrawal, focus on activties outside the workplace.
	Making a significant contribution.Encapsulated in the American exression: 'Planting a shade tree for others to sit under'.	Frustration and a growing sense of the pointlessness of work.
EXTERNAL FRAMES OF REFERENCE – NEED TO CONTRIBUTE IN TEAMS		
ESTEEM/STATUS	The need for recognition and prestige. The basis of self-respect. Knowing that we count for something.	Loss of confidence creating a poor self-image, self doubt, shame. A feeling of being an undeserving victim.
SOCIAL	The need to be a valued member of a group. The confirmation that others find us likeable.	Loneliness, withdrawal, feelings of low self-worth and insecurity. Sometimes a need to hit back.
SECURITY	The need to know that our world is stable and predictable. Confidence that gains made can be conserved.	Tension, anxiety, fear, panic. Self-absorption.
ENFORCED SELF-ABSORPTION		
PHYSIOLOGICAL	The requirements of healthy functioning of the body and self-preservation	Pain, physical discomfort, illness, even death.

Need strength — *Have maturity*

Figure 3.1 Making more of Maslow's hierarchy of needs model

opportunities for mischief are immense. After the natural sigh of relief that those who lost their jobs did not include me I begin to wonder whether I shall be unaffected next time. As I do so my sense of security is threatened and I begin to feel anxiety, tension and fear. Worse I find myself in an organisation in which human resource is severely limited and in which whole layers of management who would have previously acted as a buffer between me and possible error are no longer there. I must accept greater responsibility and greater burdens of work at higher personal risk. Any sense of insecurity which I feel is exacerbated. But there is worse to come.

While I am feeling anxious and tense, I have less time to establish close and mutually supportive relationships with my peers, partly because many have gone, and partly because we are all now simply too busy for the development of a social system. Thus I am likely to feel a sense of loneliness in the workplace if my need for social interaction is strong.

The result is liable to be withdrawal and increasing insecurity. Thus a vicious circle of insecurity is set up from which I cannot break out. I cannot break out, but I can lash out. If like many I respond to these circumstances by hitting back at the perceived cause of my unease, it is the organisation at which I am likely to strike. My sense of insecurity will limit my perceived power to act so my attack will be subtle. I will, in Bob Mager's apposite phrase, 'fire the company'. I will withdraw my cooperation when I dare, and when I dare is likely to be when it's most obviously needed.

Handling redundances

Suppose that I am not the survivor of a headcount reduction, but one of the rapidly growing new breed of 'disposable workers'. I have no long-term relationship with the business. Few perks, no pension, no planned future for me: I am there to be used when required, and at all other times it is assumed that I will find myself another employer – or go hungry. The Henley study referred to in the next chapter suggests that for the majority of us to belong is vital. We need to feel wanted. If I have no reason to feel loyal towards my short-term employer, I am likely to feel that I am an undeserving victim of the system, and the system to me is most immediately represented by those companies who use me when it suits them and condemn me to insecurity when it doesn't.

I may have remained at the lower levels of the hierarchy, but similar arguments would pertain at every level. The simple fact is that if we create feelings of insecurity and low self-esteem we will demotivate.

So, given the financial realities of survival in today's, and almost certainly, tomorrow's economy what are we to do within the context of internal and external pressures (Fig. 3.2)?

If delayering, downsizing or any other euphemism for firing people in considerable numbers has occurred or is to occur we need to think it

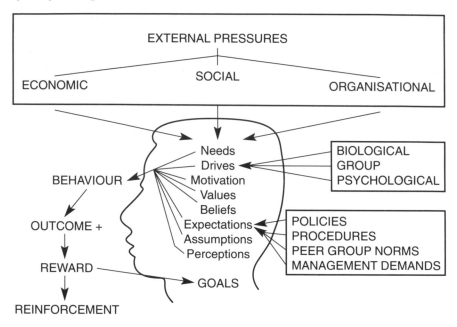

Figure 3.2 Man is a wanting animal

through. We must treat those who are leaving in a way which demonstrates that they are still worthy of our concern. We must offer those who choose or need to go on working more than outplacement. We must provide them with alternatives and we must help them to assess which alternatives are right for them. We must consider families and their needs. Those who find that their breadwinner is no longer employed are certain to be subject to stress and even those families where the time has come for happy retirement may need professional help to adjust to loss of status and activity. Spouses often need help in optimising the opportunities which exist for a richer married life when all that they see is a partner constantly 'under their feet'.

To make it clear to those that remain that old employees are truly valued, activities which have a bottom line value to the organisation should be designed so that separated and remaining management and employees do them together – such as meaningful training. In my own scheme which goes under the name of 'Outpacing Outplacement' state-of-the-art sales training serves the purpose of showing the world that all employees are valued. The remaining management and sales teams learn advanced influencing techniques to ensure that the company can continue to prosper while their ex-colleagues sit side by side with them learning how to promote themselves to prospective employers, building their saleable skills or how to sell their services or products as newly self-employed entrepreneurs.

Figure 3.3. indicates how redundant staff can be trained for life 'on the outside If this all sounds rather an expensive way of firing people, consider how expensive it may be to do it badly. To do it right may cost a few thousand pounds for each ex-employee, to do it wrong may just cost the company through low morale.

Building up the remaining work stuff

Whatever else one chooses to do, one thing is essential. Those left behind are a new team with a new task regardless of how long they may have been with the company. As such their primary need is early success. Success will build their confidence, cohesion and commitment as nothing else will. I shall have more to say about this when we examine team building and leadership.

Assessing motivation levels

Having established some of the factors which can damage motivation it may be useful to consider how motivated your team is likely to be. Figure 3.4 is a simple model which I have used with considerable success as a consultant and as a line manager. It brings together the work of several behavioural scientists, mainly Lawler and Porter. It has four simple steps.

1. Low motivation. If the group see no reward for them there will be no motivation to perform. If the group see only rewards which they do not value they will not be motivated to perform. If they see only rewards which others believe they 'ought to want' they will not be motivated.

2. No motivation. If the group values the potential reward, but sees little chance of achievement there will be no motivation. Often it is seen as being better not to try than to fail.

3. Demotivation. If the effort required to achieve the reward is seen as insignificant in relation to the value of the reward, oddly enough people will not bother to try. Similarly effort for too little reward will seldom motivate.

4. High motivation. Motivation is high when:

– rewards are apparent, available and achievable;

– targets are challenging, but possible;

– when the effort required to achieve is perceived as being consistent with the value of the reward.

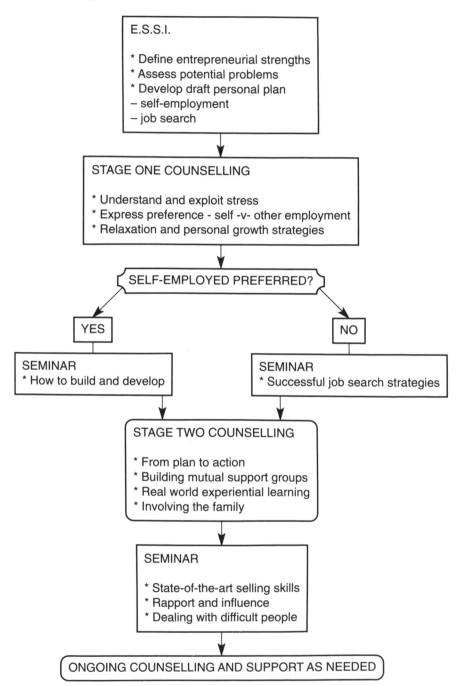

Figure 3.3 Outpacing outplacement: new career-building support programme

GROUP MOTIVATION TEST

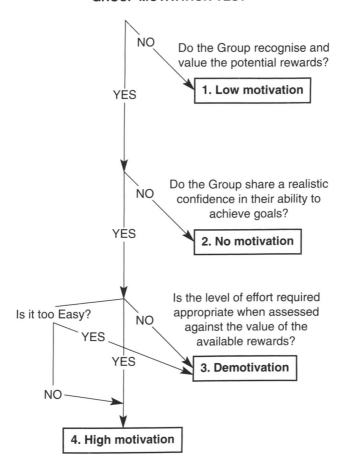

Figure 3.4 Motivation and reward: level assessment

JOB PURPOSE AS A MANAGEMENT TOOL

As argued above the current belief in empowerment will founder unless those who are to be newly empowered are released in a disciplined environment. In the long run that discipline must become a committed self-discipline. Bob Mager's ideas have been around for a long time now. They have stayed around, unlike many fads and fancies, because they work. They work for the individual and they work for the organisation. They lead people to monitoring their own performance and aspiring to the highest standards.

Figure 3.5 indicates how they work. For every job in the organisation a **job purpose** is established. This is a simple expression of the outcome for which the organisation is prepared to pay a wage or salary. For example, car sales-persons in a retail automotive dealership may have as a job purpose cars sold. In the ultimate that, and that alone is what they are paid for. Similarly an air-line pilot is paid to ensure a safe flight. Nothing is as important as the safety of passengers, crew and aircraft, so that is a valid job purpose.

The job purpose can only be established by management and should always be reconsidered when an existing job becomes vacant. It may be that the required outcome changes over time or even ceases to exist. Reconsideration can be of value when the job is to be filled. The employee should not be involved in establishing his job purpose or the definition will be distorted by the employee's preferences, but the employee should play a major role in the next phase.

Key elements are those things which must be done in order that the job purpose be achieved. They exclude by definition and by practice additional extras, no matter how attractive to employee or manager. They concentrate attention on doing the right things which as Drucker has been known to remark is more important than doing things right. Most jobs would have no more than six or seven true key elements. For my car salesperson they would be:

- prospects contacted;
- customers met and made comfortable;
- customer needs assessed;
- product presented;
- product demonstrated;
- objections handled;
- sale closed.

Similarly the airline pilot may have:

- flight planned;
- flight plan lodged;
- crew instructed;
- take off procedures completed;
- take off;
- contact with air traffic control maintained;

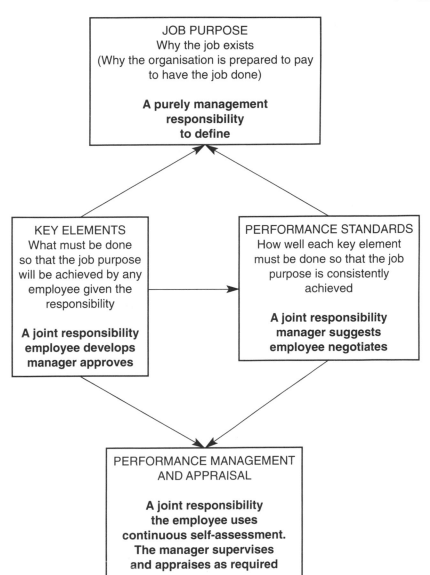

Figure 3.5 Job performance management – empowerment

Note: the requirements of the job, and not the strengths or weaknesses of the job holder, dictate the key elements and the standards to which they must be performed. Whether the job holder is a new hire, an old hand or a clockwork mouse, the key elements and the job performance standards for the same job remain the same.

- flight path maintained;

- landing;

- taxiing to indicated gate and brakes applied.

Establishing key elements which are relevant to the job purpose is the joint responsibility of manager and subordinate. Limiting the key elements to the essential activities which make a significant contribution to the satisfaction of the job purpose does not mean that the individual is expected to do nothing else. Additional contributions to the attainment of the goals of the organisation are encouraged, recognised and rewarded, but by focusing attention on the requirements of the job purpose in isolation as the esssential requirements of performance reduces the likelihood of more congenial activities being given precedence over more important ones.

Thus, if I may stay with my automotive dealership, a car cleaner also has the responsibility for collecting road tax discs. His job purpose is 'cars cleaned', but riding into town in a new demonstrator, perhaps doing a little shopping, and then collecting a few tax discs is probably preferable as an activity to washing and polishing cars. The consequence is that it is not unknown for the car cleaner to prioritise tax disc collection at the expense of the firm's ability to provide their customers with clean serviced cars at the agreed time. The employee must understand that trips to town are secondary to the responsibility for car cleaning and must not be allowed to put at risk the attainment of the purpose for which he is employed.

Job performance standards are the quantifiable part of the system and the assurance that quality requirements are met. Again it is essential that the subordinate and his manager take shared responsibility for establishing complete, essential and measureable standards.

The job purpose, key elements and job performance standards are always driven by the needs of the job and not by the experience or skills of the individual. If the same job were to be done by a newcomer, an experienced hand and a clockwork mouse all three elements of the performance management system would be identical.

Allowance is made in **job performance appraisal** for lack of experience, training or other acceptable factors, but the standards are the standards. If they are not being met today it is again the joint responsibility of the manager and subordinate to ensure that they are met in the near future. Figure 3.6 shows a typical job performance appraisal worksheet.

Remember, every employee (and that includes every manager at every level) is entitled to:

JOB PERFORMANCE APPRAISAL WORKSHEET			

Job purpose: _____   Date of appraisal: _____

Name of job holder: _____

Appraised with (manager): _____

Key elements	Necessary job standards	Actual performance	Reasons for discrepancies and agreed actions

Figure 3.6 Job performance apprasisal worksheet

- Know what is expected of him;
- Work in an environment free of task interference;
- Receive feedback which is accurate, timely and job-related.

Experience shows that the introduction of this system of job performance management leads to increased self-confidence, commitment, self-discipline and accelerated personal growth. It is the ideal pre-cursor or companion to a policy of empowerment.

POTENTIAL PITFALLS OF PEOPLE MANAGEMENT

- Assuming that what motivates me will necessarily motivate you.
- Failing to relate rewards to performance.
- Failing to provide rewards at a time when they will be firmly linked in the recipient's mind with the detail of performance.
- Underestimation of the power of either tangible or intangible rewards.
- The long-term use of fear as an agent of change.
- Failure to identify frustration and failure to provide either a solution or an outlet.
- Basing job performance management on standards rather than goals.
- Trust given too early to the immature.
- Trust withheld from those who have earned it.
- Boxes to tick and interviews which are one-way 'telling sessions'.
- A grossly simplistic view of human behaviour.
- Inconsistency of leadership style which is based less on an understanding of the needs of the task to be done and the people involved than it is on what management believe that they can 'get away with' in today's circumstances. Thus leadership fluctuates from autocratic to *laissez faire* on the winds of change.
- Penalising performance by moving the goal posts.

4 BUSINESS PROJECT TEAMS AND TEAM BUILDING

'Team building will depend on participation of all kinds, feedback on the assessment of output, a sense of fun and excitement.'
Francis Kinsman

'Elaine Garzarelli, Queen of the Quants, uniquely predicted the market crash of 1987 by working entirely alone analysing data.'
Robert Heller

In the company of the near future, teams will come to be viewed, of necessity, in a somewhat different light than they are today. The current view is that teams mean synergy (co-ordinated action), and synergy in turn means results, which leads to the assumption that if the secret of team building could be found, all problems would be solved by committed and synergistic activity. Sadly it is not that simple.

IN-BUILT REACTIONS TO TEAM WORK

As Amanda Sinclair has convincingly shown, not all people work best in teams. There are many who, in isolation, splendid or otherwise, perform near miracles of output, while there are others for whom, according to a recent report by the Henley Centre, team interaction is important:

> *'Occupation remains highly important in defining how people view their status in society and their relationship with others. And as the physical interaction with other people in the workplace is an important aspect of this self definition, they are unlikely to want to be isolated from it on a permanent basis.'*

So we have a potential conflict between the simplistic, team-building solution which seeks to incorporate even the maverick into teams in which their performance will be at best below par and at worst disruptive, and the irresistable economic logic which will lead to increased use of outworkers, telecommuters and New Temps, many of whom will be excluded from the decision-making process and will long for the warmth and security of the social group. How are we to address this potential minefield?

The short answer is threefold. First the manager must have a clearer understanding of what really happens in groups as opposed to what too many trainers, academics and consultants believe happens. Second managers must carefully address the feelings and needs of individuals whom they seek to develop into groups. **The loner** must be recognised and his special needs respected. This does not mean that the loner has no part to play in the success of teams. Frequently success is dependent on the maverick's unique and timely contribution, but management must find ways of allowing the individualist to come into the team, make his contribution and then return to the solitude which he craves. The third idea is even more contentious and I am likely to be accused of being sexist by the female reader for a degree of stereotyping, while I will be castigated by those motivated by machismo for daring to suggest that the feminine approach has much, indeed most to offer in the new world of teams.

Female logic

Recent research in the psychology of the sexes raises questions and concepts which are likely to be of increasing value as the post-industrial society emerges. People need the freedom to be individuals and everywhere they are forced into teams while, paradoxically, those who need the company of others are being required either not to belong at all in any meaningful sense, or increasingly to belong at a distance. So where does the sex factor come in?

It comes in through differences in communication style between men and women. In the jargon of the trade, women communicate to build symmetrical relationships while men seek to clarify and establish asymmetries between people. Let me define my terms before we get into deeper water.

A **symmetrical relationship** is one which is based on equality. It is underpinned by the assumption that people are at base the same, connected and equal. It is characterised by mutual concern and a caring attitude each toward the other. Its goal is one of long-term mutual commitment, warmth and support. It is more characteristic of women than of men.

An **asymmetrical relationship** is one which is founded on a belief that people are unequal. People are perceived as being different and that difference is expressed in status, hierarchies and pecking orders. Communication is either a means of probing to ascertain relative status or, where relative status is clear, a way or reinforcing the differences which exist. Where sympathy exists between two people in an asymmetrical relationship it tends toward condescension rather than true concern. Such relationships are more typical in general of men.

Where a status difference exists it is inherently adversarial. He who has status, seeks to impose it, while he who lacks position looks for opportunities to rebel. The irony is that in corporations where it has been the norm to translate poachers into gamekeepers by promoting the rebel to management, the newly-appointed ex-street fighter is often seen to be the most assiduous in insisting on full implementation of the rules which he so recently treated with such scorn. Look at those in the field of industrial relations who have come from a militant union background for transparent examples.

Even in childhood the sex differences are reinforced. We admire the boy who shows 'leadership' while we are irritated by the girl who is perceived, for showing similar traits, as being 'bossy'. Research into children at play shows that while girls somewhat democratically, tend to make suggestions about games and activities, boys quickly establish pecking orders in which the powerful deliver their instructions to the gang.

In the post-industrial knowledge-based society there will be enhanced value in the feminine approach. Relationships at a distance will not include the same day-to-day opportunities for reinforcement (see the Paradigm of Exchange model) that sitting cheek by jowl offered. Feminine styles of communication will help to build long-term relationships resistant to distance and a decline in the obvious rewards of membership. Meanwhile the growth of the role and importance of the knowledge worker will create a new individualism and antipathy to status differences which will require a deep and genuine understanding to ensure that essential input to the team is timely and complete.

This depth of understanding without conflict is typical of the feminine approach to communication. But it will not, of course, be enough to undertake a sex change. Communication style will have to be sensitive to the needs of others, firmly based on the world as it is, and supported by carefully acquired and consistently practised skills. Those skills and the femine sensitivity which underlies them are the key to influence, and they are described in more detail in Chapter 9. The remainder of this chapter is concerned with clarifying, in greater detail, what really happens in teams. I suspect it may carry a few surprises for the trained and untrained alike.

TEAM BUILDING IN ACTION

There has been at times an overemphasis on a simplistic approach to team building. Here, as always, Mant's admonition to the manager to think 'what's it for' may be critical. The reasons why teams choose to come together have been well understood for decades. Teams elect to come together because it is their view, reinforced by experience that by working in concert they can achieve more than the sum of their efforts working as individuals. In short people work in teams because they see in team membership their best opportunities for success.

Trainers and management development gurus have, as usual a word for it, and that word is synergy. To build a team is seen as being the equivalent of providing the lever and fulcrum with which Archimedes claimed that he would move the earth. With certain well-defined reservations this approach to team building has much truth. But the manager who listens only to the siren whispers of the management developers without access to the exceptions is doomed to disappointment and possibly worse.

The first reservation has been most succinctly expressed recently by Amanda Sinclair. To the annoyance of some of the team building snake oil vendors she has pointed out the simple and inescapable fact that while some work most happily and productively in teams, others don't. To naïvely assume that the dragooning of such people into teams without regard for their emotional and practical preferences is to conduct an experiment in socialisation rather than to take intelligent managerial action. What is more it is an experiment that will fail partly because the longed-for socialisation will not occur and partly because the pressures created by the effort will lead to a dilution of the contribution which the individual would otherwise have been able to make as an individual.

A second and equally important reservation concerns the unsophisticated search for **consensus** (general agreement and unanimity) which has characterised some areas of management thinking in recent years. Participation in the decision-making process can lead to enhanced commitment in the implementation of the decision. It can also lead to bad and stupid decisions which will be an unmitigated disaster if implemented.

The situations in which consensus decision making is the best strategy are known. Their importance is growing because of the rapidly changing nature of the world. For example, the cost of poor decisions is growing, if anything, faster. Under these conditions it is essential to the well-being of the firm that the manager understands when participation is appropriate and when it is not.

The German example

German industry has probably the best record for team building and partici-pative management in the western world. Their success has enabled them to compete effectively in global markets against the might of America and Japan. Do not be misled by the well-publicised current problems facing Germany. Reunification has exacted an enormous price in terms of extend-ing enlightened employment law to the East where there is little or no chance of immediate economic return. Under such circumstances it is not surprising that some employers seek a temporary respite from what, in today's circumstances is an over-expensive policy. This does not mean that the policy is wrong. It has been shown to work for forty years. It will work again, but it will take time and in the short term the cost will be high. But Germany's record remains impressive regardless of present difficulties.

The Germans developed teams which direct their aggression consistently outwards towards competition. That is how they win. Yet does not the aver-age British or American manager tend towards seeing his German colleague as somewhat inflexible and autocratic? It looks to be something of a para-dox: inflexible creativity and autocratic industrial democracy.

There is often much to be learned from apparent paradox. The models in this section will help to develop and reinforce that learning.

The basic philosophy behind team building activities is to build winning teams. Any leader who fails to realise that his role is perceived by his fol-lowers as being simply one of enabling them to come out on top will not keep his position for long. But do winning teams go on winning? Consider, before turning to the models as an example.

Lessons to learn

IBM have been a winning team to a degree unprecedented since the war. They have established a position of world market leaders which should, by any common sense measure, have been unassailable and held more than sev-enty per cent of their chosen market sector in thrall. Yet in the past two years their billion dollar losses would have established world records were it not for the even more dramatic haemorrhages of General Motors. Now it seems that commentators are forming a disorderly queue to read their obituaries before Big Blue is even laid to rest, so certain are they that a funeral is in the offing.

I am grateful to a recent participant on one of my training seminars for drawing to my attention another unrelated recent example. In 1992 Leeds United won the British football championship beating Manchester United into a very creditable and close second place. In 1993 Leeds failed completely to repeat their successes of the previous year, while Manchester, buoyed up by their earlier near success made the relatively minor adjustments which enabled them to romp away with the championship.

Consider if you will the position of Great Britain in world trade. No one, will deny that our position has deteriorated from that of global dominance to something which approaches terminal decay. How has a country which has provided the world with so much slipped so far? I shall show through the models which follow that our dependence in the distant past on our Empire for profits and prosperity was simply too far extended. It was the ease of our continued success which carried the seeds of our decline. The same model will show that it may be Australia, rather than America, Japan or Germany from whom we probably have most to fear as the global economy moves from smokestack through science to information.

A model which covers the decline of corporate giants, international sports teams and great nations is powerful. Some might think it too powerful to have relevance to their needs. Let me set your mind at rest. This model is relevant to your needs if you limit your team activities to co-operating only with your nearest neighbour or even if you have declared so strongly in favour of individualism that, like Aspirin Lil, you 'Don't get on wiv nobody!'

Winner, loser or simply making progress, sometimes forward sometimes in reverse, these models will have explanatory and predictive power specific to your position.

EMPOWERMENT

Because of the increase in the strength of specialist knowledge and the growing recognition that business is holistic and integrated, the movement in many companies toward the empowerment of the individual will find its most powerful outlet in team behaviour. The individual will be empowered to make a valid, creative and viable contribution to the team.

To empower teams and enhance the opportunities for creative advance by individuals you need to:

1. Communicate and clarify wide-ranging goals which are widely spaced in time.

2. Clarify team membership so that people recognise themselves as being part of a team. (Japanese companies provide uniforms in the shape of the ubiquitous overall to emphasise that the team extends throughout the company.)

3. Select and specify tasks suitable for team applications.

4. Clarify and re-clarify team roles and short- and long-term goals.

5. Build cohesion through team success and recognition of that success. Develop a 'common language' through the use of common tools as well as through words and phrases. Create and sustain shared values, beliefs and expectations. Establish realistic and equitable group norms (rules and rituals) and maintain them over time.

6. Identify the external 'enemy'. Make creative and constructive use of 'us and them'.

7. Combine work and social activities to bring the team together in a range of activities. Hunt suggests that the manager might usefully take as his example the great world religions. They meet regularly for rituals and, on an average of four times a year they come together for a great festival. That has historically melded people into teams for which they are prepared to die. It is worth thinking about.

8. Be open with conflict. Foster 'working conflict' – 'no matter how good your team may be; we can do better' but beware of 'warring conflict' – 'you may think that you are smart, but we are smart enough to pull the rug from under you' whether you find it in the team or directed toward outsiders. (Competitive edge comes lastingly from excellence, not from sabotage.)

9. Continue to provide leadership. (See Chapter 5)

10. Remove de-motivators such as fear and insecurity from the working environment. (See Chapter 3)

11. Remember that all of the research over many years shows that group decision making is highly variable and potentially expensive. Use it when you *know* that it is the appropriate tool. (See models in this chapter)

Do all of the above points, do them well, and you will have completed a first step in building and sustaining winning teams. But you will have done nothing more than taken the first step. Great journeys may, as the proverb says, start with but a single step, but if they go no further no progress is made. The models which follow are designed to keep you moving in the right direction.

The siren of success

Let me try to whet your appetite a little further before all, as they say, is revealed. Success is a two-edged weapon. Without it teams are in trouble. With it they can carve out trouble for themselves.

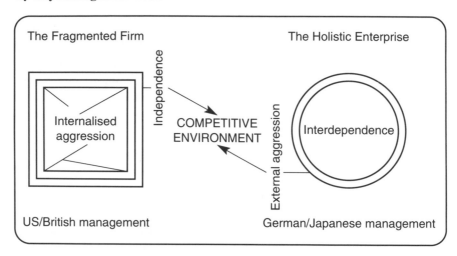

Figure 4.1 A 'level playing field' or 'killing field'?

Teams that fail turn their aggression inwards and ultimately self-destruct. Teams that succeed often lose the will to fight at all and in a highly competitive world there is no future in passive resistance. So if losers melt and winners freeze who ultimately is the winner? We must be alert to these pitfalls as we advance in our learning.

Team building

EXCELLENT Teams are developed and used in situations where a team approach is valid and the individual is respected both within and outside the team. Values and goals are shared and commitment to specific outcomes is high. The advantages and shortcomings of consensus are well understood and participative decision-making is used only in appropriate circumstances. Above all there is recognition that many perform relatively poorly in the team setting and have a strong preference to work alone. The contribution of the loner is valued and encouraged. Information is willingly and quickly shared with all who could benefit from it.

AVERAGE The organisation is driven by the belief that the team approach is to be favoured in all circumstances and much time, energy and money is spent on the study of group dynamics and the development of effective working teams. Organisational development focuses on team-building as does training. Occasional poor-quality decisions resulting from a policy of always seeking consensus are regarded as an appropriate price to pay for a growing cohesiveness within the firm. Teams are seen to hoard knowledge as if they believe in the old adage 'power flows to he who knows' and there are occasional signs of 'warring conflict' between groups.

UNACCEPTABLE No proactive approach to team building exists other than the departmental structure imposed by the organisation chart. A sense of 'us' and 'them' is encouraged as management express the view that 'competition keeps people on their toes'.

Project teams

EXCELLENT Team effort is solidly integrated around well-defined projects. Team members are selected so that they meld together as a team and bring a proper balance of skills and knowledge such that every member's contribution is individual and valued. Leadership is recognised in terms of both social and task parameters. Responsibility for the timely and complete delivery of the project lies with the team members, but they are not physically or psychologically separated from their other peers and the team becomes neither exclusive nor incestuous. Commitment to the success of projects is at a constant high level.

AVERAGE The effective use of project teams is diluted by the comingling of status and seniority needs with skill, knowledge and psychological traits indicative of effective membership. People are generally committed, but the politics of the situation put some restraint on the ability of the team to exploit the full potential of each member. Some project groups work well, others experience severe problems of group dynamics which can only be resolved by external intervention.

UNACCEPTABLE Individuals drafted into multi-functional workgroups tend to join as representatives of the operation from which they come. Hidden agendas and parochial concerns dominate the interactions and little real work is done. Seniority and status rather than skill or knowledge defines who does what and outcomes are unacceptably variable.

DESCISION BY CONSENSUS

A tricky area of team operation which is frequently over-simplified by those who ought to know better is the area of consensus. Management gurus leap to the barricades with cries of 'consensus', 'participation' and 'involvement' on their lips. Unsophisticated trainers offer consensus as a 'good thing' and what is more, they think that they can prove it. Can so many be wrong?

Unfortunately the level of 'proof' which is offered has its limitations. Consensus is an efficient and effective way of reaching decisions under certain very specific conditions. It is by artificially creating these limited conditions that trainers have the 'proof' which they desire. They are excellent exercises, I have used them myself frequently, but they are carefully and cleverly designed to create the one situation in which consensus is the best approach. I describe one such exercise in detail in Chapter 6.

The scenario is one in which a decision of some importance must be made where previous experience is largely or wholly irrelevant. Since there is unlikely to be a member of any training group who is an expert in moon exploration or desert survival this requirement is met by the exercise. The desired results are achieved with the consensus decision being better than the best individual decision. So far so good. In a rapidly changing business environment in which past experience of individuals becomes an increasingly unreliable guide to future action consensus has an important role to play. Where the relevant information is fragmented and its distribution through the team is uncertain, the importance of consensus is emphasised. But it doesn't end there.

Consensus is a time-consuming and expensive tool. It ought to be applied more on the basis of need than on the ideological convictions of any individual. What follows is a road map of consensus decision making which will be expanded when we consider decision making in Chapter 6.

Individual psychological profile

The traits of the team leader are an important consideration. If motivated by the effective use of organisational **power** or the need to build developmental and nurturing **relationships** the leader will find it relatively easy to promote and support consensus decision making beliefs. If the key motive of the leader is that of **personal achievement**, however, patience may well be exhausted by the length of the process and he/she may well find it difficult to accept any less than ideal group outcome. I strongly recommend all leaders to read and carefully consider the works by David McClelland listed in the bibliography.

The leader must also perceive that the level of risk implied by a group decision is sufficiently low to be acceptable. This usually means at the personal level that he has a high tolerance of risk and ambiguity.

Although the level of self-reliance of the leader can in theory be at any level, studies of **delegation** tend to suggest that the more self-confident the leader the more he is inclined to delegate. As with delegation, so with consensus.

The leader's **trust** in his subordinates and their ability to reach an optimal decision in the interests of the organisation without luxuriating in revenge cycles or hidden agendas must be high. The leader retains **accountability** for the outcomes of his group. Until he trusts their capacity and commitment he would be unwise to try consensus as a means of reaching important decisions. It is less a case of 'let my people go' than it is is of 'let my people go when they are ready – and they are ready when I say they are'.

The nature of the task

Ideally the decision to be made should be one in which the past is no guide to the future. Consensus works best in conditions of uncertainty and complexity. Simple decisions should be taken simply and economically and that usually means by one qualified individual.

Where a truly novel result is required there is always a strong case for consensus decision making. Many approaches to creativity, from brain storming to synectics work best when used by enthusiastic groups intent on having fun. (See Chapter 6 for further models of creative problem solving and decision making techniques.)

For the manager intent on the development of his team consensus decision making may be an appropriate tool. If the manager chooses to use consensus in this way, that is his business. Perhaps he/she should also make it their business to ensure that both team and leader are ready for the experience and that the risks to the organisation are acceptable.

Consensus decision making can be time consuming and frustrating in the extreme. The need is to reach an outcome with which every member of the team can happily live and that requires involvement, patience, sensitivity to the feelings of others, but perhaps most of all commitment to the success of the team and the organisation. Without that commitment attempts at consensus can be little more than an expensive route to chaos, parochialism and revenge for real or imagined past wrongs.

Location of essential information

The quality of any decision is dependent on the accuracy and relevance of available information. Sometimes that information is widespread within the group and, in situations of genuine novelty, even the holders of information may be uncertain of the value of what they know, think or believe. Where this is true you have the ideal situation to justify the expenditure of time and energy which is necessary in seeking consensus.

A check list for consensus decision making is provided in Chapter 5 (Fig. 5.4). Every tick in the first column of answers is an indicator that consensus should be avoided, each mark in the second suggests that consensus may be a significant contribution to team building and decision making.

If what I have written has made you wary of consensus in situations where it could be inappropriate I am delighted. If I have put you off moving toward developing the environment in which consensus is a tool which is applied with regularity and confidence I have done you a disservice. Consensus, as I have said before, will have a growing importance in an age of rapid change. My concern is that it should not be tried in situations where it is bound to fail and, having failed, be rejected. Harold Wilson tried an untimely experiment in consensus politics. It led directly to inaction and economic decline, and later to Thatcherism and economic extremes. Since empowerment will be an essential attribute of the organisation of the future, its structure alone will be enough to dictate a role for consensus. The planned and evolutionary move toward appropriate consensus is that important.

HOW TEAMS ARE MADE

To investigate the development of teams the simplest model of all is the smallest possible team. Two people who, from time to time, act co-operatively toward the achievement of a shared goal.

The psychological model of relationships known as the Paradigm of Exchange states that any relationship between individuals will be maintained only so long as the cost of maintenance is less than the rewards inherent in the exchanges. In simple language that means that you and I will continue to get on well together for as long as we both get more satisfaction than pain from the relationship. Figure 4.2 demonstrates the concept in a simple work situation. This rather simple psychological theory is basic to the growth of teams. Work teams come together for a simple and singular reason. They want to win. In order to enjoy success they are prepared to accept the costs in the sense of rules and norms, some loss of personal identity and recognition and loss of freedom to go it alone. That means that the reward is critical to the ongoing cohesion of the team – success must be directed. It must be focused on the attainment of shared goals within a framework of shared values, but even that is not all.

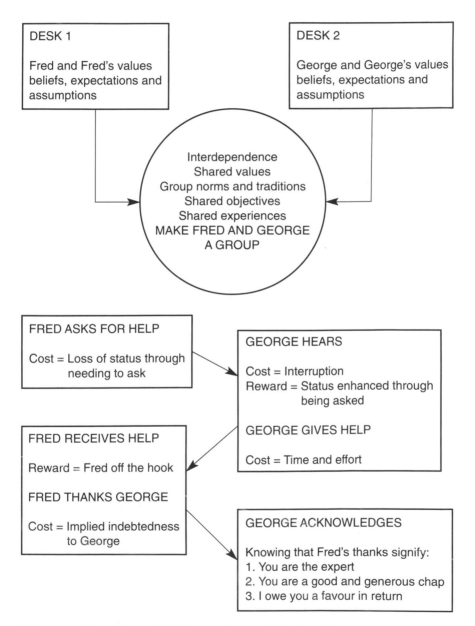

Figure 4.2 Paradigm of Exchange theory of relationships

THE POWER OF WINNING

If teams come together in order to enjoy success, then the more success the better the team – yes?

Well yes, but... If a winning team is constantly challenged by new situations, maintains a high level of creativity and avoids the trap of thinking that the new situations are really 'just like' the old then there is no reason why it should not go on winning indefinitely. As it continues to win it will continue to grow in cohesion, warm personal relationships and recognition by all members that they are part of a team. It will be confident, committed and effective in all predictable situations. Unfortunately research suggests that it usually doesn't work that way. Teams tend to approach a new task as if it were a previous one repeated. They will believe that they have the winning formula and will apply that formula to the new task. It isn't their fault, its a minor law of biology. If we see a partial cue that says 'remember me, my presence indicates that this is how it is', we cease looking for information and swing into action. It saves a lot of time and it is hard-wired into us. It makes us victims of snake oil salesmen and creatures of habit. Biologists call it the 'click-whirr response'. Click – there goes that cue again, whirr – this behaviour always works in situations such as this. If the differences are small enough and unimportant enough the old behaviour will serve us well. As it serves us it becomes more deeply entrenched. When we really need to change we truly believe that we know best and suddenly we are another Bedford Truck – out of business.

Now losing teams tend to melt. As a trainer and consultant I have to do very little to witness examples of this by the score. In the training situation all I have to do is to make some scathing remarks about a piece of work, for example a drawing taking about half an hour to complete and the team breaks up before my eyes. Not immediately perhaps: before attacking each other they strike out at me, but I rarely have to hold out against them for long before one member attacks a colleague. With the first internal schism the floodgates open. Bickering and dissent become the order of the day.

So if losing teams melt and winning teams are in danger of freezing we ask ourselves again, are there any certain long-term winners? If you want certainty I am sorry to have to tell you that research and experience are against you. You can, however, place a fairly safe bet. In most business situations the team that comes a close second is the team to watch. Their achievements in getting to second place can be presented as a victory thus building cohesion and confidence. The fact that they are still aware that they have some distance to go, helps to keep them flexible in their thinking and flexible thinking is an important tool in moving up on the rails. Of course when they finally get their noses in front there is the problem of keeping

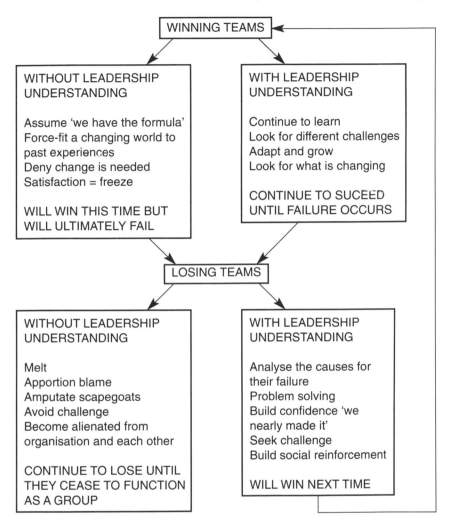

Figure 4.3 Winning teams freeze, losing teams melt

them there, but since their winning formula has been flexibility they stand an excellent chance of valuing creativity well into a challenging future. With apologies to Bob Townsend, those who are second may or may not try harder, but what they often do is to try smarter – and if they can maintain that smartness they can go on winning.

So if you have a winning team right now, or a losing team that you are anxious to get into the winner's enclosure, try to get them both to think of themselves as being a close second runner – that way you can win and keep on winning – indefinitely.

Strong teams and troubled meetings

There is a strong cultural belief that really strong individuals tend to be gentle. In society it is often true because large and strong children are under considerable pressure from parents and teachers to restrain their potentially destructive exuberance and strength. With groups things are different. Winning teams have a tendency to believe that their success gives them the right to dominate others. Losers, on the other hand, seek their salvation in an attempt to knock the winners off their perches. Like the foes of the gun-fighter heroes in the legends of the west they are as likely to try back-shooting as they are a frontal assault. Thus the venue of the most ordinary business meeting can become a gladiatorial arena (Fig. 4.4).

In inter-group meetings representatives of any team may see themselves as delegates who have been given the responsibility to win for their side. Whether it is the winning team sallying forth to do a little more empire building on the back of recent success, or the loser with a hidden agenda to pull the rug out from under the others at any opportunity, each has the clear choice. They can return to the group as a hero or a traitor. A hero is one who has, for preference, bloodied the enemy or, at worst, protected the narrow interests of his team. A traitor is one who has bowed to the needs of others, including the needs of the organisation as a whole, and has sacrificed narrow interest to the benefit of the whole. Figure 4.4 demonstrates this scenario.

Many deny that this happens or, to be more accurate they concede that it is typical of others, but fail to see it in themselves. The danger of hidden agendas is that they remain hidden, and are even denied by those who exercise them. Revenge cycles are easier to spot, but they may be difficult to trace to an ancient wrong, perceived as a wrong only through the distorting lens of self-interest. If male communication is, as psychology is suggesting with increasing force, aimed at probing relative status, informal and, from others' point of view, undeserved status is likely to be subject to all the probing which is going.

Informal status relationships are a major problem for organisations. An organisation is, by definition, a planned and integrated structure designed to achieve shared goals. No part of the organisation has no contribution to make. All contributions are essential, and where all are essential, none is more essential than another. It is a logical fallacy to argue that a sales department is more important than finance, or finance is more important than production while they all exist. When human resource management is truly less important than research and development it is because human resource development no longer has a role. If and when that moment comes get rid of HRM. Meanwhile maintain a true democracy between functions and teams.

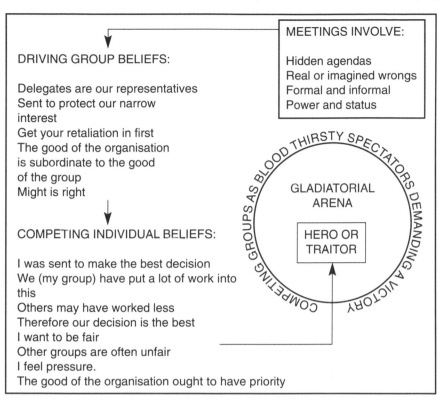

DRIVING GROUP BELIEFS:

Delegates are our representatives
Sent to protect our narrow
interest
Get your retaliation in first
The good of the organisation
is subordinate to the good
of the group
Might is right

COMPETING INDIVIDUAL BELIEFS:

I was sent to make the best decision
We (my group) have put a lot of work into
this
Others may have worked less
Therefore our decision is the best
I want to be fair
Other groups are often unfair
I feel pressure.
The good of the organisation ought to have priority

MEETINGS INVOLVE:

Hidden agendas
Real or imagined wrongs
Formal and informal
Power and status

BLOOD THIRSTY SPECTATORS DEMANDING A VICTORY

COMPETING GROUPS AS

GLADIATORIAL
ARENA

HERO OR
TRAITOR

Figure 4.4 The trouble with meetings

This is easier to say than to do. It has been recognised for many years that in the average organisation any group which initiates work for another is perceived as being more important – often with disastrous consequences. One of the great contributions of Deming to the effective conduct of busines within organisations is the concept of the internal customer which should sound the death knell of the status hierarchy. If each group sees all other groups as 'customers' then everybody is valued for their contribution and all are treated with respect.

One temptation in an organisation which is perceived as having winning and losing teams is that of giving the winning team jurisdiction over the losing. It is assumed that if the winning team absorbs the loser the latter will improve its performance as a result of the guidance of those who are perceived as 'having the formula'. Sadly this seldom works for at least three reasons. First the boss of the winning team usually has neither knowledge of, nor interest in, the working needs of his new acquisition. Second, teams are both self-indulgent and exclusive, none more than the winners of the moment, and they close ranks against outsiders whom they see as being foisted on them. Third, the members of the absorbed losers now really feel like losers. They have lost their previous identity and have become a second class satellite of the team which they are expected to emulate. If your Marketing Director does such a great job in marketing that you are tempted to give him responsibility for an ailing Research and Development operation, think very carefully about it. You may damage your winners while achieving little in your attempt to bring your losers up to par.

Refuse to have losers in your operation. Encourage and reward constant attempts at improvement by all and treat your losers as close seconds moving up on the rails as often as you realistically can.

A note on aggression

Konrad Lorenz sees aggression, on flimsy evidence, as an inescapable behavioural trait of humanity. Competition is, however, something which most of us enjoy. When we are denied the opportunity to compete with others we compete with ourselves.

Some years ago a group of behaviourists, smarting under the unfair label of 'rat psychologists', devised an experiment to compare rat and human behaviour. In behaviourist experiments rats have frequently been taught to run mazes for prizes of food. By scaling-up a rat maze and using cash to reward human subjects it was possible to conduct maze-running experiments simultaneously for rats and humans. The humans and the rats duly ran their mazes, collected their rewards and the experiment came to an end. Rats were removed to their cages and people were told that the experiment was over. The rats apparently accepted the news with equanimity, the people went on running. The human subjects were thanked for their efforts and reminded that the experiment was over, but the people went on running. Finally the laboratory was locked and access was barred to the human subjects. They broke in and went on running. This slightly grotesque farce is sometimes used to make exaggerated claims about the tenacity of reinforced behaviour. (A bird trained to peck at a coloured disc for a reward will continue to do so up to three million times after the reward is withdrawn.) I prefer a more human and simpler explanation. I suspect that the people involved saw a challenge in being able to run the maze in ever shorter times and, for as long as the challenge remained were keen to compete if only against themselves.

Side with Lorenz and the ethologists if you will and think in terms of aggression, or stay with my more muted concept and call it competition, but whatever you decide expect competition and plan accordingly. Internal competition is fine, if and only if it can be kept at the level of working competition. The evidence is, however, that keeping it there when you have losers who are hurt is difficult. As Fig. 4.1 shows, Japanese and German firms identify external targets and channel aggression toward them. As the mouthwash advertisement says – 'It's still working!' Try it!

PITFALLS OF TEAM BUILDING

- The team becomes divorced from the organisational goals. It creates its own rules while bending or breaking those of the organisation. It denies access to 'outsiders' even when desperately short of people and resources. It tries to cope with its own internal and often limited means regardless of circumstances. And it becomes jealous in the protection of information which it holds, denying access to that information to the rest of the organisation. It begins to believe that it can succeed outside the objectives, strategy, rules and philosophy of the company.

- Consensus is sought for political and ideological, rather than for process, reasons.

- Winning teams may be allowed to freeze and losing teams may be allowed to melt.

- Either task or socio-emotional leadership may be abdicated by the leader allowing informal leaders to emerge. Where competing informal leaders seek to impose their influence on the group the team may split into warring groups.

- Conflict is ignored, underplayed or mismanaged.

- The team identity is too vague. Structure is too loose and membership fluctuates without visible or credible reason.

- The superordinate purpose of the team and the contribution made to total organisational goals is underemphasised.

- There is insufficient social interaction through 'get-togethers'.

- The team contribution is unrewarded and unrecognised.

- Team building is not perceived as being important to the company, but is played at by a management who see the team as another opportunity for manipulation.

- A status heirarchy which contradicts the company's formal structure exists.

● Conflict within and between teams is fostered by a management which believes that through conflict comes performance. It does, but if and only if, the conflict remains at the 'working' level. 'Warring conflict' readily replaces 'working conflict', usually at the instigation of the losers, and invariably reduces standards.

5 LEADERSHIP IN A RAPIDLY CHANGING WORLD

For the last four or five years the word 'empowerment' it seems has been on every guru's lips. Such has been the pressure to clamber on the same band-wagon wearing a different costume that other words have been coined including the awkward but ingenious concept of 'disimprisonment'.

Manz and Sims in their book *Superleadership* define the superleader as 'one who leads others to lead themselves' putting another word into the jargon lexicon.

LEADERSHIP IDEALS

It all sounds wonderful. It is as if a whole world of self-motivating and com-mitted people are out there, simply waiting to be set free so that they may most effectively and joyfully put their myriad talents to productive use. It sounds wonderful, but is it true?

The answer as usual has to be that it all depends how you look at it. If you believe as some appear to that all that management has to do is to let go and release a flood of creativity and commitment, then common sense, careful research and probably your own day-to-day experience are against you. All of the reliable research of which I am aware suggests that a simplistic and sudden move toward the new dawn of an organisational democracy is likely to lead to disaster of one form or another.

Suppose, for example that the workgroup that you choose to 'release' are relatively immature. By this I simply mean that either they have not worked together successfully on enough challenging projects to have built a strong sense of mutual trust; or that the task is changing in a rapidly changing envi-ronment: or that membership of the group is fluid; or that the group has a new, or relatively new, leader. Any of the foregoing makes a group imma-ture, but there is more.

It may be that the group have shared success in a range of challenging assignments. They may trust, respect and like each other. The leader may be well established and may have contributed considerably to the success which the group has shared. Membership of the group may have been unchanged for a long time. We may have here the ideal task force superbly led. Is this a case where it is time to 'let my people go'?

Not if the leadership has hitherto been strong, charismatic and successful. Not at least without a good deal of planning and a careful strategy.

The reality

Let's look at what happens in real life rather than in an academic's fancy. Members of the group build expectations of the way that things are in their world. And in their world thus far leaders lead, followers accept leadership and it works. Any sudden withdrawal or change of leadership is likely to be seen as an abdication of responsibility by the leader. Possibly it will be portrayed within the group as a typical management ploy to get others to share their work without paying them for the added responsibility. At worst, the move to democratisation will be resisted, at best it will be suspect and may seriously reduce the level of trust which has been built through shared success. And as usual, that isn't all.

Within the group there will be those who, at various times have demonstrated that they have some, if not all of what it takes to be a leader. With the formal leadership reduced or taking a backseat, they will either push themselves, or allow themselves to be pushed to the position of informal leadership. The group is effectively back to stage one. They have a strong leader but it just happens to be the wrong person. Nothing significant changes for the group, but the erstwhile leader is now a person without a role and if they attempt to exercise their position they will almost certainly split a previously cohesive group into old leader and new leader camps.

That, believe me, is the best case scenario for a sudden letting go of leadership. Let's look at the worst case. Suppose that the group are, for the reasons given above, immature and unready for autonomy, what then?

The chances are that such a group will be completely demoralised by any sudden attempt at, to use another buzz word, participation. They will run around like headless chickens if they are not shocked into a state of catatonic inaction. They will need leadership and they will have insufficient knowledge of each other to know where to find it. They will feel threatened and worse, they will feel betrayed. Any inability to lash out at the leader or the organisation which has left them in this state is likely to mean that aggression is inwardly directed, either towards others in the group or towards themselves in an orgy of self-doubt, low self image and self-punishment. The group will cease for all practical purposes to be a group.

So am I arguing for the strong leader? For the never-ending application of autocratic control? No I am not. You see, people are complex and autocracy doesn't work for ever either. What is more, in a post-modern, information-driven society, despotism will be even less effective than it has been in its generally ineffective past.

Knowledge workers with highly specialised skills of crucial value to the organisation will not take kindly to autocracy. Outworkers will be serving at least two masters and will be able to play one off against the other if either client or domestic leadership styles cause them pain. Intrapreneurs will be able to withdraw their efforts along with their goodwill if they don't like the way that they are treated. Telecommuters will simply not be there to be watched, try as you might, technology will, whether you like it or not, free people to a degree unprecedented.

The practicality

So if giving people their freedom is fraught with organisational danger and keeping them under a tight rein will become even less effective in the future than it has been in the past, what is the manager to do? Fortunately the answer has been slowly emerging since the work of Tannenbaum and Schmidt, Bales and others in the late fifties. People must be freed, but they must be freed at a rate which is appropriate to their individual and group needs. They must be freed in a flexible way which enables the manager to evaluate the effectiveness of each step and adjust his strategy according to the outcome. People must individually and gradually experience the opportunities and satisfactions of increasing freedom and they must be rewarded for each step on the road which is successfully trod. Above all the implementation of empowerment must be supported by training, education, risk free practice and excellent communication. In short, freedom must be planned, implemented and monitored.

The demand for effective leaders has been met differentially but with often similar effect in America and Britain. Individualism in its manifold guises has dominated leadership thinking, and there is no surprise in this because leadership is an individualist concept. In America there has been a tendency to admire and promote the organisational infighter and then to try through simplistic management development strategies to turn the tiger into a pussycat. In Britain we have combined American ideas with our continued idolisation of the gifted amateur. We get the worst of both worlds as we stick firmly, despite all of the available evidence, to the notion that although we are happy to attend American-style seminars and will listen politely to the gurus, we know deep down that leaders are born, not made, and charisma will finally win out. Meanwhile our leaders, a near sublime combination of the urbane and the cutthroat either stay at home to complain that they would 'play the game' if only the playing surface might be levelled, or they migrate to the States where their buccaneering will reap its ultimate reward.

Elsewhere leaders are made, and sometimes even good leaders emerge.

LEADERSHIP IN ACTION

Let me try for a definition of leadership.

> *'Leadership is the ability to realise the potential in others and direct skills, knowledge and capabilities of a group toward pre-determined results. It does this through directing the group's attention toward means of fulfilling their needs which are identical to, or consistent with known objectives.'*

In short leadership is what leaders do. It is not what they are.

Such is the interest in leadership that there have been more than 5000 recognised major studies this century. The world has been hungry to learn about leadership, so I should have little difficulty in outlining what is known. Ironically, but not surprisingly, the evidence is clearer on what is not the case than what is. We know, for example, that there is little support for any trait theory of leadership. Psychology shows that good looks and an apparently strong personality may give the lucky individual a flying start, but unless the leader is able to bring the group early success, the charismatic honeymoon is of short duration, as political leaders tend to discover after the magic hundred days.

A theory which goes under the slightly disconcerting name of Idiosyncracy Balance suggests that we all get our equivalent of the hundred days, charismatic or not. In simple language it works like this. Have you ever seen someone raised to a position of leadership within an organisation and thought something along the lines of: 'He looks a total nerd to me, but I guess he must have something going for him or they never would have given him the job. Perhaps I had better give him the benefit of the doubt and just see what happens'?

That is Idiosyncracy Balance in action. You withhold judgement for a while and either the new leader performs and you concede that those above knew what they were doing after all, or he fails and your first impression is reinforced. Success or failure is a function of the leader's ability to bring success to the group. With each success his balance of credibility grows, with each bloody nose it declines. If he does nothing in an attempt to avoid risk, it slowly seeps away and he finally loses out, although he may have a somewhat longer tenure than some. Thus an inactive Prime Minister may last longer than an ineffective Chancellor, but their ultimate fate is likely to be the same. They are destined to eventually become leaders without followers.

So, not only is there little support for Trait Theory, the evidence is that what little advantage charisma brings to the fortunate few is short-lived and is balanced only by the determination of most observers to give even the more homely of us the benefit of at least their earliest doubts.

The psychological view of leadership

There is some evidence that those who don the mantle of leadership with greatest ease tend to come from a specific background. There is a positive imbalance of leaders who:

- Are the first born in their families with younger siblings to boss about from an early age;
- Are early achievers who cease to be motivated exclusively by the need for personal achievement and become effective within teams from a relatively early age;
- Display high energy;
- Are forward planners who know from an early age what they want and create flexible strategies to ensure that they get it;
- Are goal- rather than standard-directed in which the leader who seeks to get a 'first' at college perceives the high achievement as a goal rather than a standard and is therefore devastated by an upper second which is deemed a failure;
- Are politically sensitive and able to use group dynamics;
- Are self-reliant;
- Are field independent which means that they have the ability to extract the important facts or data from a broad and complex situation;
- Use internal rather than external frames of reference. That is they rely on their own judgement, only deferring to other's views when it is politically expedient to do so.

All of which adds to the credibility of the view that leadership is what leaders do, not what they are. By and large it is unsurprisingly the case that those who have had the greatest opportunity to practise the art or science of leadership in their lives tend to be better at it.

In a changing world, the detail of what leaders do becomes increasingly important. The upthrust of the individual who may not enjoy managerial or leadership status in the form of the knowledge worker means that the formal leader will be directing the work of those whose capacities and value to the organisation are at least equal to their own. The advent of telecommuting means that leaders are under a greater compulsion to get it right first time because the opportunities for overseeing activity and checking the effect of leadership will be few and far between. Simple 'carrot and stick' approaches can no longer work in a world in which the stick can't be wielded and carrots become prohibitively expensive. Yet the need for effective leadership is becoming greater not less as the only practical way to move hitherto dependent employees toward self-leadership and empowerment.

LEADERSHIP AND CREATIVITY

Back in 1954 Carl Rogers was considering leadership and creativity in tandem. Leaders of the future will need to demonstrate both areas of skill to an unusually high degree. He suggested that to perform both functions to optimal effect the individual must be:

- Open to experience and ready to learn from the now, rather than become a prisoner of the past;
- Self-reliant when it comes to evaluation and judgement rather than dependent on the approbation of others.

Ability to play the leadership game

In short the leader, and specifically the creative leader must be sensitive to the immediate and future situation and be ready to make and implement their own decisions. (Including the decision as to when to let others make the decisions.) In this the question ought to be asked: 'Does empowerment pay? Is there a bottom line justification for for "letting my people go"?' Tony Miller whom you will meet again in the chapter on training and development is devoted to measurement. His continuous monitoring of his company's empowerment programme to date shows that against an initial training investment of £55,149 the company received quantifiable benefits directly relating to empowerment of £980,000. This was in the first eighteen months and excludes the indirect benefits of 9 per cent increase in productivity with a 15 per cent increase in sales revenues and a reduction of absenteeism through sickness to less than 0.14 per cent, or one day in three years. Get it right and the returns are enormous, but getting it right includes measuring the results.

What it takes

Empowerment, or sharing responsibility, does not mean abdicating responsibility or abandoning the team to their own multifarious devices. It means a planned development of people's ability to make and implement decisions in an ever-widening range of situations. To develop people this way takes firm and resolute leadership. It requires leaders who:

- Retain a full understanding of what is happening;
- Set a clear, unambiguous direction for their teams, and ensure that people remain on course;
- Offer support, open doors and clear the way for action without taking over from those delegated to do the job;
- Make decisions which others cannot, either because of lack of time, information or knowledge;
- Continuously assess performance, reward progress and support individual and team development;
- Build trust through shared success and share information and knowledge whenever it is possible to do so.

In summary the role of the effective leader now and in the future will not be totally different from that of the best performers of past. Two things will be different, however, and they are critical. The leader in a post-industrial society will need to be more sensitive, more skilled and have greater understanding of the process than did any of his forebears. The second point is the bottom line of leadership for the nineties and beyond into the foreseeable future. The poor leader has, in the past and right up to the day before yesterday, been able to survive through the shrewd and impenetrable defences of bureaucracy, and spending more time protecting his backside than leading. Those days are over. Today's leader faces a scarcity of knowledgeable and potentially irreplaceable people who will not countenance the third rate from those in positions of power. Power is being eroded through the loss of control which was reinforced in smokestack industry by direct reporting, maintenance of sanctions and rewards and exclusive technical and organisational knowledge. Increasingly the leader will be expected to do nothing other than lead. Leadership is becoming a profession. From today the leader will succeed or fail by his specific leadership skills to a degree hitherto undreamed of. Those skills and their sensitive application are all that stands between the manager and the abyss.

Some proven planning aids follow which simplify the present and future situational analysis. I hope that you will be willing to use them in the interests of your development and survival.

Leadership style and behaviour

EXCELLENT The prevailing Leadership Style of the organisation is sensitive to the needs of the company, its culture, mission and goals, the expectations of the employees and the community and the needs of the management team themselves. There is flexibility in the face of a rapidly changing business and social environment, but the style is seen as being both consistent and fair because the response to change is timely and the evaluation of the situation is accurate. Managers take a pride in their leadership skills, are fully trained and are committed to life-long learning as the basis for unending improvement. Feedback on the effect of the evolving style is actively sought from subordinates, peers and superiors. Managers take the responsibility for being an exemplar of desired behaviours and are active and much-copied role models.

AVERAGE Managers are trained and have been supported in analysing and evaluating their preferred leadership style and its relevance to the job to be done, the work environment and culture and the needs of the work force. The established style is both a function of and a determinant of the organisational culture. Flexibility is limited to moving coherently along a continuum from 'Tell' to 'Delegate' as the situation and the assumed capability of employees appears to indicate. The Chief Executive serves as a role model and most members of the management team adapt and adopt styles consistent with his/her own.

UNACCEPTABLE Managers' leadership styles reflect only the idiosyncracies of the individual's comfort zone. Any consistency between style and the situation is purely fortuitous. Little concern exists other than to use managerial behaviour to emphasise differences in status and to impose the values of the formal heirarchy and ensure the strict adherence to rules, procedures and policies by all.

THE LEADERSHIP MODELS

In the post smokestack economy three things will be essential to the art of leadership. Consideration must be given to the total situation. The needs of the task, the organisational structure and the socio-technical system will have to be fully understood with a better than passing understanding of the external environment thrown in. The developing and changing needs of the people involved, not just the led, but also the leaders will have to be sensitively appraised and then related to the changing expectation of the customer. And finally the purpose of leadership, and therefore influence will need to change over time.

As has been argued above, knowledge workers will have, at least in their area of specialism, a higher capacity and a greater degree of knowledge than their leaders can aspire to. Telecommuters will be geographically removed from the centre and will not be subject to close monitoring. Intrapreneurs will have much to give to the organisation, but will be able to withhold their bounty if they feel bad about the way they are led.

This means that leadership will move ever further from competition for power and closer to skilled relationship building.

Rosalind Coward in her book *Our Treacherous Hearts* argues convincingly that women have traditionally left senior positions for domesticity and child-rearing to escape from the organisational demand to compete for status. The information-driven organisation will need its male leaders as well as its female to apply the feminine sensitivity and relationship-building skills to leadership. The models which I have chosen are not new. They are, however, those which have consistently offered the best route toward sensitive application of the right leadership style at the right time. I believe that they will continue to do so.

There has been a longstanding view that the best leaders are those who are seen to be firm but fair. To achieve this all that you need to be able to do is to be flexible and consistent at the same time. This is not the paradox it may appear to be. Only if you are flexible as a leader can your style be appropriate to all of the influences indicated above. Only if your style is invariably consistent with the changing situation as it unfolds will you be perceived as being consistent. It really is as simple as that. Have a range of skills available to you which enable you to get it right, first time every time, and they will say of your decisive and sensitive leadership that it is 'firm but fair'.

Forces at work in leadership

The team looks to the leader to bring them success. Tannenbaum and Schmidt saw success being intimately related to the ability of the leader to apply the style of leadership which was appropriate to what they called the 'three forces'. The forces in the environment, the forces in the group or work team and the forces in the leader himself.

Forces in the Environment

- What is the nature of the task?
  - simple or complex?
  - novel or routine?
  - enjoyable or disliked?
  - high profile or day-to-day?
  - high risk of errors?
  - high or low value outcome?

- What is the economic, social, legislative climate?

- What is the present work environment?
  - available resources?
  - current level of technology?
  - hierarchy, both formal and informal?
  - are there structural or cultural considerations which must be taken into account?

- What are the time considerations?

Forces in the Work Team

- Has the team enjoyed previous success in a similar task?

- Are the team an established workgroup?

- Have the team enjoyed autonomy in task management and decision making before?

- Do the team fully understand and share the goals?

- Are the team values implied in the task?

- Is the team ready for further development in autonomy and decision making?

- Have the team demonstrated commitment and the ability to meet deadlines?

Forces in the Leader

- Has the leader a track record of success with this team?

- What is the leader's preferred style or 'comfort zone'?
  - autocratic?
  - democratic?
  - laissez faire?

- Does the leader trust the group sufficiently to live with their outcome?

- Is the leader under time pressures?

On the balance of the above the team leader can decide on the appropriate leadership style for any situation, depending on the level of maturity, as in Fig. 5.1.

He may decide that it is appropriate to *tell* the team what to do. That is he can issue clear and complete instructions, set unambiguous goals and priorities and establish and maintain effective monitoring procedures. He may equally decide to use a *tell* approach in the interests of time, particularly in an emergency. To take an extreme example, if bullets are flying it is perfectly reasonable for a normally democratic leader to simply shout, 'Get your heads down' and, for the duration of the emergency, wave goodbye to democratic decision making in the interests of the general good.

A small move away from the autocratic end of the scale is achieved when the leader chooses to *sell* the decision. To ensure the commitment of the group the leader may decide that it is appropriate to spend some time convincing the team that there are benefits to them in doing what he wishes them to do.

Where the judgement and commitment of the team permit such an approach, the leader may decide on the best course of action and *test* the decision for group acceptance. It goes without saying that this approach is only available to the leader who is prepared to reconsider the original decision in the light of the response of the group.

Consulting the group means that a genuine period of consultation takes place and any outcome truly reflects the inputs of fact or feeling from group members. It is not an opportunity for a pretence of involvement to be followed by the implementation of the action which the leader had in mind from the beginning. People are very sensitive to such game playing and sooner or later they respond to it effectively.

The *join* approach is used where the leader has sufficient trust in the group to sit down with them as a first among equals to reach a truly democratic outcome. The effective leader is fully aware that this approach is costly in the expenditure of time and requires from him exceptional skills ranging from a degree of self-effacement to the ability to ensure that every team member has every opportunity to express his views in full. He must also be able to deal with the situation where one team member holds views which are at variance with those of the rest of the team and which are a bar to the achievement of consensus. The psychology of such situations is known and the effective leader controls the situation in such a way that the adverse possibilities do not materialise.

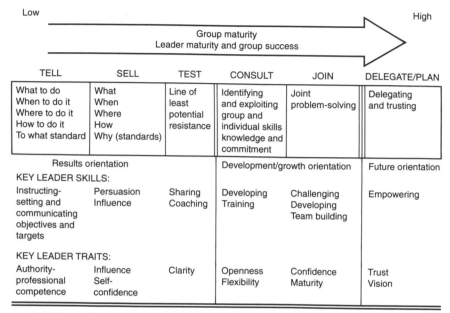

TELL	SELL	TEST	CONSULT	JOIN	DELEGATE/PLAN
What to do When to do it Where to do it How to do it To what standard	What When Where How Why (standards)	Line of least potential resistance	Identifying and exploiting group and individual skills knowledge and commitment	Joint problem-solving	Delegating and trusting
Results orientation			Development/growth orientation		Future orientation
KEY LEADER SKILLS:					
Instructing- setting and communicating objectives and targets	Persuasion Influence	Sharing Coaching	Developing Training	Challenging Developing Team building	Empowering
KEY LEADER TRAITS:					
Authority- professional competence	Influence Self- confidence	Clarity	Openness Flexibility	Confidence Maturity	Trust Vision

FORCES DICTATING/INFLUENCING STYLE

Figure 5.1 Situational leadership: progression with development of maturity

Handling deviation

Where there is a perceived deviant in the group, the individual holding the maverick opinion becomes the centre of interest. His views are listened to with care and are logically discussed. Should this discussion lead either to the group as a whole moving toward the deviant opinion, or the maverick being convinced by the group, all is well. The group regards the extra time and effort spent in reaching an outcome to be worthwhile because either their superior logic has been tested and has prevailed, or the deviant's creativity has led them to consider and accept a better outcome than would have otherwise emerged. Either way the deviant remains a valued member of the group.

Consider, however, what happens when logic fails to lead the group to a happy outcome. The first stage appears to be harmless enough. There is a period of *seduction* in which the deviant is offered inducements to persuade him to accept the group's view. In British and Australian groups, in which a clear sign of affection is the friendly insult, the whole group continues to make the deviant the centre of attention with a varied programme of attempted bridge-building and jokes at his expense. If this works the deviant will find that although his return to full group membership appears to be in a spirit of humour and without cost, there is tacit recognition that the next time he steps out of line the outcome will quickly degenerate to the next stage.

The third stage is one of naked *aggression* in which being the centre of attention is far from comfortable. Insults cease to be friendly and are openly intended to wound. By now the deviant has no realistic chance of persuading others to his view. He can only hold out or submit. If his choice is to submit all may appear to be fine. The insults and emotional pressure will cease and there will be often a good deal of tension release which will be expressed in a return to joking, although no longer necessarily at the expense of the former dissident. Some group members will noticeably not join in any joking. Now the deviant has really put the group to some trouble and, sooner or later, he will pay for it. Reason and seduction will be very shortlived the next time he steps out of line and he may well find that relations with some members of the group are strained even when he is assiduous in 'keeping his nose clean'.

The fourth and final stage is not to be even contemplated by any leader who wants to be at the head of an effective and cohesive group. Failure to return to the fold during the aggressive period closes all doors. The final stage is one of *amputation*. The deviant is out of the group now and forever. Organisational structure may indicate that he is a member of the team, but he will have no credibility, no opportunity to make a contribution and no action on the part of the leader will lead to his re-instatement.

I hope that this excursion into the psychology of deviance within a group is sufficient to convince the leader that in any situation occuring at the *join* stage, the key responsibility of the leader is to manage group dynamics so that the discussion remains at the logical, or at worst the *seduction* stage at all costs. If the cost is one of eventually silencing the deviant and losing the potential value of his contribution, then so be it. The alternative is so dire that it should not even be contemplated.

Empowerment is more than mere delegation, but delegation is a necessary precursor to empowerment. Many managers tell me that they find it difficult to delegate effectively. That is in one way hardly surprising. Effective delegation requires, in the early stages, the application of every style in the Tannenbaum and Schmidt repertoire. The following notes may be useful.

DELEGATION OF WORK

Delegation differs from mere work assignment in that it infers the transfer not only of the responsibility for completing the job, but also the authority to decide 'where', 'when' and 'how' the job is completed within the constraints of an agreed timeframe. It differs from empowerment in that it limits the decision-making authority of the delegatee to the prescribed task. None the less, delegation needs careful planning with planned communication. The following checklist will enable the manager to think through the best strategy for effective communication and control of delegation.

Thinking it through

To get a clear idea of exactly what ought to be delegated and avoid misunderstandings, consider:

- Why is it necessary to do this job?
- What problems will be averted by doing the job well?
- What skills and abilities does your chosen subordinate bring to the task?
- How much freedom are you prepared to allow?
- What benefits will the subordinate experience as a result of accepting this responsibility?
- How much time can you afford to commit to positioning, training and monitoring your subordinate during this assignment?

To relieve yourself of the need for supervision and control, consider:

- How will the subordinate know that the job is accomplished?
- What are the specific indicators of success?
- What specific results do you expect and require?
- What potential problems may arise?
- Which may be avoided?

- Which are unavoidable?

- What would be the danger signs should things be going wrong?

Since the employee may have as much work as they can carry, consider:

- What is the individual's normal response to stress?

- Which tasks can be re-assigned?

- What priorities and deadlines can be changed?

This is important, as it may avoid piling on the last straw by at least rearranging the load.

To avoid potentially costly errors, think about and note any effective and useful tips on how to do the job which your subordinate may not know about or may overlook.

The subordinate may have doubts or fears in their mind, so to prepare the way for a positive response plan how you may best introduce the idea of delegating the job:

- What benefits will come to the subordinate from taking this responsibility?

- What assurances or reassurances may be useful in putting the subordinate at their ease?

- What previous good performance is this an opportunity to recognise?

Making the assignment

When you have planned to delegate you still have to communicate effectively to your subordinate. When talking it through the following sequence will be helpful thus ensuring that your subordinate approaches the task in a positive frame of mind:

- Checking that no major concerns are uppermost in their mind;

- Thanking the subordinate for recent good performance;

- Explaining how this assignment fits with demonstrated skills and experience;

- Relating the assignment, where possible, to a specific objective or to known career plan which is important to this individual.

Provide all necessary background understanding by reviewing those current conditions which are relevant to the job.

Give the assignment

- Explain the task;

- Spell out the level and limitations of the authority delegated;

- Specify any constraints on freedom to act;

- Clarify the level of authority;

- Detail your own role as supervisor of this project;

- Specify the required results;

- Warn about any known potential problems;

- Pass on any useful hints or tips without implying that you are infringing the subordinate's freedom to do the job their way.

Ensure through appropriate feedback that you have made your intentions clear. Close the discussion after making it clear that you are available for advice or support if needed.

LEARNING FROM THE EXPERTS

Ken Blanchard has achieved fame and fortune through the series of books *The One Minute Manager*, *The One Minute Salesman*, etc. With his partner, Hersey, he designed and developed the approach to leadership which I am convinced will remain the foundation of effective influence in the information society. Their approach has many parallels with the work of Tannenbaum and Schmidt, but the devil, or in this case perhaps the angel, is in the detail. I would like to describe that detail in practical terms.

Hersey and Blanchard's approach is close to that of Tannenbaum and Schmidt's in several important respects. They share the view that the effective leader must be able to call upon a wide repertoire of flexible leadership styles. They also have in common the fact that they take a pragmatic rather than an ideological viewpoint. No style is seen as being intrinsically better than any other. Each is 'good' to the extent that it is right in the light of the parameters of the total situation. Appropriateness and adaptability are the measures of the value of any style and those measures can only be applied if the situation is sensitively and accurately assessed.

Where the four great thinkers begin to diverge is in how the situation is to be assessed. Hersey and Blanchard focus attention on one of the three forces. They suggest that the situation is best analysed through the maturity and track record of the team. Task, leader and team dynamics are all brought together in their thinking. For example if the task is a new one, it is new *for this team.* If the leadership of the group changes, it is the potential effect of that change on the team and its performance which is important.

As with every important thinker about leadership in recent years Hersey and Blanchard see growing maturity and autonomy as a function of success. To put it at its most basic, a team becomes capable of assuming more responsibility as a direct result of their track record; the relationship is not, however, a simple linear one. Early success is not a justification for early license.

Start at the beginning

Assume if you will a new group, facing a new task under the direction of a new leader. The group need is for success. If they achieve success they will cohere and move forward in confidence. The leader needs success to reinforce his leadership of this group and to deny access to any potential rivals in the form of informal leaders. The organisation requires success – the achievement of goals within the overall strategy is why functional groups are formed.

High task, low social

It really does not matter too much whether the team like each other or enjoy each other's company at this stage. That, like so much else will come with success. Given that there are a limited number of hours in the day and that focused action is most likely to be effective action, the leader should concentrate his attention on the task and accomplishment. Which means:

- Setting clear, challenging and unambiguous goals;
- Establishing and communicating clear priorities;
- Developing and insisting on effective process;
- Consistent monitoring and feedback on progress.

Social leadership will be low key and will consume relatively little time. It will be limited to encouragement and recognition of satisfactory progress toward goals. If the time constraints are such that something must be sacrificed, the social leadership activities will always be subordinate to those which are specifically task and goal directed.

In short, the leadership style will be one which is high on task and low on social requirements. Here readers may recognise a clear distinction between this approach and that of Bales, Fleischmann and Blake and Mouton, all of whom argue that social and task leadership skills should always be maintained in a state of balance or even synergy. Hersey and Blanchard argue that in the real world such a balance in the early days of team development is unnecessary and probably impossible. Through effective task management the team will enjoy early success. That success will be, in the final analysis, all the social 'stroking' that they will need.

High task, high social

Stage two of the life of the group follows and builds on early success. The role of the leader now is to maintain or increase momentum, avoid the team either falling into a rut of 'we are winners – we have the formula' or of letting confidence outrun competence to the degree that the group are tempted to take on more than they can handle, or to develop highly idiosyncratic ways of doing things in a display of unjustified machismo. That means that the effective leader will retain a firm grip on the reins. He will continue to tell people what is expected of them and will monitor and supervise their performance. He will continue in short to be high in task management. But things have changed and the intelligent leader will reflect that change by spending an increasing amount of time listening to people, providing support and encouragement for their efforts and facilitating their involvement in problem solving and decision making. This stage requires the leader to be actively involved at a high level in social leadership. Ensuring that the team keep on track and progress toward autonomy is tough, the leader will experience no busier and probably no more fulfilling period than this.

High social, low task

Success in phase two of the life of the work group brings its rewards for the leader and the led. Now the team have a proven track record of success in the tasks which they undertake. As members of a winning team which has avoided the temptation to fall into a rut, they have demonstrated commitment and flexibility. Through day-to-day success they probably now understand more of the detail of what is expected of them and how it may best be achieved than their leader can hope to alone. This will be increasingly true as firms in the information society put more and more dependence on knowledge workers. They have earned the right to increasing levels of autonomy through their commitment to corporate goals and their proven ability to achieve them. And the leader has spent time developing on a planned basis their increasing involvement in decision making and problem solving. Now the leader can relax, but only a little.

Continued highlighting of task would be offensive to those who have demonstrated that they now know the job in detail. The wise leader will now greatly reduce his emphasis on task accomplishment and leave that to the skills, knowledge and motivation of a committed team. Leader emphasis throughout this phase will be on social leadership skills and facilitating further individual and team growth.

Low task, low social

The strategy for stage four in the development of the group is the one which gives many unsophisticated leaders pain. At this stage the group have enjoyed consistent and growing task success, they have increasingly participated in the problem solving and decision making process, initially in areas which were strictly related to the job in hand, but as their skills, confidence and commitment grew they have become involved in wider and more challenging issues. At the same time the team has grown in cohesion and members have demonstrated the ability to handle internal and external problems and conflicts without undue difficulty. What is there left for the leader to do?

Managers complain about the lack of what the jargon of the day calls 'quality time' – what I, old fashioned as I am still prefer to call 'discretionary time'. Well at this stage in the life of a group you have it in abundance. The team neither need nor would welcome your interference in the accomplishment of the task, they have been doing that successfully without you for some time. Similarly they have no need of a leader to manage their social or developmental interactions. They are at the zenith of team performance and they know it. Some leaders faced with this situation panic and tighten the reins just for the sake of something to do. They then find that they have just designed the ultimate way to demotivate a winning team. The wise, or well-trained, (it comes to the same thing), leader lets go. He does not abdicate all responsibility of course, he still maintains a watchful eye and is available if needed. But he interferes as little as possible and in the mean time he uses that quality time that so many managers feel that they need, to plan new challenges for himself and his team. As he introduces new tasks, new organisation and new challenges he moves the team back to phase one and the cycle begins again until his obvious leadership capacity is recognised and he moves on to ever greater things, and creative use of quality time to think.

Organisational check-list

The above four phases involve the following leadership functions in varying degrees:

- **Task behaviour**
  - structure
  - control
  - monitor
  - supervise

- **Social behaviour**
  - praise
  - listen
  - facilitate
  - develop

I have described the life and development of the work team as if it were linear and unidirectional. Unfortunately, unless the leader is unusually gifted, uniquely lucky, or both it doesn't quite work so smoothly. The group makes progress and backslides a little. Problems arise which even a hitherto autonomous group are unable to resolve. In short, progress is usually of the 'three steps forward - one step back' variety.

I am also guilty of a second simplification. Since groups are made up of individuals, it is easier to predict the behaviour of groups than it is of individuals, but that does not mean that the individual may be ignored. Fortunately the individual who is out of step with the rest of the group can be treated exactly as described for the group at the stage at which the individual currently is operating. If one person is a little more competent and confident that their colleagues give them more social support allied with a little more autonomy. Use them, if you can do so without creating embarassment as a role model to the team. If I, on the other hand make slower progress than the rest of my group, be ready to give me tighter direction and control until I am ready to move forward. I will make faster progress and will feel more secure.

If the group slips back make them become more directive and task-oriented until they are back on track. Flexibility in accordance with the current situation is the secret of leadership.

Leadership style plan

In order to recognise the phase of leadership acquired, the following questionnaire will quickly highlight the appropriate action.

Has anything important changed:
  Leader?

Task?
Group membership?
Culture?
Company values?
Business environment?

For any 'yes' consider moving to a more directive style in the short term.

Has group experienced worthwhile success in the current circumstances?

If 'yes' consider moving toward a more supportive style permanently.

Is the group riding high in terms of confidence and competence?

If 'yes' consider initiating a new level of challenge and returning to more directive style until real evidence of success in new circumstances is seen.

Are any members of the group 'out of step'; showing either considerably more or considerably less confidence and competence than their colleagues?

If 'yes' encourage the fast trackers by giving more support and less direction, while encouraging the slow developers by giving lots of individual direction and support. For the exceptional fast tracker be prepared to delegate fully, but professionally – no 'throwing in at the deep end' – delegation needs direction and support and a slow withdrawal.

Trends in leadership style

I have concentrated on the work of Hersey and Blanchard and of Tannenbaum and Schmidt because I believe that important as their ideas have been for the last twenty years, they have yet to reach the zenith of their utility. The information age is one in which leaders of lower technical capacity will be managing the task accomplishment of highly skilled, highly paid, scarce and highly mobile knowledge workers. At the same time they will be responsible for maintaining team awareness between those who are physically separated as they telecommute rather than waste time travelling to a central location. They will need to judge when to give intrapreneurs their head, and free them to optimise the use of the company's expensive but limited resources to maximise return on investment. These models provide the best current hope of moving into a new age under control. They have been proven in the field and carry none of the silly ideological baggage which mars so many alternatives.

One final point worth repeating before moving on. The relationship between leader and led is changing and will continue to change in the forseeable future. The leader of the nineties and beyond must give the team success, but that is only the start of things. In a post smokestack society the leader cannot rely on positional power to succeed, nor can he depend on the distribution of rewards and sanctions.

Leadership will cease to be a matter of imposing a higher level of status when the balance in the value of contribution shifts and combines with changed and growing expectations. The macho leader of the past will become the professional leader of the future or he will perish. The way is open for the leaders who will replace the 'masculine' approach of defining and defending status with the 'feminine' style of building and maintaining mutually fruitful relationships. These models, thoughtfully applied, will unite the benefits of both sexes and, in the longer run will ensure the development of empowered and trusted teams and individuals.

Leadership style and culture

The influence of individuals, particularly those who are in the most senior positions, is often so strong in organisations that their personal leadership style becomes a role model for the greater part of the management team. Research and common sense suggest that this is most likely to happen when the style of the role model is highly visible and limited in range.

Clearly important business strategies such as empowerment and TQM (total quality management) are difficult if not impossible to put into effect if the organisational leadership style is hostile to them. An autocratic organisation in which people have been punished for acting on their own initiative may talk of the importance of empowerment, but they will not experience it. A macho corporation in which feelings have had to be repressed will not drive out fear nor move toward TQM.

Figure 5.2 is a simple but useful tool to establish whether there is an organisational style, and if so, whether it is appropriate to the present corporate plan. It is based on the repertoire of leadership behaviours which are specified by Tannenbaum and Schmidt. 'Test' is omitted because it is rare this is preferred to 'tell' or 'sell' at the corporate level.

The ability to clearly identify a specific leadership style as typical of the firm is of itself an indication that the essential requirements of flexibility and

LEADERSHIP STYLE

OUR SUPERORDINATE GOAL (The present most important reason for this group's existence): ------------------------------

IN THIS ORGANISATION AT PRESENT:		TASK / PEOPLE / MANAGEMENT	TICK	
We **tell** people what to do		The TASK requires:		
		Creative and committed input from all involved	(a)	Each (a) ticked indicates the usefulness of a more PARTICIPATIVE style
Management decides and **sells** their idea		Simple routine work only	(b)	
		Self-sacrifice of time, autonomy or earnings capacity by those involved	(a)	
We ask for opinions and **consult** before taking any action		Tangible rewards are high and valued by the group	(b)	Each (b) ticked suggests a more CONTROLLING style
		The PEOPLE involved are:		
We **join** as a team to make key decisions		Competent and self-confident	(a)	
		Over-confident and inexperienced	(b)	
Key decisions are **delegated** to the lowest level fully competent to decide		A mature group used to working together	(a)	
		A new group, or under new management	(b)	
		Used to success as a team	(a)	
		Used to near misses or failure	(b)	
		MANAGEMENT are:		
		Flexible and fully trained	(a)	
		Rigid and bureaucratic	(b)	

Figure 5.2 Leadership style harmonisation

appropriateness may not be met in important situations. Logically, however, if an organisational style is perceived as existing at all, the quickest way to progress toward an adequate degree of flexibility will be through moving that style, in the short term, in an appropriate direction.

To use the tool simply tick the style or styles which predominate in your organisation. If several are ticked, well and good, it is unlikely that the organisation is stuck with a style which by definition must be wrong for many situations. That is not to say, however that the range of styles are necessarily sensitively and appropriately applied.

If a single style predominates there is reason for considerable concern. First the style will almost certainly limit the short term ability of leaders to develop and apply a flexible approach, and even if they are successful, their style may be perceived as falling into line with that which predominates because the dominant overall style has created an expectation of 'That's the way things are around here.'

The right hand half of the model enables the manager to establish, if the organisation must have a single consistent style, the style which fits with the current or desired situational analysis.

As with all such simple tools the more people who use it the more statistically reliable the outcome will be. With that in mind I suggest that the model be copied and used in the settings of Organisational Development Workshops or training programmes.

The person in the middle

Within the organisational structure any manager or leader is under different and sometimes conflicting pressures. They are perceived by those to whom they report as being a conduit through which their demands may be fulfilled. At the same time they are seen by their subordinates as a person who has access to the higher echelons and who has a responsibility to them to pursue and attain their aspirations. Add normal peer pressure requiring the individual to demonstrate solidarity with the group and the model is complete.

This model (Fig. 5.3) has been used constructively by some members of Japanese management. They have argued and practised that since anyone in an organisation is a member at the same time of many teams there is no reason for any sense of 'us and them' no matter how many lines of reporting there may be. By bowing to the inevitable they have successfully enhanced two-way communication through the organisation by making it team-to-team.

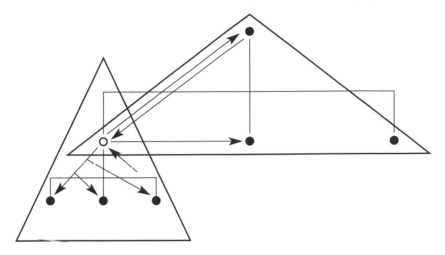

Because the leader is seen as a member of the management group by peers and superiors, leaders are expected to influence the subordinate group in the interests of management. At the same time, perceived as 'our leader' by the sub-ordinate group, they are expected to influence 'management' in the interests of the 'workers'. Neither group necessarily accepts that the manager has a duty to the other, and any behaviour seen as favouring the other group is perceived as 'treasonable'. Japanese industry has to some degree recognised this dilemma and used it to drive two-way communication.

Figure 5.3 The manager as person in the middle

THE MOTIVATION TO LEAD

Some years ago David McClelland a leading American psychologist investi-gated the special motives which drive leaders to lead. He found three, but they are not equally potent. It may well be that any individual is motivated to a greater or lesser degree by any or all of them. They are:

- **N-Ach.** The motivation toward high standards of personal achievement. A commitment to the quality outcome.

- **N-Aff.** The need to develop good personal relationships. To nurture, sup-port and develop others and defend their interests.

- **N-Pow.** The motivation to use organisational power and resources effec-tively. A need to use what is available to get things done.

As I have written above, the three motivators are not equally distributed among the most successful leaders. The evidence is that if you really want to be a high flyer your chances are best if you are motivated primarily by one of them. But which one?

When training groups are discussing this area of leadership I sometimes hold a straw poll in guesswork. When I do, N-Ach., the desire for personal achievement wins hands down. That shouldn't surprise me, it's eminently plausible. In fact it is so plausible that McClelland himself thought at first that the desire for personal achievement would drive the most effective leaders. But consider this.

I am a man driven by the need for personal achievement. Nothing but the best satisfies me. If I take up a hobby I want to be perfect from day one or very soon after and I am prepared to make any sacrifice to reach the very highest standards in the shortest possible time. I carry the same drives and needs into the workplace. Because of my commitment to quality outcomes I am appointed leader of a group of good professionals. How good will I be at delegating work to those below me? How effective will I be in allowing my subordinates to develop through making mistakes and learning to solve the ensuing problems? As it happens I can tell you because the description above applies pretty well to me.

I delegated because, with a well qualified team, I knew that I ought to, but when they started to work, did I allow them to get on with the job? I watched and as I watched I grew increasingly uneasy. They weren't doing things exactly as I would have done them. My uneasiness would turn to something akin to panic as I concluded that the outcome would fall short of what I believed to be possible and necessary. Without fully comprehending the harm I was doing I used to find myself pushing my subordinate out of the way with a cry of 'Let me show you.'

Thus N-Ach. is the key motive of the entrepreneur, particularly the one man band. Fine for a consultant (or one who writes on management concepts) but a dangerous primary drive for a leader who is reliant on the development of his people.

Contrast the situation with that of one who is motivated by N-Aff. Arnold wanted to be liked by everybody. He was never known to say 'No'. Whatever the request, he answered in the affirmative. He was the ideal model for the advertisement for the hamburger restaurant where their tag line is, 'You've got it!'

If an unqualified subordinate came to Arnold and said, 'I would like to do that.' Arnold replied, 'You've got it!' If another colleague said 'He's not qualified, he can't do that.' Arnold said 'You've got it. I'll tell him.' He didn't tell him, of course. That would have been too tough for a guy who wants to be liked by everybody. He just left chaos to sort itself out. Similarly he rarely kept a promise because he had so often promised the same thing to two different people or promised two incompatible things at the same time. He never understood why he wasn't liked, he tried so hard to please everybody.

So if N-Ach. and N-Aff. don't lead it must be N-Pow. It is the drive to use the organisational resources including its people effectively to attain predetermined results that makes for the best and most successful leaders. If you want to be a leader you must think about your personal attitude to power.

Those who prefer co-operation to competition have trouble with the concept of power. Again let me refer you to the waste of skills and experience which has occurred because many women of great talent are not prepared to play political power games to continue their journey to the top. But the concept of power is changing.

In a smokestack economy power was dependent on the position of the individual in the hierarchy, their control over rewards and sanctions and their understanding of the political system. In an information society increasingly it will be true that power flows to those who know, and in the leadership setting what they will increasingly know is how to form and maintain longstanding relationships, how to act as a role model for desired behaviour and how to get the best consistently out of people who are free to fire the company any time that they are less than satisfied with the way that they are used.

SUMMARY

Leaders in a smokestack economy have not been called on to be leadership professionals. As the post-modernist society extends its influence further and further into industry and commerce the subtle skills of true leadership will become increasingly important. Those skills require a sensitive and accurate appraisal of the situation and the sense to apply the most effective technique from a substantial repertoire. The leader of the nineties and beyond must be acceptable to those that are led.

Those who aspire to leadership might usefully ask themselves four questions.

1. What do I have going for me that puts me above the herd?

2. Am I prepared to work at leadership as if it were a profession?

3. What are the key beliefs and values which I want to communicate to my followers that they can commit to?

4. What are or will be my sources of power and how can I use them?

PITFALLS OF LEADERSHIP

Leadership fails when:

- Insufficient regard is paid to the total situation.

- Leadership positions are used to reinforce status differences.

- Individual leaders are unable to operate beyond their comfort zones.

- Leadership styles are ideologically biased.

- Leaders fail to realise that feelings are facts.

- The dominant leadership style of the organisation is at odds with the needs of the strategy.

- Leaders lack flexibility and sensitivity to the needs of work groups.

- Informal leaders are allowed or encouraged to emerge.

- The philosophy is that leaders are born not made and training in the skills of leadership is ignored.

- When leadership training is of poor quality.

- Leaders are denied the opportunity to create early success for their groups.

- Leaders fail to communicate worthwhile and acceptable values to their teams.

- Leaders are motivated by wanting to be loved.

- Leaders are motivated by the need to have their personal achievements recognised rather than those of the team.

- Leaders regard their position as one of personal rather than organisational power.

6 PROBLEM SOLVING AND DECISION MAKING

Chapter 5 has argued, I hope cogently, that the leader needs to develop his own and his people's creativity as he introduces a programme of planned empowerment. But there is more to problem solving than either creativity or participation.

It is essential for the practising manager to have at his immediate command a range of problem solving processes so that he may apply that which is appropriate without delay or costly error.

USING CREATIVITY

You leave home early one morning. This is to be a big day. You have a meeting which, if it turns out as you hope and expect, will end in your being given a significant opportunity to advance your career. It is vital that you give a good impression, and you know that the person who you must impress above all has a mania for punctuality. He has even been known to bar late-comers from meetings with the words:

'We have done perfectly well without you so far. I see no reason why we should need you now. Good day.'

On such a day, and when you are to have an opportunity to impress such a man, you leave the house early – and your usually reliable car won't start.

If your arrival at the meeting at the right time is solely dependent on getting your car to start, creative techniques are of little use to you. You, or someone with the requisite knowledge needs to trace the fault, correct it, and get you back on the road in the shortest time possible. You need a combination of technical knowledge and rational process which will identify likely causes, isolate the most likely, correct the deviation and test the solution. The role of creativity in such a process is limited in all probability to overcoming the possible need for non-available parts, as in the time-honoured replacement of torn fan belts by ladies tights or stockings.

If however, you neither have, nor have access to the knowledge or skill required to diagnose and repair a fault in an internal combustion engine, the nature of your problem changes. Now your need is not to repair the car. That is unlikely to be achieved in the time which you have. Your problem is how to get to your, perhaps distant, meeting using an alternative means of transport and do it in time. For this you may need all the creativity you can lay your hands on.

So we have two types of problem. A deviation from norm where we need to address the unique cause from among perhaps many possibilities and rectify it; and a situation where we need to identify and implement a novel and attractive solution beyond our normal experience. Is that all?

Not quite. Everyone who has had even the most limited exposure to marketing is aware of the Product Life Cycle. The demand for any product or service is finite. Typically it builds slowly, then increases rapidly as the benefits and availability of the product become better known and then demand falls away, often as rapidly as it once rose, until it finally peters out. The wise company invests in product development to lengthen the life cycle or introduce timely replacements before the business fades to nothing. To bring a totally new product or service to an enthusiastic marketplace demands creative problem solving, but a totally new offering is not always the most effective or economic approach. You can often increase enormously your market opportunity, with a pleasing increase in revenues and profits by making incremental changes to what you already have. Letting your product or service grow and evolve, if you will. To enjoy these benefits requires a third and different kind of problem solving skill.

So we have three key, and different areas of managerial problem solving and three different, but mutually consistent approaches. Is that all we need?

I think not. There is another and very important type of decision to be made. That decision is 'Who is best placed to solve the problem or make the decision?'

The evidence suggests that the answer to this can be complex and it impinges firmly on Leadership, Motivation and Team Building. There is little doubt that where people are involved in the problem solving or decision making process they tend to be more committed to the outcome. On the other hand, desirable as group involvement is, ideologically, and in some cases practically, why is it that we believe so firmly that a camel is a horse designed by a committee? Please bear with me while we explore this interesting question.

Consensus decision making in groups

Managers who have attended training programmes where consensus decision making exercises, (The NASA Exercise, 'Lost in the Desert', 'Lost in the Jungle', etc.) have been used are frequently sadly misled by the trainers. Each of the exercises mentioned above is carefully designed to show that in the very special situation which the exercise addresses, full participation by the group and a decision arrived at by consensus is the most effective way to proceed. So far so good, but as I have already indicated the exercises are specially designed to facilitate that conclusion. They have limited relevance to real life.

For the sake of those who have not experienced it, let me describe briefly the NASA Exercise. You, that is the participating group are told that you have crash landed on the dark side of the moon. Your space suits are undamaged and you are uninjured. Your mother ship or base is two hundred miles from your point of impact. You are to trek the two hundred miles. Before you set out you are given an inventory of items which have survived the impact and your task is to rank these in terms of their importance in helping you to survive your journey and reach your base. You complete this rank ordering twice. Once individually and without any talking. This is scored by the trainer in terms of the variance between your scoring and that of NASA experts. (The higher the score the greater the 'error'). You are not advised of your score, but you are now asked as a team to redo the exercise as a group consensus task.

In well over 90 per cent of trials the consensus score proves to be 'better' than both the average individual score and the best individual score. In almost all cases the consensus score is substantially better than the average individual effort. An impressive demonstration of the power of consensus decision making ? Well not quite.

The task, rank ordering of items to support a trek across the dark side of the moon is not something which the average manager undertakes every day. That is why it has been chosen. It is unlikely in the extreme that the group will include an expert with personal experience of the conditions and terrain on the dark side of the moon. The group as a whole however, thanks to television, books, newspapers and radio is expert. Almost every member will have seen or read something which is a meaningful contribution to the pot of knowledge. Frequently those holding the relevant and important pieces of knowledge will be sublimely unaware of the significance of what they know until it is brought out in conversation and someone cries 'Eureka!'.

The second vital factor is that these exercises are used in the relaxed democracy of the training seminar. The group is, in formal terms at least, leaderless. Each individual has an equal personal standing with the real leader of the team, the trainer, and each is equally motivated to contribute to a 'bit of fun'.

These are the conditions in which consensus is efficient and effective. In many real world situations any unsophisticated attempt at participative leadership is sunk by a combination of the leader's lack of real confidence in the team, the team's lack of self-confidence and the control of essential data by one or two 'experts'.

A tool for analysing a complex situation is given as Fig. 6.1. In simple terms, if you tick or circle 'YES' or 'NO' appropriately for each question, a mark in the first column is an argument for the leader making the decision herself. A mark in the right hand column suggests the use of consensus.

Since consensus is a complex area of managerial psychology, let us try to avoid oversimplifying it by considering each question in a little more detail.

Do you know what information is required to ensure a quality decision?
If you, as leader know fully and precisely what data is essential it is generally more cost-effective to accumulate the information, analyse it and make the decision. Passing the decision to the group will probably lead to a great waste of time in pursuing irrelevancies, wild ideas or hidden agendas. At the end you will almost certainly be forced to cut short discussion, and if emotions have become roused you may need to make a unilateral decision anyway, leading the more sensitive members of the team to believe that you have been playing games with them.

Do you have all the information necessary to make a good decision? If you have all the necessary data, involving others in the decision needs to be justified. (For examples see below.) The most cost-effective and safe strategy is to make the decision yourself.

Do you know who has the relevant information and expertise? If you do, you have a choice of either consulting that individual before making the decision yourself, or delegating that decision to that individual. Involving others is a potentially high risk strategy in which it is possible that your expert's view will be lost in a welter of information.

Do you know where the relevant information will be found? Again a choice, but a limited one. Either amass the data yourself and make the decision or delegate the acquisition of information and, if you wish, the decision to an individual or team. As usual, action by a single person is more cost-effective.

Is this a low risk situation, suitable for the development of team decision making skills? As leader an important part of your function is to develop the team. You ought to be constantly on the lookout for opportunities to accelerate that development without commercial risk. In the early stages, if the risk

INFORMATION		
1. Do you know what information is required to ensure a quality decision?	Yes	No
2. Do you have all the information necessary to make a good decision?	Yes	No
3. Do you know who has the relevant information and expertise?	Yes	No
4. Do you know where the relevant information will be found?	Yes	No
RISK		
5. Is this a low risk situation, suitable to develop team decision making skills?	No	Yes
6. Is this a high risk situation where failure will be costly?	Yes	No
7. Is commitment from every member of the group critical to the successful implementation of this decision?	No	Yes
8. Do the group have sufficient appreciation of the goals and desired outcomes?	No	Yes
GROUP MATURITY		
9. Has the group a strong track record of success as a team?	No	Yes
10. Has the group successfully made decisions like this before?	No	Yes
11. Does the group tend to rely on strong leadership behaviour?	Yes	No
12. Have the group's previous successes been mainly driven by the leader's personality and enthusiasm?	Yes	No
THE SITUATION		
13. Is this an evolving situation where previous experience is likely to be the best guide to decision making?	Yes	No
14. Is this a totally new situation where previous experience is likely to be irrelevant?	No	Yes
15. Is this situation so new that team members may not even be aware that they have picked up useful and relevant information?	No	Yes
16. Would you, as leader feel confident in leaving this decision to the team?	No	Yes
17. Can you commit yourself in advance to 'live with' any decision which the team comes to?	No	Yes

Figure 6.1 The case for consensus decision making: a high score in the right-hand column suggests consensus is needed rather than personal action

is so minimal that you can live with *any* decision, that is the ideal situation to hand the decision making authority to the group. Later they will seek challenging tasks which imply greater risk. Be sure that when you provide such tasks the group is prepared for them through adequate safe prior practice.

Is this a high risk situation where failure will be costly? Your primary responsibility to the organisation and ultimately to the group suggests that you think long and hard before passing this decision down to the team. To put it bluntly, in the last resort you can delegate authority, the responsibility for outcomes remains yours. You must be careful not to put at unnecessary risk the wellbeing of the company, the group or, if it comes to it your own leadership position. Groups have a habit of dumping leaders who get them into trouble. (See Idiosyncracy Balance, Chapter 5)

Is commitment from every member of the group critical to the successful implementation of this decision? This is almost a mirror image of the last note in that if commitment is essential you should think very hard before you deny the group the opportunity to take part in the decision making process. There can be little remaining doubt that involvement helps to generate commitment. The type and degree of involvement will depend on a complex web of factors including the maturity of the group, their track record and the importance of the decision. (Chapter 5)

Does the group have sufficient appreciation of the relevant goals and desired outcome? Until they do, involvement in the decision making process is the equivalent of playing snooker with both hands tied behind your back. It is simply not a meaningful activity.

Has the group a strong track record of success as a team? Has the group successfully made decisions like this before? In general winning teams want and can achieve more triumphs, but before delegating the decision consider whether there is any danger that your group may have got into a success rut. They may be heading for disaster by assuming that they have the winning formula and all problems are just like those which they have previously solved. If this situation is significantly different is their track record to date relevant?

Does the group tend to rely on strong leadership behaviour? Has the group's previous successes been mainly driven by the leader's personality and enthusiasm? Contrary to the bland solutions of the idealists, people need to be weaned off dependence slowly and carefully. Throwing people in at the deep end produces more corpses than swimmers. If the expectation is that you will provide strong leadership, change the expectation before you change the behaviour.

Is this an evolving situation where previous experience is likely to be the best guide to decision making? Where precedent is the best guide the cost-effective decision making strategy is to have the decision made by he or she who has the best knowledge of the past and the most accurate appreciation of the emerging needs of the business. In many situations that person will be the manager.

Is this a totally new situation where previous experience is likely to be irrelevant? Is this situation so new that team members may not even be aware that they have picked up relevant and useful information?

This, if you will is the NASA Exercise situation. You will almost certainly get a richer input of information and a better decision if you involve as many people as possible and provide sufficient time for the optimal decision to emerge. The leadership role in this situation is one of facilitator ensuring that everyone has sufficient opportunity to express their views and share their knowledge and ideas.

Would you as a team leader feel confident in leaving this decision to the team? Can you commit yourself in advance to 'live with' any decision which the team comes to? Unless your answer to both of these questions is an unequivocal 'YES' are you yet ready to delegate? So much for the use of the group in decision making situations. Now let us examine problem solving.

Problem solving in organisations

EXCELLENT The focus of the organisation is consistently on problem solving rather than blame fixing. Problem solving is engaged in by all of the people involved and all are trained in appropriate problem solving techniques. Because of a high standard of consistent training the appropriate problem solving technique is available and used for each situation. Potential problem identification and contingency and avoidance planning are routinely part of all plans. People at all levels in the organisation are empowered to take risks in pursuit of excellence and higher levels of performance because the ready availability of effective problem solving team and individual skills ensures the mitigation of losses and increases the likelihood of incremental progress.

AVERAGE All employees are trained and practised in at least one proven problem solving technique. There is some danger that problems are force-fitted to the technique rather than techniques being applied which are specific to the problem. Management Training staff are used by line management to conduct problem solving workshops on an 'as required' basis. The responsibility for introducing the appropriate tool lies with Management Training which can lead to inappropriate applications when training specialists either favour or only know a single technique. The organisational culture encourages participation by all relevant people in problem solving. Risk, however, is reduced to a minimum by ensuring that no innovations are introduced without proper authorisation.

UNACCEPTABLE Problem solving is the sole province of management. It is assumed that 'intelligent people can solve problems without fancy techniques' and no particular training is given. There is no attempt to predict potential sources of problem and the approach is characterised by the concept 'if it ain't broke don't fix it'.

Research and development

EXCELLENT A steady flow of ideas is always available for evaluation, testing and product development. There is no 'creativity gap' and this innovative approach is carried over into the constant improvement of processes. All employees contribute to the generation of ideas and each recognises and fulfills a personal responsibility for the reputation and sustained growth of the organisation. The philosophical basis for our creativity is our commitment to satisfy changing customer needs consistently and at minimum cost.

AVERAGE Ideas are occasionally raised either informally or through the formal Suggestion Scheme. Relatively few employees take it upon themselves to initiate suggestions and good workable ideas are few. There is a dependence on the Marketing Division to identify and communicate changing customer needs.

UNACCEPTABLE We offer a good product or service right now and can see no reason to dilute our approach to the market by introducing anything new until the demand for what we have today is exhausted. In the worst scenario rights to new developments are acquired and patents established not to exploit improvements, but to attempt to stop others from introducing new ideas into the market place and maintain the status quo.

APPROACHES TO PROBLEM SOLVING

If there were a problem solving hall of fame the names of Kepner and Tregoe and Prince and Gordon would be held in the highest esteem. The value of their work, the first pair in the field of rational process and the second duo in creative problem solving, is second to none. Kepner, Tregoe, Prince and Gordon have taken our natural sluggishness and developed systems which make problem solving, if not always easy, at least predictable and economic. To have rationalised creativity is a major intellectual feat.

A general model of problem solving

Both major approaches to problem solving imply a simple and common model. First it is necessary that someone sees the situation as a problem. That is that a less than desirable situation exists and it is believed that there is a way, if it can be found, of creating a more desirable or even ideal state. Reality or perception, if you or I believe a problem to exist we are likely to seek some form of solution or amelioration.

The fact that a problem may be either imagined or real implies the need for problem ownership. If you feel that you have a problem then it is a problem to you regardless of my sense that it is nothing to worry about. I am reminded of the story of the schoolgirl who confided in Einstein that she had difficulty in understanding geometry. Einstein who at the time was trying to pull together the threads of the geometry of space-time as it would apply to a unified field theory, (a theory which would include all of the workings of nature), shook his head sadly, 'My dear you should have my problems.'

A charming story about a charming human being, but hardly helpful to a little girl who couldn't remember the difference between congruent and similar triangles. As I say, you have your problems and I have mine and ownership is a necessary precursor to problem definition and effective implementation of a solution, as are the assumption of responsibility for the outcome and limitations on the power to act.

As I rather more than hinted in the introduction to this chapter, the type of problem dictates the style of problem solving technique which is likely to produce the best result. Let us be more specific in the analysis of problem type and the appropriateness of a technique.

Problem type	Probable technique
Deviation from established norm	Kepner Tregoe (Return to standard)
Quality or consistency problems in manufacture warehousing or distribution	Kepner Tregoe Synectics (Invent new process)
People problems	Synectics Brainstorming (Both with a serious spicing of understanding of human behaviour)
Repair of machines or systems	Kepner Tregoe
Innovation	Synectics Morphological analysis Brainstorming
More than one problem owner	Synectics
Potential problems	Kepner Tregoe
Financial results	See chapter 7 – Cascade diagrams.

As general 'rule of thumb' the more diffuse the problem and the more creative the solution, the more likely is Synectics to be the best approach. The more defined the problem, the more likely is KT to be useful. Morphological analysis and cascade diagrams are generally specific to their areas of new product development and financial improvement respectively. For problems which are unusually complex, or which are part of an advanced technological environment other specialist approaches such as Soft Systems Methodology may be preferred.

Situation analysis

> 'When sorrows come, they come not single spies but in batallions.'
> William Shakespeare – *Hamlet*

As with sorrows so also with problems. It is necessary therefore to assess the environment in which they occur to establish priorities for their solution. If, in the immediate environment something is serious in its effect, liable to get worse if not resolved and puts the problem holder under pressure, it ought to be addressed as a matter of urgency.

Problem analysis

Most problem solving methods demand that at some point the 'w' questions are asked and answered.

- What is happening?
- When is it happening?
- Where does it happen?
- Who is involved or affected?
- Which items or processes are involved?
- Why does it happen?

Possibilities

It is tempting to say that problems of necessity have causes, but this is not necessarily so other than in the most trivial way. If something has gone wrong, there is a cause or a series of causes, but my problem may be that I see an opportunity that I am unable to exploit immediately. In any case there are potential solutions from which we will wish to select the most desirable.

Evaluating possibilities

To establish the most likely cause or causes requires a detailed comparison with what is known about the situation. Solutions, however, need to be considered in terms of the relationship between costs and benefits. The effective implementation of the solution may well depend on its attractiveness to the problem owner and novelty as well as its feasibility.

Select preferred alternative

Where alternative strategies are available selectivity is essential.

Test and implement

Probable causes need to be tested so that the likely solution can be implemented at minimum cost with maximum expectation of success. Just as a plane is a little off course for much of its journey, but lands safely at the right place, solutions need to be kept under some sort of review. Under the banner of total quality all processes are subject to assessment and continuous improvement.

CREATIVE PROBLEM SOLVING USING SYNECTICS

Although Synectics can be usefully applied by one individual acting entirely alone, it has certain design features which make it peculiarly appropriate to team operation. Because the selection and ownership of problem and solution lie in the hands of a single individual, the client, it carries none of the dangers inherent in inappropriate searches for consensus. The role of the team is that of assisting the client through idea generation and the creation of an environment characterised by enthusiasm and fun. Decisions remain the responsibility of the client.

Synectics is a carefully structured, step by step, logical approach to developing creative solutions to complex problems.

It is at its best a team activity in which a lively atmosphere is intended to ensure that emotions are given their full weight in reaching an attractive solution.

There is a third role beyond that of client and team member. A team leader assumes responsibility for process leadership and making all the emerging ideas visible to the group by being the appointed scribe. There is no reason why the leader should be in any way the most senior member of the group, but just as the client or problem owner has always the final say in matters of content, the leader controls the process absolutely regardless of hierarchical status.

Applying Synectics

Synectics requires that the problem is owned to ensure effective and committed implementation of any solution, but it requires more than that. It demands that the perception of the problem is and remains that of the problem owner. That perception may well change over time, but it changes if and only if the problem owner chooses to recognise such a change.

The process starts therefore, in the group problem solving session, with the problem owner defining their problem as they see it. Figure 6.2 underlines the twin concepts of **ownership** and possibly idiosyncratic but binding personal **perception** and this stage is known as the PAG, or **Problem As Given.**

The PAG has four key elements.

1. The problem specification and background from the perspective of the problem owner.

2. The problem owner's ideal or preferred solution if they have one. This solution is not constrained by any considerations of feasibility. The client has the opportunity to wish or to dream, the eventual role of the group is to provide the ideas which will develop a solution as close to that dream as practicality allows.

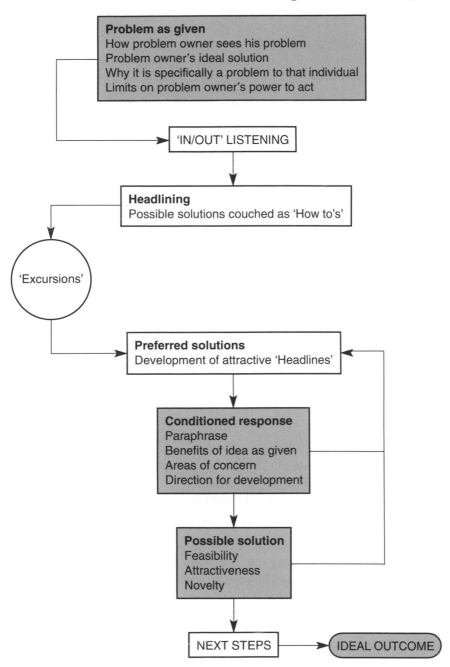

Figure 6.2 A skeleton for problem solving by Synectics

3. Why it is a problem to the individual who owns it. Those aspects of the problem affect him or her personally.

4. Limitations on the problem owner's power to act in implementing a chosen solution.

While the client is expressing the PAG in their own words and at their own pace, the group practise in/out listening. One of the great fallacies of management and sales theory lies in the belief that by a massive effort of will, one can listen evenly and with total concentration for as long as it takes. The human brain does not work that way. While we listen we think, and while we think we are distracted. We tune in and tune out as we listen, remembering the early part of what was said, the end and those scattered items from the middle of what was said which particularly caught our wandering attention such as names, especially our own, thoughts and ideas which logically link together and, I am saddened to report, the occasional vulgarity.

Synectics, just as it goes with the certainty of emotional overtones in problem solving by proactively keeping emotions to the forefront and positive, goes with the way that the brain works. The problem solving group is encouraged during the PAG to use the certainty that minds will wander by scribbling down key words related to thoughts that pop into their heads as they listen. These often unconnected words and phrases and half-born ideas provide the basis for the next step in the process.

When the problem owner has completed the PAG to his satisfaction, the group leader invites the group to provide 'headlines' each of which is recorded without comment or discussion on sheets of flip chart paper so that they can be displayed around the walls of the room. A **headline** is in the form of a short and, at present meaningless 'How to' statement such as:

HOW TO USE GRASS CLIPPINGS

HOW TO HINGE THE WALL

HOW TO REMOVE THEIR LEGS.

The energy of the process is maintained by avoiding explanations or evaluation. Indeed the group would be hard put to it to explain or evaluate anything for the simple reason that those expressing the headlines often have absolutely no idea what they mean. Some, however will catch the imagination, particularly the imagination of the client, and it is from these apparently unpromising foundations that truly creative and novel solutions to the problem will emerge. The greater the energy, silliness and fun of this part of the session the better. Headlines should flow in a breathless stream as one apparently daft idea triggers another. The leader will decide if there are enough nascent ideas emerging. If not, the group will be taken on an excursion.

An **excursion** is anything which will free up the minds of the group and thus lead to greater creativity. It always has the feeling of a non-competitive game. One simple and favoured example is for the team to make up a lively and action-packed story by each adding in turn to a tale begun by the leader. To increase creativity and ensure liveliness and action, both within the tale and within the team, it is essential that inputs are of variable length with each team member struggling to add their contribution seamlessly to that of the predecessor as soon as they stop talking. Another ruse to increase pace and flexible thinking is that there is no speech in the story, everything is action and movement.

When the laughter subsides the leader returns the group to the light-hearted business of creating further 'how to's'.

When enough 'how to' ideas adorn the walls the client identifies those which appeal and invites their creators to explain them in more detail. With the creative energy really flowing by this time a great deal of ingenuity is released and fantastic ideas emerge which begin to offer some vague promise of feasibility. Gradually or even quickly an idea emerges which, often for some still unknown reason, grips the attention of the client to the extent that he or she believes that this among all others carries within it the germ of an idea which would be the most fun to implement. The process now is sensitively changed to ensure the development of a feasible, attractive and still novel idea which will solve the problem.

The team bend their considerable ingenuity to giving birth to an idea which meets the criteria and which has a recognisable progenitor in the crazy 'how to' which had an inexplicable but real appeal. This is a major exercise in team building. We become attached to our ideas. We tend to feel that when one is rejected we are rejected with it. By choosing a different one to pursue all others have, for the time being at least, been put to one side. This is not a major problem at this stage, because few of the ideas had been developed beyond the embryonic stage, but from this moment on although the sense of fun may continue and even develop, the group will be engaged in the hard graft of serious idea generation and each will have a major emotional investment in his own contribution. Many of those contributions will be rejected in real-life problem solving because they either are impractical or unattractive. A technique to maintain the commitment of all in the face of rejection needs to be found.

The technique which has been shown to work is that of 'Conditioned or Positive Response'. Designed by a psychologist to reduce the potential for marital discord, it is a reliable tool in any situation where ideas are evaluated and selected.

Before any evaluation, the idea is paraphrased by the client to ensure that he has fully understood what was meant. The creator of the idea will accept or amend the client's interpretation until there is certainty that no misunderstanding can creep in and colour judgement.

The client is then required to identify and express a minimum of three benefits which would result from implementing the idea as it stands. This serves the dual purpose of ensuring that little is rejected without adequate thought and reassures the creator that the idea has real concrete merit.

By expressing specific areas of remaining concern which are not fully satisfied by the idea as it stands the client is able to direct the development of the solution which most closely approximates to his ideal.

Each amended solution is subjected to the same process of paraphrase, positive evaluation and re-direction until, either the client is satisfied that the optimal solution has been identified, or that no further progress is possible in which case they turn back to the displayed 'how to's' to start the process again.

The emergent solution is subjected to two final tests. First it is considered to ensure that it is at the same time feasible, novel and attractive. By 'attractive' in this case I mean that the client can hardly hold back his enthusiasm to implement it without delay. Finally before 'going and doing' it is prudent to undertake a financial evaluation.

- How much will it cost to implement, buy or install the solution?
- How much will any solution cost to run?
- How long will it take to pay back any investment?
- What effect will it have on the returns which are required?
- What effect will it have on staffing levels, training needs and productivity?

Remember that nothing should be done in a business unless:

- There is a good business reason for doing it;
- It will pay for itself in a reasonable time;
- It can be explained in simple language to those who will have to make it work.

Thus the process of Synectics takes us from the rarified altitude of creativity back into the real world of application not with a bump, but a profit.

RATIONAL PROCESS USING THE KT MODEL

Problem solving does not by any means always call for creativity. Often the situation is that something which ought to be right has gone wrong and the only need is to find the fault and fix it. Figure 6.3 provides a simple worksheet for doing just that. KT (Kepner and Tregoe) problem solving is aimed at finding effective, efficient and economic solutions to deviations from norm. Wherever what should happen is not happening although it has happened in the past, reach for KT.

There is no excursion into the dizzy heights of creativity within KT, it sticks solidly to rational analysis.

- What is the problem or deviation?
- Where is it experienced?
- When does it or did it occur?
- How old is the process or product when the problem first occurs?
- How often does it happen?
- How big is the problem?
  - how much?
  - how many?

Answer these questions fully and you have specified the problem in detail. You know precisely what is going wrong. In fact, although you may not recognise it you know something equally important. You know what is not happening. It may seem odd to think that with alligators biting at your nether regions there is mileage in considering what is not happening, but if you are to correct an out-of-step situation you need to find a cause and research shows that the cause often lies in the distinction between what is and what is not, happening.

Thus in your analysis for every fact that indicates what is happening you need to consider what is not. Let us consider a simple example.

Implementing the KT model for problem solving

You manufacture and market yellow widgets. For years you have produced the yellow widget on your antiquated production line with never a moment of worry. Recently you introduced a new product. You expect that your new puce widget is about to take the widget world by storm. You have cranked up the production facilities to build both puce widgets (the new star) and yellow widgets (your cash cows). After a major research and development investment cash is short, so the old and new lines are produced on the same machines. Since the only difference between them is their colour there is no logical reason why they should not be produced in turn without difficulty.

DEVIANCE OR DEFECT: _____

SPECIFYING QUESTIONS	Defect IS experienced	Defect IS NOT experienced	Distinctions between IS and IS NOT	Changes which could explain distinctions
IDENTITY What is the unit with the problem/deviation? What is the problem?				
LOCATION Where in the process is the problem observed? Where on the unit is the problem observed?				
TIMING When was the problem first observed? When in the life cycle of the unit is the problem first observed? With what frequency is the problem observed? When specifically is the problem observed?				
MAGNITUDE What is the extent of the problem? How many units are affected? How much of any unit is affected?				

PROBABLE CAUSE(S) OF PROBLEM: _____

Verification by: _____

Figure 6.3   Outline for KT problem solving model

You schedule the production of puce widgets in the mornings and yellow in the afternoons. Business is good and the workplace is humming at a whole new pace. In the quickened pace of the old widget making machinery you can almost hear the acceleration of the growth of your bank balance. But from the start things begin to go wrong.

Every morning your happy workforce turn out puce widgets exactly to specification in ever-increasing numbers to meet a growing market demand. At the start there was a small problem with the late afternoon runs of yellow production – some of the end of shift widgets were emerging from the machines not pure and bright yellow, but a vulgar and ugly orange. At first you were happy to live with it, a little increase in the scrappage rate was a small price to pay for the success of puce in the market place, but now it is becoming serious. It seems that as production of lovely puce widgets increases you can barely get an hour of production of the yellows before the ugly, and unsaleable, orange begins to appear. Fortunately you have been on a Kepner-Tregoe problem solving and decision making seminar so all is not lost.

A quick glance at your notes and you are in problem analysis mode. You complete a worksheet, Figure 6.4, and the problem is defined.

The following points emerge:

1. The problem started with the introduction of the puce widget.

2. The more puce widgets made the greater the problem.

3. The growth in the demand for puce widgets has been met by speeding the line rather than by investing in new plant.

4. Only yellow widgets are affected.

5. Yellow widgets are always made later in the day than puce.

6. There is no material difference between yellow and puce widgets other than colour.

From the above you might isolate the following as possible causes:

1. The ancient widget making machines are unable to cope with the increased production volume and are possibly overheating, causing discolouration.

2. Some colouring matter is left in the machines after the manufacture of puce units which is adulterating the colour of the yellow.

The second possibility seems to be unlikely since the first few yellow widgets are unaffected and one would expect that they would normally be most affected by the adulteration since it would be at its maximum when they are produced.

DEVIANCE OR DEFECT: _ _ _ _ _ _Yellow widgets change colour in production_ _ _ _ _ _ _

SPECIFYING QUESTIONS		Defect IS experienced	Defect IS NOT experienced	Distinctions between IS and IS NOT	Changes which could explain distinctions
IDENTITY	What is the unit with the problem/deviation?	Yellow widgets	Puce widgets	Colour and time of manufacture	Previously only one colour produced at lower volumes
	What is the problem?	Discolouration -yellow turns orange	Any other colour	As above	Production of yellow widgets changed to afternoon only
LOCATION	Where in the process is the problem observed?	Completion of yellow production	Early in Production process	Inspection	Numbers affected increasing with increased production of puce
	Where on the unit is the problem observed?	All over	In limited areas or on parts of unit	Whole unit equally affected	
TIMING	When was the problem first observed?	When puce widgets were introduced	In the good old days when we only made yellow widgets	Introduction of puce widgets and speeding up old production process	Puce widgets
	When in the life cycle of the unit is the problem first observed?	During manufacture	During storage or distribution	Manufacturing process extended	Production volume and timing
	With what frequency is the problem observed?	Daily	Intermittently	Cause is likely to be something which happens daily	Puce widgets
	When specifically is the problem observed?	The latter part of yellow production run, but getting earlier as production of puce increases	In the mornings	Time of day	Yellow widgets made following puce
MAGNITUDE	What is the extent of the problem?	An increasing number of units	A decreasing part of production	Problem appears to increase in line with production of puce	Volumes, timing and speed of line increased
	How many units are affected?	See above	On any puce products	See above	Puce widget production increased
	How much of any unit is affected?	All	Part	Cause affects the whole of any unit	

PROBABLE CAUSE(S) OF PROBLEM: _ _ _ _Overheating or colour remaining_ _ _ _ _ _ _ _ _ _ _ _ _
Verification by: _ _ _ _ _ _ _ _ _ _ _ _ _ _ _ _ _

Figure 6.4 The Yellow Widget problem – example of KT analysis

The probable cause is, therefore, that of overheating. The cause can be verified by slowing down production and seeing if the problem goes away. (Oh dear, it looks as if we may have to invest in some new widget making machinery.)

The tale of the yellow and puce widgets is a simple one, but the technique behind it is powerful. It is a technique which has been successfully applied in areas of complex high technology with advanced ballistic missiles which were going astray and with almost every type of deviation which occurs in business and commerce. If a similar technique were available to economists, economic theory might produce results that would lift it from a position of something like equality with astrology as seems the case today.

SUMMARY

Describing two advanced techniques can be little more than a refresher or a stop gap. Advocates of both Synectics and Kepner-Tregoe methods conduct regular in-house and public training programmes and I cannot emphasise too strongly the advantages in attending both and using the powerful techniques which you will learn. Both offer the additional advantage that they enhance team building activities – KT by providing a shared 'language' between different departments and specialisms and Synectics by bringing people together in an enjoyable activity with a serious and valuable outcome while avoiding the potential problems which are inherent in a premature search for consensus.

Practical advice in problem solving activity

- Be sure that you have adequate power to act.
- Ensure that if major change is required those that will be affected recognise the problem and desire the solution.
- Plan the implementation carefully after testing your solution.
- Establish if help is required.
- Identify champions for change.
- Identify potential problems.
- Plan avoidance and contingency strategies.
- Implement
- Monitor implementation.
- Change methods if necessary, but keep goal firmly in mind.

PITFALLS OF PROBLEM SOLVING

- All problems are submitted to a single problem solving technique regardless of type.

- Blame apportionment is seen as being more important than problem solving.

- Whatever the problem, those who are involved in the problem solving process seek to protect their own backs even at the expense of finding a workable solution.

- Groups are inappropriately excluded or inappropriately included in the problem solving process.

- There is no ownership of the problem.

- Problem solving skills are developed in high risk situations.

- Senior management invites employees to work to solve problems and then rejects or ignores their ideas.

- Management uses the problem solving process as a method of manipulation to get its way by 'delegating' difficult problems and coming in with their preferred resolution when the group are struggling.

- When the problem is not recognised as a problem by the problem owner.

- When the problem owner is dragooned into a solution which they neither desire nor like.

- When the problem owner's power to act is lacking.

- When the solution requires resources beyond the organisation's capability to supply.

7 FINANCE MANAGEMENT

Some of the most important, least understood and most feared tools of management are financial. The financial wellbeing of the company is the essential prerequisite to growth and survival. All managers need to have a good working knowledge of how key financial ratios can help them in the day-to-day management and decision making of the business.

FINANCIAL TOOLS

It is seldom realised that the **balance sheet** is a tool of great importance. It is a model. A model of the business, frozen at a single moment and showing, at that moment, the company's ability to go on trading and justify continued or additional investment.

The **profit and loss account**, similarly offers a picture, couched in financial terms, of the effectiveness of the organisation's buying, selling, product or service building and cost control activities. It also indicates the availability of profit on a month-by-month rolling basis which, through distribution or re-investment in new assets, justifies the confident perpetuation of the capital base.

The profit and loss account and the balance sheet are inseparable in the sense that in the management use of ratios to aid decision making and control they are used together, with information from one source being brought together with information from the other to create a meaningful pool of information.

Take a simple example. To encourage the continued investment of capital in an enterprise is it essential to be able to demonstrate that the assets, paid for through that investment are being effectively and efficiently used. Efficient use lies in the generation of an acceptable level of profit through the exploitation of the assets. If an acceptable level of profit is not generated, the assets might as well be sold or diverted to some other, potentially more profitable purpose. The profit is shown on the profit and loss account and the assets of the company are detailed on the balance sheet. Neither on its own is a particularly meaningful figure. Together they tell an important story of how well resources are used.

The **cash flow forecast** is the last of the three musketeers of management accounts. It predicts the movement of funds in and out of the business and identifies times when the outward flow dictates the need to borrow to satisfy short term needs. It is a basic 'law' of borrowing that short term capital, such as an overdraft facility should be used to cover short term needs such as working capital, (for stocks, debtors and immediate cash needs), while long term loans – including mortgages – should be used to finance long term needs, (premises, plant and equipment amortised over several years).

Budget control

Before moving on, a word about the financial tool with which the majority of managers are most familiar, the departmental budget. A budget is best seen as a tactical plan to achieve worthwhile objectives written in financial terms. It is a working document not a financial constraint. As such there should be no tendency on the part of companies to follow the time-dishonoured path of: 'We are ten per cent adrift in our budgeted sales volume. All expense budgets are to be cut by twelve and a half per cent, (in case it gets worse!)'

What ought to happen is as follows:

- The ten per cent shortfall in sales volume is analysed and specific and true causes are identified.

- A realistic decision is made as to whether, in changing market conditions, the original objectives are still attainable.

- A decision is made whether such objectives, if attained, are worthwhile in terms of immediate return and long term contribution to the business plan.

- An assessment is made of the additional cost of achieving worthwhile objectives in the current and forseeable market conditions.

- A re-assessment is made of whether the attainment of the objectives remains worthwhile at the now higher cost.

- Budgets are either reduced, retained or increased on the basis of the ability and value of achieving established goals.

In my years of experience as a consultant and businessman I have been assured from time to time by finance officers that something like the above has taken place. I have yet to meet the marketing or other specialists with whom they have conferred before slashing budgets across the board. And if they haven't asked those who know, how did they find out?

As a general rule: if an objective was realistic and worthwhile when you set it, it is still worthwhile if it can be achieved at an acceptable increased cost. If it isn't, you should be able to point to specific changes in the market which either make achievement impossible or too costly.

DEFINITIONS

In a short chapter there is insufficient space to do justice to the subtleties of either management or financial accounting, but it might be useful to the reader who has little experience in this field if some basic concepts were defined in everyday language. Those who seek a deeper understanding, and all managers should, might like to consult a thorough and workmanlike book; *Key Management Ratios* by Ciaran Walsh, Pitman Publishing (1993).

Assets

What the company owns with which it conducts its business. These are divided into two types:

Current assets (working capital). The value of stocks, money owed by debtors (accounts receivable), cash on hand or at the bank and securities which could be immediately turned into cash should the need arise. These are assets used on a day to day basis in running the business and are also known as working capital.

Fixed assets. These are the assets which it would take a long time to turn into cash and which would not normally be sold unless the company was being wound up or subject to some other major change. Fixed assets include the buildings (if owned), the land they stand on and plant and machinery.

Liabilities

Are what the company owes to its various creditors.

Current liabilities. These are debts normally repayable within twelve months or on demand. They might include outstanding sums owed to creditors who extend facilities to the company for goods supplied, overdraft facilities, tax payable this year from previous years of trading and similar short term debts.

Long term liabilities. Mortgages, debentures and other loans which have terms longer than one year.

Net worth (equity)

Is the arithmetical difference between the assets and the liabilities. In a healthy firm assets would exceed liabilities and the net worth would be positive. Because the net worth of the company is what would be owed by the company to the owners if the assets were sold and the debts payed, it always appears on the same side of the balance sheet as the liabilities. On old fashioned balance sheets, since the total liabilities and the total assets always balance it was possible to read off the value of assets by reading the bottom line on either side of the page.

Capital employed (funds employed)

Is normally defined as the sum of the fixed assets and current assets less the current liabilities. From what has been said about liabilities and net worth above I hope that it is clear that subtraction can be avoided by simply adding net worth to long term loans. Return on capital employed is a vital ratio which shows how well the resources are being used. To work out ROCE you simply divide the total sales revenues by capital employed and multiply the result by the percentage net profit. For example, if your business was small, having a capital employed of £100 from which you generated sales of £300 and on those sales you made 10 per cent net profit; you would enjoy a highly acceptable ROCE of 30 per cent. (Acceptable that is if you could live on £30 per year and leave a margin for re-investment.)

Solvency

The degree to which the debts of the company can be fully covered by the assets. A solvency ratio of 1:1 would indicate that although the company could meet its commitments by selling or otherwise realising its assets, there would be nothing left for the investors. A company is insolvent if its assets are insufficient to allow it to pay all of the monies which it owes.

Liquidity

A company's liquidity is a measure of the degree to which it is able to provide cash for its day-to-day funding. A company, in general terms, remains liquid as long as it holds cash, or items which can quickly be turned into cash which are sufficient to meet any unexpected call on its resources leaving a surplus adequate for its working capital needs.

SOME IMPORTANT FINANCIAL RATIOS

Return on investment

An important, and popular (with accountants) measure of the long term future of the business. As in the case of ROCE it is established easily by dividing the total sales revenue by the owned investment (net worth) and multiplying the result by the net profit percentage. By excluding debt from the calculation it underlines that if a company can create sales and profit from borrowings in such a way that the profit is greater than the total cost of servicing the loan, it is in the company's interest to borrow. If, in our little ROCE calculation above we had no borrowings, and we found that by borrowing £100 we could double our sales and maintain our net profit margin we would enjoy a ROI of: £600 divided by £100 times 10 per cent, or 60 per cent. Most impressive, but with the same caveat as before. When the cost of borrowing fluctuates wildly as in recent years, accountants prefer to use ROCE rather than ROI. Escalating interest and bank charges can quickly exceed any additional profit in a volatile economy.

Enterprises which hold large and expensive stocks and turn them over very slowly, such as jewellers, need unusually high profit margins to justify investment since the investment cannot, by the nature of the trade, be turned over quickly enough to have a worthwhile multiplying effect. The strategy of the High Street chain jewellers in recent years has been to buck this trend by reducing margins and prices, increasing sales volume and stock turnover to produce a high return on investment without high margin.

Conversely when some businessmen moan that they would, because of low profit margins, be better off with their money left in a building society to accrue interest, they frequently overlook the effect which capital turnover has on their overall return. If you can turn your investment over enough times in terms of sales volume, a low net profit can be very acceptable. Thus the concept of 'pile 'em high, sell 'em cheap'.

Return on working capital

In situations where it is impossible to define the share of total capital which might be properly charged to a commercial department, for example the parts or service department of a motor dealership, it is common to work out the ROWC in the same way as the examples above. Obviously if the sector expected, say, 18 per cent ROCE, there would be a considerably higher expectation for ROWC from each contributing department or the overall justification for investment would not be realised.

Net working capital

The difference, hopefully positive, between total current assets and total current liabilities. If all current (due within twelve months) debts were to be paid off, net working capital would represent the residue which would fund the continuation of the business without recourse to selling the family silver in the form of premises, plant or equipment. The ability of the company to expand its operations and take advantage of opportunities which arise to trade profitably is often determined by its level of net working capital and since a basic goal of the company is to grow, this year's net working capital should be more than last year's.

Current Ratio

Provides the answer to the question 'how much net working capital is enough?' The current ratio is established by the simple arithmetical task of dividing current assets by current liabilities. An answer of two or better generally is taken to indicate that the company has access to sufficient money to carry on and expand trading in most circumstances, but only just. With the reservation that capital and assets should never be so much in excess that they are in effect standing idle, a higher current ratio is desirable. Something around 2.5 would probably delight the average accountant.

Quick ratio (acid test)

In an emergency it may be that the key factor is not how well liabilities are covered so much, but more a case of how quickly can the firm get its hands on cash. By and large inventories, whether in the form of finished, but unsold goods, part finished goods, or raw materials, would take a considerable time to turn into cash. What is more, part finished goods might well need a cash input before they could be made saleable. Quick assets are, therefore, the difference between current assets and inventories. Thus they represent those resources which are in the form of cash, or can quickly be turned into cash. They would include actual cash and marketable securities as well as accounts receivable. By dividing quick assets by current liabilities you have an indication of the company's ability to meet its obligations in an emergency and survive to trade another day. A ratio of better than 1:1 would indicate a good chance of emerging bloodied but unbowed from a crisis.

Expectations, or better requirements, vary in different sectors and in different countries at different stages in the growth of a company. Whereas I was always taught to look for 25 per cent ROI in the retail automotive industry in the United Kingdom, Japanese banks frequently express themselves to be perfectly happy with 8 per cent in the early years of a new enterprise.

If you want to use ratios effectively you need to:

- Identify the levels appropriate to the better performers in your business sector;

- Understand the special circumstances which affect the levels achieved and the degree to which they could be changed with creativity and flair;

- Learn more about ratios than this book has space to teach, either by acquiring a specialist book, or by attending a good training course.

Capital structure

EXCELLENT Sources of funding and the overall financial mix are such that capital is consistently available at the lowest possible cost and utilisation ensures optimal growth in share value in all conditions.

AVERAGE The general sourcing and utilisation of capital leads to acceptable results for shareholders and share values show an overall tendency to rise in all but the most difficult of conditions. Better planning could lead to results closer to the optimum.

UNACCEPTABLE The business is at risk because borrowings are at a maximum, the cost of servicing the debt is unacceptably high and any downturn in business activity is likely to threaten the company's ability to trade profitably and repay interest.

Asset growth

In theory the organisation exists to ensure asset growth which in turn leads to greater shareholder value. In practice the growth in asset value, if out of line with current trading results and therefore present share value, can attract the unwelcome attention of asset strippers who mount an unwelcome bid for the company and, if successful, wind up the business and make a quick and substantial profit on the sale of assets. That's why 'junk bonds' were born.

EXCELLENT A sufficient share of profit is re-invested in the growth of the company each year and resources are increased to facilitate the early achievement of the business plan. Assets are, however, acquired strictly against business needs and the organisation continues to run as a tight ship. The budget for each asset acquisition includes a specific training budget to ensure effective use and an early return on investment. Where possible the acquisition of plant and equipment is preceded by the training of key personnel in its use. Levels of return on capital employed continue to be better than the industry norm.

AVERAGE Assets are acquired when required as indicated by a shortfall in quality or delivery or an increase in downtime and maintenance costs. Where possible employees are encouraged to be creative in the use of existing assets and they take pride in producing timely output of an acceptable quality using equipment which is not entirely suitable either by age or design. Occasionally production is lost through breakdowns of old equipment or the problems which come from the use of no longer suitable premises.

UNACCEPTABLE The primary concern of the Board is to maintain the level of dividend in the short term at all costs. To this end the organisation is starved of investment and *in extremis* borrowings are used to maintain dividends for the current year rather than to ensure the future survival and growth of the firm.

Return on capital employed

EXCELLENT The return on the capital employed in the company is maintained at a high level by constant monitoring both of the rate at which capital is turned over and the level of net profit enjoyed on sales. The top management team constantly monitor the performance of other comparable companies and timely and appropriate actions are taken to keep us in the forefront of our industry. All employees are aware that our ability to compete and to keep them in employment is a function of their expertise in using all resources effectively. Employees frequently make valid suggestions as to how costs may be curtailed and productivity and sales increased.

AVERAGE We do what we can to ensure that resources are used effectively and that sales margins are optimised. We have regular blitz-style cost-cutting exercises and reward employees for worthwhile suggestions. Much of the time, however, the focus is on maximising sales revenues without regard for profit or for the efficient use of investment.

UNACCEPTABLE Trading is carried out at the price that the market will bear without concern for the efficient application of investment.

FINANCIAL MANAGEMENT MODELS

In spite of the deep concerns which many capable managers have, the basics of financial management are simple and can be readily understood. The models in this section are designed to emphasise the basic simplicity rather than to offer a complete course in management accounting.

Whether you are collecting information to solve a problem, assessing the viability of a company or contemplating a change of tactics in a volatile business environment, the use of financial data is, at base, limited to comparing one figure with another, or carrying out one of the four basic calculations of arithmetic. It is seldom more complex than adding two numbers together, subtracting one number from another, multiplying two numbers or dividing one by another. The models have been designed to underline this concept of doing one simple thing at a time.

In my early days in business, finance directors of client companies would tell me that they had made a decision which they would be happy to explain, but which was somewhat complicated. The implication was that I, a non-specialist, would not understand. Fortunately I had been taught to respond with two words. The words were: 'Try me.' Those two words have stood me in good stead across the years. I commend them.

The balance sheet

The oddest thing about the balance sheet is that it is only true for the tiny period of time for which it was drawn up. It is as close to being a snapshot of the business as is possible in a written document. As soon as anything happens in a business, or simply with the movement of time a balance sheet ceases to be entirely true. It is, nonetheless, an important source of information and an important model of the business. The balance sheet tells three important things.

It establishes what the company owes – whether to suppliers, banks or investors. It states what the company owns. And it tells you of the plight of the owners of the company were it to be wound up by selling what it owns and paying all that it owes. What is left, if anything, is the owners' equity in the business. So if it is that simple why all the confusing detail of balance sheets as they appear in real life?

Ironically the detail is there for the express purpose of making things easier. For example it is one thing to know that a company has liabilities of £100,000, it is quite another when you can see that only £10,000 of the total indebtedness is repayable within the next twelve months while the rest is in

BALANCE SHEET	
LIABILITIES(What the company owes)	ASSETS(What the company owns)
CURRENT LIABILITIES – Money owed to suppliers – Short term loans and overdrafts, etc. FIXED LIABILITIES – Long term loans including preference shares, debentures and mortgages. NET WORTH or EQUITY What would be left for the owners of the company if they sold what they own and paid what they owe, and consists of the positive balance between the LIABILITIES and the ASSETS plus any RESERVES built from profits of previous years.	FIXED ASSETS – Property – Plant and Machinery – Transport, etc. CURRENT ASSETS – Cash in hand or at the bank – Stock – Money owed by customers, etc. INTANGIBLES – Goodwill – Patents owned etc.

*Figure 7.1 The three lines which make balance sheets balance: a 'snapshot'
of the Company which provides a summary of assets, liabilities
and ownership.*

the form of a long term loan which is repayable over twenty years. The total debt may appear to be overwhelming to a small company while that which is current is relatively small, and that which might be subject to immediate repayment is tiny indeed. It is to enable those who can use it to get this information that the detail exists.

Accountants attempt to balance the needs of detail and clarity with those of conciseness and on the average balance sheet they have done so very effectively. The balance sheet is a tool. It is a useful and relatively simple tool. All managers should seek to be able to use it.

To use the balance sheet the manager needs to undertake five simple steps:

1. Consider your purpose in analysing the balance sheet. Are you seeking to identify trends over a period of time by comparing balance sheets drawn up for a number of successive years? Or do you seek to assess the company's strength at a single point in time, or both?

2. Calculate and compare, if appropriate, the key ratios.

3. Look closely at any information which looks unusual. Balance sheet ratios or trends which are distinctly different from each other or from what you have learned to expect may tell you a great deal.

4. Become a detective and look for hidden trends. The fact that things are simple does not mean that they have to be obvious.

5. Relate what you find to the business environment as you know it. Try to make sense of what you find in your own world of practical business.

Remember that there are no ideal ratios for balance sheet performance. Different business sectors, different stages in the maturity of a company and even different national cultures dictate fashionable or pragmatic levels of performance. Look and compare, vertically with historic results and horizontally with the results of others in the same sector in the same period. That way the figures will begin to make sense.

When you make horizontal comparisons be aware that circumstances vary from company to company. Even in the same industry at the same time no two companies will have quite the same financing structure or turnover mix. Expect differences and use your knowledge of the business to draw meaningful conclusions.

Even what may look like a poor ratio may make sense in the light of your knowledge of the business. For example high borrowings are a sign of pending disaster if they are the result of a continuing inability to correct losses, but if they are made within the framework of a strategic plan for planned growth after the careful analysis of new market opportunities they may be an indicator of prudence and a harbinger of new prosperity.

Evaluating competitors' financial performance

If you want some solid guidelines as to the ratios which the top companies are enjoying, let me again recommend Ciaran Walsh's *Key Management Ratios* which will give you the information which you seek. But remember that even a top company's balance sheets are only true for one moment of time, so get it while its hot!

You will no doubt have heard of 'creative accounting'. This book is too brief to deal in any kind of detail with the cosmetic activities which are possible, even if I knew them all, which I don't, but the practical manager might look for such things as:

- the sudden and timely revaluation of property;
- overvaluation of stocks by a policy of not writing off obsolete items;
- inflation of assets by the continued inclusion of bad debts far beyond any hope of payment.

Any of the above may be used *in extremis* to make the company look better than it is. The manager may fruitfully ask 'why?' and 'why now?'

How do key ratios relate to each other?

It seems an odd thing to say, but sometimes I feel that the way in which the various factors of finance fit together verges on the beautiful. Take a look at Fig. 7.2. Net working capital is defined as current assets less current liabilities. Current ratio which is indicative of a company's liquidity is found by dividing current assets by current liabilities. The so-called quick assets on which the company ability to survive a financial crisis could depend are nothing more complicated than the current assets without the stocks (which would take some time to turn into cash). And the famous acid test ratio which means so much to accountants everywhere is merely the quick assets divided by current liabilities. Always taking things just two at a time, and always the most simple of arithmetical calculations and all falling neatly together. That is why I think that it's beautiful!

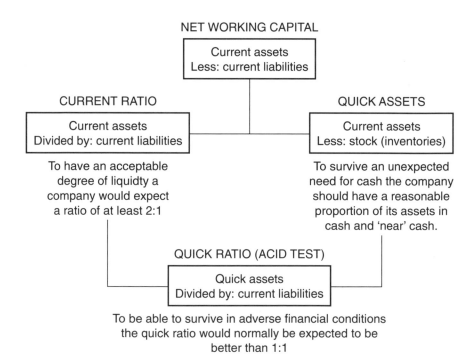

Figure 7.2 Not only are key financial ratios simple mathematically, they fall into family groups

I used to try to persuade managers that management accounting was more than just beautiful, it was fun. I ran a training programme which I called *The FUNdamentals of Finance*. I don't think that anyone believed the title until one day when I was working in a location where the equipment was archaic and looked as if it had been bought second hand from a down-market junior school. There were no flip charts or dry wipe boards. All that was provided was a blackboard of the interesting kind which is made of some form of cloth, which stands about eight foot high and revolves vertically. I had given the group an exercise to do and took advantage in the lull in my lecturing to write a very complex balance sheet on the board ready for the next session. Obviously I didn't want to distract the group from their labours so I wrote the complex figures on the reverse. When the time came to use them the fun began. I had overlooked the small but vital fact that the top of a section of blackboard at the front became the bottom when it was turned to the back. I began the lecture, spun the board to show my carefully written and detailed balance sheet – upside down. At last they found something to laugh at in financial management!

Funding

The small Fig. 7.3 sticks to the theme of no more than two things at a time and gives an overview of where the money comes from to conduct the business.

Capital is either long term, or it is short. Long term or permanent capital is either supplied by the owners of the business or it comes from outside. The owners provide capital through the purchase and retention of ordinary shares and by ploughing back profit into the business. Long term loans are normally in the form of debentures, which are a sort of fixed term share at a specific interest rate, or in mortgages and long term bank loans. It is a truism, as explained above, that long term or permanent capital is used to provide long term or permanent assets or resources.

Short term or working capital comes from the overdraft facility, (which can be reduced or withdrawn without notice) and from suppliers who offer credit terms. Not surprisingly working capital is used to provide the resources which are used in the day-to-day conduct of the enterprise.

Fig. 7.3 shows why Drucker and others have very rightly warned against the pursuit of short term profit as the key objective of the business. There is little point in conducting a business which is unprofitable with little hope of long term survival. Profit is a necessary prerequisite to the survival of the business and the purpose of capital is again twofold.

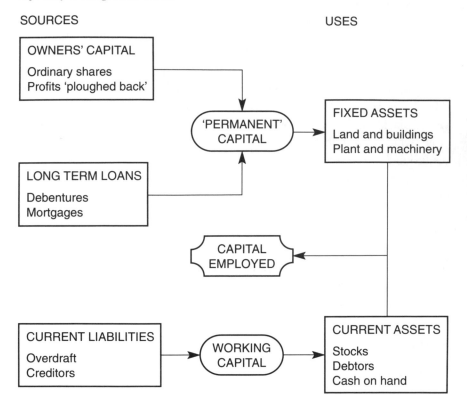

Figure 7.3 Sources and uses of capital

First capital must be used to provide a net profit. Second it must be turned over sufficiently often to provide an acceptable return. As it does so it generates further capital by the re-investment of profits retained in the business and continued and increased external investment. Return on capital is a prime business ratio and the way it relates to sales, capital employed and profit is demonstrated in Fig. 7.4.

Financial problem solving

Most financial problems are of the 'not enough' variety. An inadequate return on investment, insufficient profit or low sales dominate the thinking of the manager. The chart, Fig. 7.5, again encourages the manager to think in pairs. If ROCE is too low for prosperity one of two things must be true: either the turnover of capital is too low or there is not enough net profit. If net profit is too low either direct profit or overheads must be at the base of the problem. And so it goes on, two by two until you get to the root cause.

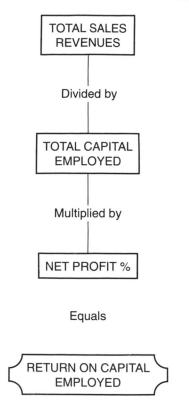

Figure 7.4 The prime business ratio of return on capital

Check list to isolate financial weaknesses and improve cash flow planning:

- Buying policy
- Suppliers – number used, level of returns, frequency of seeking and obtaining quotations
- Availability and use of discounts
- Employee attitude to costs
- Management attitude to costs
- Scrappage rates
- Quality policy
- Customer returns and complaints
- Administrative expense
- Sales expense

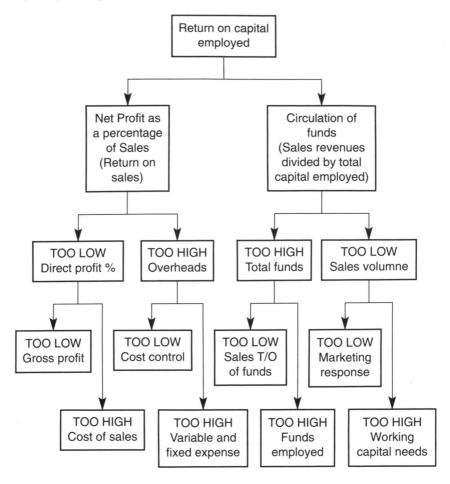

Figure 7.5 Profit improvement – cascade approach: looks at financial figures of merit in pairs to identify problems

- Customer loyalty and repeat orders
- Special customer requirements and short production runs
- Component and raw material costs
- Exchange rate variances and use of overseas suppliers
- Personnel policies and reward/sanction systems
- Sectors and markets served
- Level of prospecting for customers
- Age of product

- Stage of product life cycle
- Salespeople training policy and outcomes
- Stock levels and mix
- Sales 'made to order' as opposed to sold from stock
- Amount and value of 'work in progress'
- Manufacturing and distribution lead times
- Advertising response and campaign quality
- Sales Promotion response levels
- Company image and reputation
- Customer satisfaction indices
- Lapsed customer accounts
- Level of debtors and average age of accounts outstanding
- Company supplier payment policy
- Stock control system

Development of a simple budget

The well-established habit of taking last year's budget and increasing everything by a given percentage is unlikely to be meaningful in tomorrow's fast-moving business environment. The concept of **zero budgeting**, always starting from fresh to establish what must be spent in today's world to achieve goals has much to commend it. For those who seek a short cut to the development of a realistic budget the following will be helpful.

1. The mission, strategy and objectives of the company are central to all budgets. Budgets are there as a financial plan to achieve objectives. The objectives of divisions and departments, if achieved, will ensure the attainment of corporate strategic goals. Therefore the corporate business plan lies at the base of every budget and no budget is meaningful outside the business plan.

2. Departmental and divisional tactical plans are established to exploit opportunities and develop the organisation.

3. Sales and other forecasts are translated into revenues and costs to project income and expenditure.

4. Manpower requirements are assessed. Will staff numbers be increased? Will there need to be a greater emphasis on training? Will wages, salaries, perks or pensions be increased?

BALANCE SHEET			
Where the money comes from (income)		**Where the money goes (expenses)**	
Capital	£	Assets	£
Share Capital	10,000	Land and Buildings	25,000
		Plant and Equipment	13,000
		Furniture and Fittings	2,000
		Company Vehicles	5,000
			45,000
Borrowings		Working capital	
Bank Overdraft	40,000	Stock	40,000
Hire Purchase	5,000	Debtors	30,000
Mortgages	20,000	Work in Progress	1,000
		Cash at bank	4,000
			75,000
Reserves		Less current liabilities	
Revenue reserve	20,000	Creditors	(15,000)
Deferred Taxation	5,000	Current taxation	(5,000)
		Net Working Capital	55,000
	100,000	**Funds Employed**	**100,000**

*Figure 7.6 A typical definition of funds empoyed in the form of a balance
sheet*

5. In a sales environment will variable costs be increased as new volumes are achieved? Will promotion costs or incentives increase?

6. Will improved customer services with regard to the internal as well as the external customer increase costs in the short term, whatever the long term benefit? Will there be need to invest in new equipment?

7. Are there any known, or suspected additional costs as a result of governmental, social or legal requirements?

The budget which is produced must be flexible and directed toward the economic achievement of goals. It should be more than a target against which performance is routinely assessed. It should be a viable and vibrant plan for success at minimal cost.

PITFALLS OF FINANCIAL MANAGEMENT

- Financial decisions are made in isolation without consideration of the strategic plan or the realities of the market.
- Managers outside finance operations are excluded from financial planning.
- Budgets are limited to the assessment of performance.
- Budgets are cut 'across the board' without regard for the value of objectives.
- Cash flow is not planned.

8 MARKETING AND MANAGEMENT

Many years ago, when I first took responsibility for ensuring the development of a consistent yet culturally sensitive market plan in each of a number of international markets I was astounded to find that few of the marketing professionals with whom I had contact really understood what marketing was about. Most had some very specialised knowledge of a single aspect of marketing, perhaps advertising or sales promotion, but it was rare to find anyone who looked at marketing as a fully integrated system of beliefs and behaviours.

MARKETING IS EVERYBODY'S BUSINESS

If the professionals had gaping holes in their understanding of what marketing is, what chance was there that those whose specialisms lay in other fields would have anything other than the vaguest ideas? And I was looking for everybody in every organisation to understand about marketing. Marketing is like the old jazz number which warns: 'If you can't see Mama every night, you can't see Mama at all!' because if you do not have the whole organisation devoted to marketing you don't have marketing at all.

WHAT IS MARKETING?

Definitions of marketing have a tendency to spring up like weeds in an untended garden. But the one which says it most clearly for me is:

'Marketing is an integrated effort by the whole organisation to create, identify and satisfy customer need at a profit.'

So marketing has three aspects none of which is an option. First everyone in the organisation has a role to play. There can be no exceptions. From the way you treat the customer to the way you treat your colleagues, the marketing concept insists that what is done is done, in the last resort, to create, identify and satisfy customer needs at a profit.

Second marketing is proactive as well as reactive. It is as much about creating customer need as identifying it and reacting to it. Some years ago sales of toothpaste in the United States were, to an overwhelming degree dictated by the tastebuds of the buyers' children. Toothpaste sales were dominated by the flavours which children liked because parents bought the toothpaste which children would use without fussing and fighting twice daily. A major marketing technique was to hold tasting clinics at which the latest minty/fruity flavour would be unveiled to an epicurean world. In marketing jargon the primary buying motive was nothing less than hedonism.

One manufacturer of toothpaste was in trouble with this important market segment. The product was good. Clinical tests showed it to be very good indeed, but nobody liked the taste. They could, of course have decided not to buck the trend and simply changed the formula to produce a pleasant tasting alternative. Instead they chose to exploit the difference. They targeted not the kids, but their mothers in an advertising campaign which, in effect, said:

'We wouldn't make it taste this lousy, if we didn't have to, but we have to in order to protect your children's precious teeth.' (I have no doubt that their slogans were slicker, but that was the message.)

The result was to create a major shift in the market. Mums bought what they believed was best and took on, where necessary, the battle of the bathroom. In case you like jargon, the primary buyer motive had shifted to 'nurturing' in marketing parlance.

The third crucial feature of marketing is that it requires that the customer is satisfied, or better yet, delighted but at a profit. Any damn fool can delight customers by giving away an excellent product or by providing a superior service at no cost. Marketing demands that every employee, from the shop floor down to the CEO, actively seeks ways of optimising the profit while still ensuring consistent satisfaction. This is what makes any organisation which really understands the marketing concept a cohesive marketing team. Never let those who talk knowingly of 'above the line' and 'below the line' spend, or other similar arcane expressions, con you into believing otherwise.

If you are wondering if there is a typing error when I say 'down to the CEO', or whether I am just not bright enough to understand the 'this way up' of an organisation chart, let me reassure you. Where marketing is involved the customer is firmly at the top of any chart with customer-facing staff next in the heirarchy. The CEO is, from a marketing, or for that matter Total Quality, perspective at the bottom of the pile of relative importance.

Consider if you would another definition.

'To consistently and for all time delight the customer at minimum cost.'

The above is a popular definition of Total Quality Management. If you accept the, I believe, inescapable fact that TQM implies the active input of the total organisation team, I would suggest that it would be difficult to distinguish between the two concepts. TQM involves the wider team of suppliers and distributors as I would argue that marketing should. In short, TQM is the ultimate marketing strategy.

Market segments or sectors?

As with all specialisms marketing has a tendency to create and perpetuate jargon. Two words which are often confused, even by the professionals, are segmentation and sectorization. A market is segmented if you start with your product or service and then seek to establish which groups are likely to want to buy it. So if you design the proverbial 'better mousetrap' you assume that only a part of the world will in fact beat a path to your door, and you try to establish which recognisable segments together make up that part in order that you may target your message and direct it specifically to probable purchasers. (Incidently there was a joke current among American marketeers a few years ago which went: 'I invented a better mousetrap. All I got out of it was a better mouse.')

If, on the other hand, you start by investigating the market to establish what needs may exist which you have the ability to satisfy, you are using a sectoring approach. So the sector approach is driven by grouping similar customer needs and relating them to your capability, while segments are the identified potential buyers of your existing offering. Levitt's concept of marketing myopia, an over-narrow definition of the business, is frequently the result of a history of successful segmentation leading to the thought that 'we are, and always will be the premier pony cart manufacturer'. Very nice, unless, of course you persist in that belief long after the need for carts has been superceded by the invention and development of the car.

Product life cycle

A favourite marketing concept is that of the product life cycle. This suggests that there is a natural life-span of a product or service from *introduction*, through *acceptance* and *application* and *maturity* to *decline*. The vital role of marketing professionals is to increase the period of acceptance and maturity by decreasing the time which it takes for the product to get established and, toward the close of day, pre-empt the decline of demand. The first goal of rapid acceptance by the market is achieved by effective product launch and sales promotion strategies. The second goal of extended maturity is achieved in general by developing the product to provide new benefits or by finding alternative markets or both.

The figure 8.3 which I have freely adapted from Gilley and Egglund's excellent book *Marketing HRD Within Organisations* shows, by way of novelty, the perceived life cycle of training fads, fancies and firm favorites. The lower figure shows how I use the concept of the product life cycle to research, design and develop a new concept in sales training based on the philosophy that you can win them all. All that you need to do is understand a little buyer psychology and the realities of today's business environment, add a smattering of sensitivity to what the customer is communicating and enough flexibility not to have to regard every problem as a nail and you are in business.

Dogs, cows and stars

I believe that it was the Boston Consulting Group which many years ago introduced the terminology which defines products as cash cows, stars and dogs.

A **cash cow** is a well-established product which, for the time being at least, goes on selling and bringing in revenues and profits with little additional investment in promotion. It is usually a well-known brand with a well-understood demand and until it reaches the end of its life cycle it will go on churning in the profit which will, in part at least, finance the development of the star.

The **star** makes a major contribution to the profitable perpetuation of the firm. The star, however, often demands heavy and expensive promotion, which it justifies, unlike the dog.

The **dog** either has had, or never will have its day. Dogs are products which the market has rejected, sometimes as a result of reaching the end of the life cycle, often without ever getting off the ground.

Cows require little investment, they just mooch gently on bringing in the cash. Stars eat up investment as if it were hydrogen, and like their namesakes in the firmament they are the providers of life. Dogs, I am sorry to say, have to be left, in a harsh world to die in ditches. They are the no-hopers of the marketing zoo. As the late and to my mind very great Harry Worth used to say: 'They keep on at me to make a comeback. I don't think I've been anywhere.' Dogs are going nowhere.

PRICING STRATEGY

It continues to surprise me that I still meet managers on marketing seminars who are startled to be told that pricing is a strategic concern. It seems that there is a general belief that prices are established either by taking a wild guess at what the market will stand, giving it a try and laughing all the way to the bank if you get away with it, or by establishing the cost and simply adding a margin for profit while hoping for the best.

The pricing policy needs to satisfy, at the same time, the need for an adequate return on investment and a clearly defined marketing objective. Either of the two approaches outlined above completely ignores one of these essentials. Pricing should be taken more seriously, and the strategy should be in the hands of the professionals. Some of the better-known strategies include:

Differential or flexible pricing

Low prices are used in slack periods to generate sales and even out fluctuations in demand. With the use of intelligent shelves in supermarkets, prices can be adjusted today automatically to ensure an even flow of sales and little or no produce left on the shelves to pass its sell-by date.

Discreet pricing

This is the nearest thing to licking your finger and holding it into the wind which professionals will countenance. Discrete pricing seeks to be neither high nor low, but by being aimed at the majority of customers' willingness or ability to pay it ensures an adequate return on investment by maximising sales revenues.

The ability to pay, however, is established by careful research and is not the result of unbridled hope or a wild guess.

Discount pricing

Pricing is carefully used as a tool to attract volume business at a level where its profitability is maximised through ease of distribution or economies of scale.

Guarantee pricing

Prices are high, but so is the actual value of the product or service. Rolls Royce service at Rolls Royce prices.

High price maintenance

Similar to guarantee pricing, but in this case the superior value of the product may be more apparent than real, being based on a long and complex history of brand imaging. For example a manufacturer may sell the same goods under different labels – one of them at a premium price. I'd love to give you some examples, but my publisher would object to being sued!

Off-set pricing

Basic prices are low to attract customers, but 'extras' are heavily promoted and carry a heavy price penalty. When I was in the automotive industry many years ago it was common practice to offer a 'basic model' of a car at a highly competitive price. The dealers were not, however, expected to sell these real value-for-money models. They were required to 'sell up' from them, a requirement which was often backed up by the manufacturer with stiff price penalties to the dealer network if they failed to sell the cars which came complete with all the bells and whistles.

Price lining

No company ought to consider this strategy in a world in which quality is king. It is the old trick of reducing product quality and standards of service to accurately reflect the level of the price. A case of building down to a price rather than up to a specification. Examples could again lead to writs, so I'll resist the temptation.

Diversionary pricing

Also known as **loss leaders**, this is the concept of offering a limited range of products at a low price with the intention of giving a (false) impression of low prices overall. How often do you hear the complaint: 'Not everything is cheaper there you know' directed at a so-called 'discount store'? Such a remark indicates a situation in which diversionary pricing has been tried without success.

Skimming pricing

Intentionally creating prices so high that they put the product or service out of the reach of the majority of the market to attract profitably those few buyers who seek to buy exclusivity at any price.

I hope that there are enough examples above, some reputable, some not, to ensure that the manager from other disciplines understands that the business of pricing is more complex than 'pile 'em high, sell 'em cheap'. The most interesting thing may be, however, to reflect on how often you or I are the victims of less estimable practices.

TO MARKET WITH A PLAN

Marketing starts with a customer and ends with a delighted advocate and a profit. To achieve that it must be lived by a visualised and integrated team who are committed to a marketing strategy which is comprehensive, congruent with the values of the organisation and consistent with the reputation, image and products of the firm and those whom it serves.

The marketing plan will include, at the very least:

- Market analysis and research, including competitive analysis;
- Product strategy;
- Sales promotion strategy;
- Advertising plan;
- Congruent personal selling policies and techniques;
- A defensible pricing strategy;
- The building of company and brand image;
- Timely and relevant feedback followed by evaluation and review of plans.

In a short chapter it would be overwhelmingly ambitious to attempt to do justice to each of the above. Marketing is sustained by information, the models which follow are designed to provide a framework in which data may be processed into information. A company-wide marketing strategy is portrayed in Fig. 8.1.

Marketing plan

EXCELLENT Marketing is recognised throughout the organisation as the active responsibility of all employees. There is a concerted and totally integrated effort to create, identify and satisfy customer needs consistently and at minimum cost. All employees are trained not merely in the theoretical aspects of the marketing concept, but also in the specifics of action and behaviours which enable them to make a full contribution to the marketing effort. Workshops are regularly conducted to enable all employees to plan their contribution to exceptional customer care. We regularly analyse the actions of the competition to ensure that we can stay in the forefront of customer satisfaction.

Our marketing efforts are flexible and are planned to meet the identified needs of each sector and segment which we serve.

AVERAGE All employees are aware of the primacy of customer needs and do their best to meet them. We are strong on exhortations to ensure that all employees are aware that the customer comes first. Characteristically we spend large sums on posters and other communication devices to ensure that employees see that the company is customer-driven. We use glitzy and slick 'sheep dip' training programmes to motivate the staff to want to care for the customer.

Some attempt is made to market on an understanding of the needs of the various sectors which we identify, but much of our marketing effort is focused on the segments to which our products appeal.

UNACCEPTABLE Marketing is a specific and separate specialist function which addresses the needs of sales promotion, advertising, personal selling, public and press relations, product development and little else. Each functional area operates autonomously with little or no consideration for the effect of its activities on other organisational operations.

Our approach to the market is totally product-driven and we make little attempt to identify emergent customer needs.

MARKETING MODELS

The Marketing Plan

The marketing plan, like so much in the business begins with the mission of the company. The mission will have been designed within the corporate planning process (Fig. 8.1) to clarify what is different about the firm's offering. In short the mission states why the customer should do business with this company rather than another way round. The marketing process should, therefore, be totally consistent with the aims and ethics implied and expressed by the mission statement.

Drucker was firm in identifying the key areas in which corporate objectives of the business should be set. The primary goal of marketing must, through customer satisfaction, be that of market standing. That is not enough, however. The definition of marketing requires that market standing should be developed and maintained at a profit. For that reason the objectives of the marketing plan should address the needs of an adequate return on investment directly. Failure to do so will all too often lead to excessive expenditure in pursuit of market penetration with potentially disastrous results. Similarly, nothing will be done in even the most automated of businesses without the

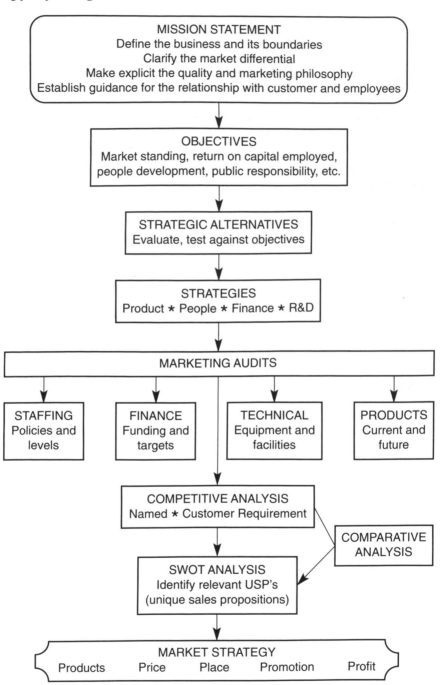

Figure 8.1 The market plan and its relationship to corporate planning

involvement of people. Marketing involves all of the people all of the time. Specific objectives must be developed which clearly indicate how all those involved will be prepared to play their marketing role.

Many companies today are responding to customer concern by emphasising the environmental friendliness of their products. In an ever more competitive environment the companies which have broad ranging and appropriate objectives which relate to public responsibility will enjoy a vital marketing edge. This is not to suggest that marketeers of the future should become pseudo-social workers. All marketing decisions should be hard-nosed business decisions, but where social concerns may be properly addressed in the interests of both society and the organisation – that is marketing.

As with corporate strategic planning, the marketeer should be creative in the development of strategic alternatives. Good products and services are costly to develop and in a fast-moving technological environment the time available to exploit them profitably may become shorter. A wide range of viable and attractive strategies will play an important role in providing the essential flexibility to be proactive in a volatile market.

Selected strategies will be those which promise to meet market standing aspirations to the benefit of customer and company. At the least they will when chosen for product or service development and research. Recruitment, training and use of people and the timely availability of necessary financial resources are also key parts of the internal strategy.

Marketing audits will be company-wide and aimed at a clear assessment of the company's ability to deliver what it promises. There is nothing to be gained from developing a promotional strategy at the end of the line which promises the earth only to deliver little more than mud. The promotional strategy needs to specify the usual four 'P's', product, place, promotional tactics and price each of which should be considered against the background of the company need for profitable sales.

Competitiveness

The next model, Fig. 8.2, provides a simple and useful tool for simultaneously meeting the needs of customer needs analysis, internal capability audits and competitive analysis.

Competitor information needs to be accurate, timely and complete for all of those who are in a position to adversely affect the company's ability to compete. This is assessed in terms of competitors' ability in effectively identifying, creating and satisfying customer need.

A SWOT analysis (assessment of coporate or departmental strengths, weaknesses, opportunities and threats), or better, if it is carried out by a relatively inexperienced team, a COST analysis (concerns, opportunites,

**COMPETITIVE ANALYSIS TO
ASSESS ABILITY TO FULFIL CUSTOMERS' NEEDS**

COMPETITORS

CUSTOMER NEED	Importance	My capability														

Figure 8.2 Competitive analysis worksheet based on assessment of ability to fulfil customers' needs

strengths and threats) should provide the areas to be exploited, and particularly **unique sales propositions** (USP's) based on those strengths. It should enable the company to prioritise weaknesses or concerns so that those which get in the way of customer satisfaction are resolved or minimised while threats to the organisation's ability to meet its goals are identified, categorised and contingent and avoidance plans are developed. Opportunities are the key to the promotional strategy and should be considered from every direction not merely to provide a rich mix, but to encourage all those in the organisation to contribute to market intelligence as relevant information comes to them from a myriad of sources. See Chapter 2 for basic principles behind a COST analysis.

There was a story which did the rounds some years ago about the chief executive of a major supermarket chain. It was claimed that prior to the opening of a new branch he would comb the local refuse dump for empty cans and bottles (this was before recycling) to establish what people bought and thus what should be stocked and what would need to be heavily promoted. I have no doubt that the story was apocryphal, but it underlines the idea that everybody has an active role to play in market intelligence.

Competitive analysis

This model enables the manager, on a single page, using the form given in Fig. 8.2, to analyse customer need, compare the company's capability to satisfy that need with that of critical, named competitors and identify gaps in the market intelligence which is available.

List the key needs of customers in the major sectors of the market in which your company serves in the left column as indicated.

In the 'Importance' column rank each need in terms of its importance to the customer using the simple coding:

H (high). Of considerable importance to potential and actual customers. A key determinant of the buying decision for many. A perceived solution for a known major problem which the sector or industry faces in the market today.

M (medium). Desirable to present and future customers, but not in the forefront of their thinking at present.

L (low). Of limited interest to customers at present, but potentially an area of recognised need in the future.

In the 'Your Company' column rank your capacity to service each specific need again using the H, M, L coding or using the following numerical grades for greater sophistication:

5 Excellent, an exemplary ability to handle market needs. The bench mark which others strive to copy.

4 Good, markedly better than average.

3 Satisfactory, considerably better than average.

2 No better than average.

1 Poor – not acceptable (if the rating 1 is placed against any need which has been identified as being of HIGH importance the company must rapidly develop the ability to meet it, or must consider a considerable change of marketing strategy.)

* The necessary information is not at present available. (If this is an important customer need it is essential to research both the company's and its key competitors' capability as a matter of urgency.)

Having assessed your own company's capability, identify key competitors by name and assess them on the same basis, using the same marking system. Where information is lacking it is essential that all which refers to an area of importance to the customer *must* be investigated and the comparison between the company's and its competitors' capability must be evaluated. To grow and prosper in a highly competitive market the choice is between equalling or exceeding the ability of the best of the competition to meet known customer needs, or developing new needs which your organisation is best placed to meet.

PRODUCT LIFE CYCLE

The concept of the product life cycle has always been central to marketing strategy. All products and services have a tendency to follow a simple and similar path from introduction through to eventual decline. After a period of early, and often expensive, exposure to the marketplace comes a period of gradual acceptance. Maturity of demand, if and when it occurs is a period of greater or lesser length in which the mature market demand continues to rise before moving into slow, but inexorable decline. The period of post-maturity decline is normally characterised by a relatively rapid falling off in demand for the product.

Investment in development and promotional budgets is usually high in the periods of exposure and acceptance, becomes moderate to low during maturity and should become very low during decline. It is a cardinal rule of promotional tactics that money is not spent to promote into a non-existent market. Development expenditure during decline may be justified in an attempt to economically present the market place with a product for which there is demand by either finding new uses for the existing product, or changing it sufficiently to resurrect buying interest. (See Chapter 6 on creative problem solving.)

My interest in education and training leads me to exemplify this with the double example shown in Fig. 8.3. The world of training and education is one in which solid research-driven practical needs constantly are in competition with the fads and fallacies of the moment. These fads frequently dominate the expenditure on training until they are found to be of little practical use. Since they were in favour with many simultaneously they are found out in all their weaknesses together. When they are found wanting they usually go into fairly rapid decline. This situation is made more complex because valid and worthwhile training is treated as a fad and may be introduced into the wrong culture at the wrong time with unrealistic expectations. Such 'flavours of a bygone month' often make a comeback later under circumstances which create a danger of perceived faddishness all over again. In short the world of training is volatile and uncertain.

As I write, in 1993, the world of training products looks somewhat as the top graph. Programmes in intrapreneuring are at the earliest stage of exposure, having been introduced only by a few companies such as IBM. The need to fully utilise all resources will, it is predicted, rapidly lead to a growth in such programmes. Similarly information technology, in the sense of what state-of-the-art technology can contribute to the competitive edge in an information-driven society, is beginning to take off.

Management development is accepted in principal, but the form which such development should take for the future is being questioned. The mushroom growth, for example, of MBA (Master of Business Administration) programmes during the eighties is now being questioned as is the transfer of learning to the workplace of highly academic concepts and ideas.

Sales training is seen as being 'mature'. In a highly competitive world there is always a demand for sales training, and in recession when the pennies have to be counted, training which it is hoped will increase revenues continues to be valued. Although it continues to ride high, sales training may in fact be on the verge of decline. Little has been done to genuinely present a new approach which gives a genuine competitive edge to those who practise it, and the change to a post-modern business society is crying out for a complete break away from the 'pile 'em high, sell 'em cheap' philosophy.

Programmes such as leadership based on Blake and Mouton's Management Grid are in decline as more sophisticated and situation-sensitive

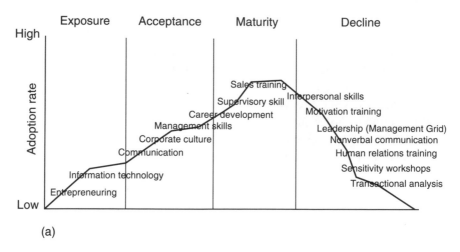

(a)

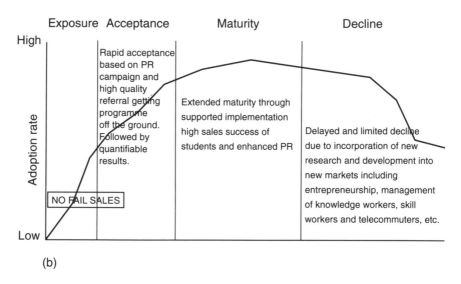

(b)

*Figure 8.3 (a) The current product life cycle of training according to Gilley
and Eggland (1992); (b) Planned life cycle of 'no fail sales' with
supported implementation*

approaches demand consideration. Meanwhile, except as a part of some of
the less effective customer care offerings, transactional analysis has almost
disappeared from current interest. This is not to say, as I made clear above,
that TA and possibly Management Grid are either inappropriate or incapable
of making a comeback. The product life cycle says little about the intrinsic
worth of the product, it speaks only of market demand over time.

As an example of how the product life cycle can be used in practice the lower part of Fig. 8.3 takes the development of a programme of my own and relates the strategy to bring it to the marketplace with the predicted effects on life cycle. It will be obvious by now that the key factors relating to the life cycle are as follows, to:

1. Use the life cycle concept to assess market potential for a new product or service;

2. Design the new product or service to offer the satisfaction of an important emerging or existing need;

3. Minimise the time and cost of early exposure and move to the earliest possible acceptance;

4. Extend the period of maturity as long as possible and delay or limit the decline of demand.

Background to the decline of sales training

As an aside, I offer the indicators which place sales training on the brink of the declining part of the product life cycle:

1. There is a continued high level of demand for sales training in principle.

2. Current offerings, in spite of grandiose claims, provide little to differentiate one approach from another.

3. There is little indication that providers have sufficient confidence in their products to offer a guarantee of results.

4. Few, if any programmes, have built in a comprehensive strategy to ensure transfer to the workplace.

5. By implication or explicitly, existing programmes support the salesperson's contention that 'you can't win them all'. No programme currently exists which is comprehensive enough to reflect the conclusion of modern influence psychology and biology that you can win them all. But to do so requires a wide range of compliance techniques which are sensitively applied.

6. Little of any depth indicates that current sales training offerings are accurately reflecting the changing needs of a post-modern business society.

7. There is little evidence that any present programme is fully sensitive to gender differences in communication and is designed to enable participants of both sexes to exploit them intelligently and congruently.

8. Few if any programmes are fully supported in the field to ensure the economic achievement of pre-determined objectives.

9. Few, if any programmes are co-designed and co-presented by teams which reflect academic and very recent practical knowledge, presented by qualified trainers who represent both sexes.

10. Only one other programme is known to exist which is equally valid for management and sales training and works well with mixed groups.

TRAINING STRATEGY TO AVOID DECLINE

By using available practical research it is now possible to avoid all the above symptoms at an acceptable cost.

A programme is designed, say, combining the best validated research with state-of-the-art materials and a planned strategy for the transfer of learning to the work situation. A fast track sales director with a reputation for training and coaching tests the programme and joins the team.

Since the total concept is new and therefore newsworthy a press campaign to increase credibility, reduce promotional costs and accelerate acceptance is combined with a word-of-mouth campaign of referral.

By insisting on, and publishing quantifiable results, the climb from acceptance to maturity is rapid. The period of maturity is extended by continued emphasis on measurable results and the growth of the use of the programme with groups of senior executives and managers.

Decline is delayed by the inclusion of new research findings as these are validated and the development of specialist courses from the main programme.

I hope that the above little case has demonstrated that the concept of product life cycle is more than an arid theory or the result of accumulated hindsight. At any stage in the life of a product it is possible to assess the position which it holds and where, without some 'proactivity', it may be heading. By actively seeking ways to extend the period of maturity and stave off decline, stars and cash cows can make a significantly greater contribution to the results of the organisation, particulary if the products outline as well as outperform the competition

ADVERTISING

From time to time in my consultancy career I have had the opportunity of training advertising agency staff in writing **'haemorrhoid' advertising**.

That is advertising which will never win any prestigious awards, but which will none the less sell products or services. It is called haemorrhoid because it is based on the concept of reaching and offering relief to those who have the pain. More to the point I have trained small businesses to develop their own advertising to increase sales while minimising the spend.

With that background in mind perhaps a brief overview will be of help to those readers who run, or are employed by, small businesses.

Direct mail

The first thing to consider is when to advertise. If your current and potential customers are so dispersed that you have little other hope of reaching a significant number at reasonable cost, that is the time to advertise. **Direct mail** is always more focused and gives you more room to say all that you have to say to those who are interested enough to read it. Always consider direct mail with long copy first. But if your market is dispersed you may well fall back on general advertising.

Advertising professionals enthuse endlessly about the delights of white space, while others assure you that people simply will not read anything more than a couple of pages. All of the reliable evidence points to the fact that long copy sells. It is much more important when designing a direct mail piece to design it to provide the detailed information that those who may be interested in your product will need to make a decision than it is to create something clever and eye-catching. I admire creativity, but I throw dozens of creative pieces away every day. Those that I read may not be so smart, but they give me information which I believe I need to make an informed decision. The same rules apply for content for direct mail as for advertising. The difference is that with a mailing piece you are not limited to x column centimetres. Make the most of it, tell the already interested what they need to know to become buyers.

However, never advertise unless you know that there is a market out there for your product. Advertising when the market is non-existent in order to try to generate interest is a quick way to Carey Street.

Media advertising

Don't advertise with media which you know nothing about simply because a persuasive salesman approaches you by telephone with an offer which will never be repeated. If a magazine, newspaper or journal invites you to take space ask for a **media pack**. The pack will give you a breakdown of readership and distribution and will normally include a copy of the publication. Study them carefully before making a decision.

You may consider using an agency. Some are wildly expensive and profligate with the client's budget, but the majority will make more of a limited budget than the non-professional can expect to.

Do-it-yourself advertising

If you decide that you will write and place your own advertising take confidence from the fact that many small businesses have done so successfully for many years. The important thing is to work within your budget and write advertisements which bring you business, not admiration.

What you write must include the following:

Heading

Your advertisement is aimed at being read by those few among the vast number in the market place who will be interested in buying your services now or in the future. It is competing with the other advertisements and editorial for their limited attention. Make sure that your header says 'READ ME' loud and clear to the right people.

You need to identify your readers by name, description, profession or shared problem. For example:

ARE YOU CALLED SMITH?

TODAY'S WOMAN

SOLICITORS AND BARRISTERS

SHORT OF CASH?

Offer

Once they have started to read, your prime requirement is to ensure that they keep right on reading until they take the desired action. They have to believe that here is the answer to their problems or the highroad to their dreams. So make it clear up front that their wishes will be granted because if you fail to convince them early, you quickly lose their attention. For example:

'You will learn the secrets of the super-rich in one fun-packed day.'

'Reduce your motoring budget by at least ten per cent.'

Evidence

Give your readers reason to believe that you can deliver what you promise and be sure that you can. Never make the asumption that there will always be another customer before long. Convey your conviction about your product. For example:

'More than a million delighted users world-wide.'

'A unique, new, but proven approach.'

'Researched and validated by Cambridge University.'

Expand on your offer

If space and budget allow, develop the benefits which buyers of your services will gain. Where possible, create a logical linkage between benefits so that belief in the first guarantees belief in the second which in turn ensures acceptance of the third and so to the end.

Facilitate action

Tell your readers what they must do to achieve the benefits you offer. Be sure to give them alternatives:

- A tear-out coupon to mail.
- The telephone number for those in a hurry.
- Your fax number if you have one.

If you include a mailing coupon make sure that some way of contacting you is printed elsewhere in the advertisement for those who see or refer to the advertisement after the coupon has been cut out.

Strategy for advertising

To determine what you may most effectively say about yourself and to get an idea of what it may cost you to say it take the following seriously:

1. Understand the business environment

- What is the economic, social, legislative and business situation?
- Who are your competition?
- What are their strengths and weaknesses?
- What are yours?
- What do you have to offer that is unique?
- Is there anything which is being underplayed by your competition so that if you were to promote it the reader would assume that you have it uniquely?

2. Opportunity analysis

- What are the opportunities right now? In the immediate future?
- Where could you make your biggest gains?

3. Position your business

- The least effective advertising is that which says: 'We do anything for anyone and do it cheaper.' Position your business to ensure that those who seek to hire you understand that they are hiring specialist expertise from a company with a defined culture and values.
- If you are a business 'which cares and goes on caring', or if you 'charge only for everything necessary, and nothing extra', or if you offer 'Rolls Royce service at Ford prices,' think how you will communicate the idea clearly in a few, inexpensive words.

4. Write advertising objectives

- Establish the number of responses that you need.
- Calculate the incremental sales which you want the advertising to bring in.
- Clearly identify the market segments which you must reach.
- Determine the key points which readers of your advertisements need to recognise and respond to.

5. Establish you budget

- Obtain media packs from those publications which you are considering.
- Establish precisely what your advertisement will cost in terms of £/1000 target readers reached.

6. Consider an agency

- A reliable agency can save you much grief. If you are clear about what you want to achieve, who you want to reach and what you want to say, an agency can place your advertisements very advantageously. But be warned, to approach an agency as a means of avoiding having to think for yourself could lead to disaster.
- Agencies are paid a commission on the placing of your advertisements by the media who benefit. If you have a large budget they may be willing to handle your account for free. In any case their costs ought to take into account the 10 to 15 per cent commission which they are paid by the publication,

7. Measure the results

- Compare the results from different publications, different positions and different days of the week.

- Consider using a scrapbook to monitor your most and least successful advertisements.

- *Never be afraid to repeat a successful advertisment – you are building business, not seeking prizes for novelty.*

8. Determine the risk

- What could go wrong with an advertisement?

THE MEDIA

Since the majority of businesses advertise through the medium of print, I have concentrated on print until now. Some readers are likely to be more adventurous and will want to investigate other media. For them a brief overview is appropriate.

In order to make an informed choice it is necessary that you:

- Know the types of media;
- Consider the advantages and disadvantages of each;
- Buy the media to your best advantage ;
- Understand some of the techniques which add an extra dimension to a medium's effect.

Understanding the media

An advertising medium is defined as being any vehicle which carries your promotional message to the targeted client. Professionals would normally list ten, of which by no means all are relevant to your needs. But for the sake of completeness I list them all.

Newspapers

Advantages

- Broad market coverage
- Readers are actively seeking information/ideas

- Permanency. Ads are torn out for future reference
- Credibility high
- Position of ad can select readers
- Illustration easy and relatively inexpensive
- Copy emphasis readily controlled by size and style of type, headlines, captions, subheads etc.
- Wide choice of size and therefore cost
- Geographically as well as demographically selective.

Disadvantages

- Circulation pattern may not efficiently cover all prospects
- Publication pattern may not meet your needs
- Competition for reader attention
- Mass medium, restricts ability to target prospects

Magazines

Advantages

- Full colour potential
- Prestige
- Effective targeting
- Many more readers than circulation figures suggest: 'pass along' readership
- Can support and be supported by, your articles, press releases and letters
- Frequently offer excellent deals to advertisers for copy close to deadline if space still unsold.
- Some, such as Management Today are the official organs of a professional body. (The IM)

Disadvantages

- Scheduling relatively inflexible – long lead time to publication
- Lacks immediacy, can imply lack of urgency for response
- Quality of artwork required may be difficult/expensive

Direct mail

Advantages

- Messages can be directed to a highly selected target group
- Messages can be any length
- Mailing personalised
- Timing highly flexible
- Continues contact with existing clients leading to potential referral and repeat business
- Can 'piggy back' with non-competing material to reduce cost

Disadvantages

- Total dependence on quality of list of contacts
- Rented lists only usable once
- Bought lists need constant updating
- Built-in resistance to 'junk mail'
- Less than 8 seconds attention average

Radio

Advantages

- High frequency at reasonable cost
- Flexibility. You can change copy right up to transmission
- Cheap to produce
- Can be highly creative
- Relatively low per listener cost

Disadvantages

- You cannot use visuals to support your message
- Lacks permanency
- Very localised and variable listener base
- Cannot put across detail effectively

Television

Advantages

- High impact - sight, sound, movement
- Memorable
- Demonstrations convincing
- Scheduling flexibility
- Closest approximation to face-to-face communication
- High credibility 'saw it on television', 'as seen on television' gives inexplicable power to attract buyers.

Disadvantages

- Production costs high
- Professional help essential to prepare commercials
- High transmission costs
- Desirable 'spots' expensive and difficult to acquire

Cinema

Advantages

- Low overall cost
- Relatively low production costs
- Large screen – colour – sight and sound
- Relatively attentive audience

Disadvantages

- Limited exposure
- Need to check carefully types of advertiser you will be associated with
- Cost per prospect highly dependent on film showing at time of ad.
- Very difficult to measure results
- Very local coverage

Good Will Gifts

Advantages

- Keeps your name in front of client for as long as gift is useful and lasts

- May last many years e.g. 'leather' or brass edged document wallets, calculators

Disadvantages

- May be expensive
- Much competition
- Message limited and static

Outdoor advertising

Hoardings large and small, the growing fleet of mobile billboards and bus shelters play a useful role in ensuring that the name of the advertiser is seen all around the place and can help to build brand awareness, but they have little value to those whose need is to build immediate business.

Transport advertising

Unless you have a thing about getting your name known with passengers on a certain bus or underground route it is difficult to see how this kind of advertising could be applied to building your business. For ads placed *outside* public transport the fact that the advertisement is moving means that the message must be brief and catchy and if your intended customers travel by car they can only see and read easily the lower rear panel.

Pulling it together

Advertising is always expensive. You cannot afford to let it become an expensive failure. Use advertising tactically where no effective alternative exists and use it thoughtfully.

Buy advertising skillfully. Where you have the flexibility, place your advertisements just before press time at bargain prices. You can save 50 per cent or more on the cost of placing an advertisement by taking advantage of the offers which papers and journals are prepared to make when they are faced with the choice of either selling space cheaply, or of reducing the number of pages in the issue.

Measure the effect of each advertisement carefully. Never rely on the ability of enquirers to remember where they saw your advertisement. If you are advertising in several publications at once and want accurate information on which is 'pulling' for you use a clip-out coupon. Put a different code in the corner of the coupon used in each publication or keep a copy and check returns to see what is printed on the reverse. (It is almost certain that no two publications will carry the same insertion on the back of your advertisement so you will have an accurate indication of when and where the advertisement appeared.)

Do all that you can to predetermine the probable effect of any advertisement before it goes to press. You will still get surprises, but at least your chances of missing an important error in style or copy decrease with care.

PRINCIPLES FOR EVALUATING YOUR ADVERTISEMENTS

1. Does the advertisement demand positive attention?

2. Is the headline powerful?

3. Does it offer meaningful benefits for my target audience?

4. Is the message clear?

5. Does it address predetermined needs?

6. Is the layout clear and easy to follow?

7. Is the overall image positive?

8. Is the stimulus for action now likely to be effective?

9. Is it clear how, when and where to respond?

10. Address, telephone number and fax clear and accurate?

11. Does my advertisement indicate why my product/service, rather than my competition's?

12. Would I spend my money in response to this advertisement?

13. How do I rate the overall impression? What will be my readers' gut reaction?

If your advertising or mailing fails

Symptom: Little response

Possible cause:
Wrong pricing, if priced

Message vague

Insufficient frequency of repetition

Advertisement too small

Wrong medium or wrong publication

Wrong placement of ad. in publication or wrong timing of transmission

Poor mailing list

Buyers simply aren't there at present.

Symptom: Good response, poor subsequent sales

Possible cause:
Poor offer

Inappropriate selling techniques

Lack of sales skills

Economic environment wrong

Wrong stage in purchase cycle

Insufficient promotional material

Style of promotional material inappropriate to offer or potential purchasers

As you can see there are many potential changes that can be made to improve the situation. Try to discipline yourself to making one change at a time. That way you can accurately identify and resolve problems.

Advertising planning sheet

Use the following checklist to plan and re-work your advertisement to greatest effect:

Header: What can I use to capture the attention of my prospective clients?

Offer: What promise can I make which will get them to go on reading?

Evidence: How can I build confidence that I can deliver?

Action: How can I ensure that they take action NOW?

Facilitate: How to contact us or order from us is clear?

Would I buy from this ad?

SUMMARY OF MARKET PLANNING METHODS

A marketing philosophy and effective marketing practice is essential to every business large or small. Marketing is not the domain of specialists who use odd expressions like 'above the line and below the line spend', it is the responsibility of everyone in every business. If I had my way, and I did

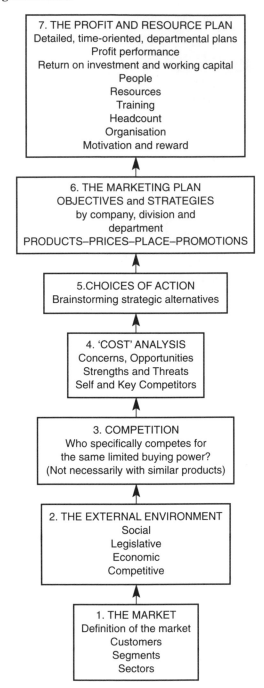

Figure 8.4 The steps to be considered in market planning

once many years ago, every chief executive would add to his title 'and marketing unit manager' as a daily reminder of the real business that he is in.

Market planning is a relatively straight-forward process as Fig. 8.4 shows, but it is less a matter of what is done, than of how it is done and by whom. Critical to the success of market planning is the role and commitment of top management. They must know and communicate:

- What the key strategic issues are;

- The outcome of their own time spent addressing key strategic issues;

- Their assessment of the environment in which the organisation is operating;

- Their detailed assessment of their main competitors and their view of the keys to success in the areas in which they choose to compete;

- Their decision as to when it is time to change the business to meet key strategic needs;

- The direction in which change is required in sufficient detail to ensure consistency across departments and divisions.

When they have done all of the above and generated in all staff and management a commitment to consistently satisfy customer need at minimum cost they can safely leave the tactical planning detail to the professionals.

PITFALLS OF MARKETING

- Marketing is left to marketeers;

- The marketing effort is totally product driven;

- The Chief Executive fails to identify himself with the marketing effort and fails to recognise his position as head of the marketing team;

- The Finance operation either sees itself as, or is seen by others as a constraint rather than as a support to the marketing effort;

- Objectives are too limited, for example, emphasis is put on sales volume rather than market penetration;

- There is no plan.

9 SALES AND SALES MANAGEMENT

I believe that in many ways the impact of the information economy will be most strongly felt in the area of sales and sales management. Customers, both commercial and consumers, are looking for a new kind of relationship with their suppliers. Gradually and all too slowly people are beginning to appreciate that the cost of doing business has to do with more than just the price of goods or the discounts offered. Companies who truly seek to offer quality, and there are as yet too few of them, are coming to understand that their ability to provide it is a function of the relationship which they have with their suppliers. GIGO (garbage in – garbage out) is coming to be recognised as an inexorable law of far wider application than the input of data into a computer.

Every step in the chain between raw material supplier and end consumer is slowly being recognised as an opportunity to add value in terms of quality of product and service. But for that value to be not merely added on an *ad hoc* basis, but specifically targeted to the known and predicted needs of the organisation or individual at every step in the chain needs planning and that planning can only occur if those involved have an enduring understanding characterised by high levels of mutual trust and openness. In short the current and future role of the salesperson must be one of building long term relationships in the initial sales process so that repeat and referral sales are assured and the salesperson's time may be applied to enhancing the quality of the service, product and relationship.

TOWARDS A NEW EXCELLENCE IN SALES TECHNIQUE

The sales manager has an unique advantage in the post-industrial society as it develops. Among managers in the smokestack economies of the past only the sales manager was expected to manage a specialist team at something more than arm's length. The skills which enabled the successful sales manager to support and enthuse a dispersed team are worth considering in the search for techniques and capabilities which will facilitate the future management of telecommuters and knowledge workers. Similarly the skills of the best sales management have always been directed at the development and accelerated move toward autonomy of the entire sales force, and it has been on the basis of individual need. This coaching skill will be an essential pre-requisite to the growth of effective empowerment. Many companies of the future will survive and prosper by making fuller and more imaginative use of all their resources, human and otherwise. As Drucker and others have pointed out, the day of the intrapreneur is at hand. The skills implicit in the highest standards of sales and sales management will enable the creative specialist to sell his good ideas at every level within and outside the organisation.

The models in this chapter are based on a total of more than one hundred years of committed research into what actually works, not simply to influence behaviour today, but to build a long term relationship where ongoing influence is assured. They are relevant to every manager who seeks effective tools for long-lasting influence regardless of his area of specialism. They are both a sales and a leadership tool. They are proven and they are professional.

Sales skills and behaviour

EXCELLENT Our sales people use state-of-the-art techniques which are fully congruent with the desired image of the organisation. We are successful in building long term relationships with our customers and we are perceived by them as a valued part of their team. We offer value rather than price and the most cost-effective solutions to our customers' problems and needs.

Our salespeople constantly prospect for new opportunities to apply their skills.

AVERAGE Our salespeople are fully trained in standard sales techniques which are generally used. There is pressure on our sales team to meet today's sales targets even if it is, from time time, at the possible expense of the long term relationship with the customer.

The sales manager is required to ensure that his sales team prospect for new customers when targets are not achieved.

UNACCEPTABLE We pile 'em high and sell 'em cheap. We employ order-takers rather than salespeople and see little value in training those who have no capacity to learn.

What is prospecting?

THE SALES MANAGEMENT MODELS

The **sales team opinion survey** (Fig. 9.1) is a simple instrument which will provide management with invaluable information. Used properly it will help to build commitment not only within the sales team, but also among customers as they experience ever higher levels of quality of product and service at realistic cost.

Its use is not limited to sales teams but with very little intelligent amendment it can be used throughout the organisation.

To use the instrument effectively it is necessary for management to commit themselves to:

1. Seek information with a genuinely open mind. This does not require that they hold no prior opinions of their own. It does mean, however, that they should be committed to take the opinions of others seriously and be prepared to reconsider their own views in the light of what emerges from the survey.

2. Regard the rights of the individuals completing the survey to be sacrosanct. No attempt, of any kind should be made to identify respondents. If any respondent takes the opportunity offered by the survey to be offensive or stupidly irrelevant, the manager might consider the maturity of his group and whether his personal leadership style is appropriate. More than that, he may consider, as a matter of urgency what he needs to do to help to build the maturity of his team.

3. Commit to implementing all that is reasonable and feasible without delay. Any changes should be announced in advance and specifically tied in to the survey in order to build confidence that views which are elicited are acted upon. When ideas emerge which are constructive, but which cannot be implemented at present they should be publicly and fully acknowledged, and the reasons why they cannot be implemented should be explained.

Implementing the opinion survey

The purpose and method of the opinion survey must be carefully and sensitively communicated to sales staff. A sample departmental memorandum is displayed overleaf.

MEMORANDUM

To: All Members of the Sales Team

From: The Sales Manager

Subject: Sales Team Opinion Survey

Each of you individually has a key role to play in the present and future growth and development of this company. Not only are your views important, but you have an absolute right to express them openly without fear of criticism or comeback.

To enhance the flow of information I would be grateful if you would complete and return the enclosed survey. I am happy that the survey should be both confidential and anonymous so please do not sign your forms and if you wish, please arrange that they all be sent to any one of your colleagues and returned to me in a batch to ensure anonymity.

The survey covers four essential areas of our business where excellence in all that we do is critical to your personal success as well as that of the company. Please take a little time to complete the survey as we in management will be actively seeking to put right anything in need of improvement and your evaluation of where we stand will be very helpful.

To ensure that communication is a two way process, I intend to feed back the results to you at our Sales Group Meeting on _____. Please have the completed questionnaires returned to me by _____.

[Your colleagues in other departments/divisions are being asked to complete a similar survey and the Chairman will report back at a meeting of all staff the date of which is to be finalised.]

This information is critical to your future and that of the company so please answer all questions as honestly and frankly as possible. Please do not feel under pressure to invent problems where none exist, but pull no punches where improvements are needed. I enclose notes to help you with the task.

Thank you.

OPINION SURVEY
Notes to help with completion

This survey is intended to be anonymous, please do not indicate your identity in any way on these forms. If you wish to retain a copy for future reference please feel free to photocopy these forms.
   The forms cover four basic areas:

   The products which we sell;
   The company and its facilities;
   The jobs people do;
   The quality of your management and leadership.

Because we need your personal opinions uninfluenced by others please avoid discussing this survey with your colleagues until all forms are completed and returned. Once the forms are all completed please feel free to discuss it as widely as you wish.
   To complete the survey all that you have to do is to circle a number against each of the sixty items. For each you have six choices available to you as follows:

1. 'Not Acceptable' – when you are personally totally dissatisfied with our efforts and/or results in this area.

2. 'Less Than Acceptable' – when you feel that we need to do a great deal better in this area to satisfy our important stakeholders, (our employees, customers, suppliers, shareholders and the community in which we operate.)

3. 'Barely Acceptable' – when you feel that we are getting by, but ought to be doing much better.

4. 'Acceptable' – when you feel satisfied, but less than excited by the standards we meet.

5. 'More Than Acceptable' – when you feel generally pleased with our efforts and results.

6. 'Excellent' – when you feel delighted by what we have achieved and you believe that customers and community are likely to feel the same.

Do not add additional notes or detailed comments to the copy which you return, but if you take a photocopy and retain it for your own records please add any notes which are helpful for the meetings which will follow. Notes are equally useful both before and after you have talked to your colleagues – if you sense a current of opinion as to the best way to address a problem, that is great. Please write it down for future discussion.

Please feel free to start completing the survey as soon as you are ready. Nobody can help you with the answers because it is your opinion we need and value, but if the instructions are unclear please ask for further information.

SECTION ONE – THE PRODUCT

How do you feel about:

Excellent ⟶ Unacceptable

1. The QUALITY of our product range	6 5 4 3 2 1
2. The APPEARANCE and attractiveness of our products	6 5 4 3 2 1
3. The AVAILABILITY of our products	6 5 4 3 2 1
4. The PERFORMANCE of our products in use	6 5 4 3 2 1
5. The RANGE of products we sell	6 5 4 3 2 1
6. Our PRESENTATION of the product range	6 5 4 3 2 1
7. The IMAGE our products present to the market	6 5 4 3 2 1
8. Our STOCKING LEVELS	6 5 4 3 2 1
9. The COMPETITIVENESS of our prices	6 5 4 3 2 1
10. Our PRICING POLICY including discounts	6 5 4 3 2 1
11. Our ADVANTAGES over competition	6 5 4 3 2 1
12. Our SHORTCOMINGS compared with competition	6 5 4 3 2 1
13. Our DISTRIBUTION system	6 5 4 3 2 1
14. Our RESEARCH and DEVELOPMENT of new products	6 5 4 3 2 1
15. The LAUNCH of new products	6 5 4 3 2 1

SECTION TWO – THE COMPANY

1. The WORKING ENVIRONMENT	6 5 4 3 2 1
2. The quality of our ADVERTISING	6 5 4 3 2 1
3. Our SALES PROMOTION activities	6 5 4 3 2 1
4. Our SALES PROSPECTING activities	6 5 4 3 2 1
5. Our CUSTOMER FOLLOW-UP system	6 5 4 3 2 1
6. Our CUSTOMER SATISFACTION research	6 5 4 3 2 1
7. Availability of critical TOOLS and EQUIPMENT	6 5 4 3 2 1
8. Our TELEPHONE system	6 5 4 3 2 1
9. Our TELEPHONE RECEPTION	6 5 4 3 2 1
10. FURNITURE, FIXTURES and FITTINGS	6 5 4 3 2 1
11. The IMPRESSION of our company we give visitors	6 5 4 3 2 1
12. The REPUTATION of our company in the community	6 5 4 3 2 1
13. Our ADMINISTRATION	6 5 4 3 2 1
14. Our RULES, POLICIES and PROCEDURES	6 5 4 3 2 1
15. Us as an EMPLOYER	6 5 4 3 2 1

Figure 9.1 Employee opinion survey designed for the sales team but which could be easily adapted for other departments

SECTION THREE – YOUR JOB

How do you feel about:

Excellent ————————➤ Unacceptable

1. Coming to work in the morning	6	5	4	3	2	1
2. Your HOURS OF WORK	6	5	4	3	2	1
3. Working LATE	6	5	4	3	2	1
4. Your HOLIDAY ENTITLEMENT	6	5	4	3	2	1
5. Your TRAINING to do the job	6	5	4	3	2	1
6. The amount of PAPERWORK you do	6	5	4	3	2	1
7. Time spent on ROUTINE TASKS	6	5	4	3	2	1
8. The fairness of SALARY and WAGE levels	6	5	4	3	2	1
9. The competitiveness of SALARIES and WAGES locally	6	5	4	3	2	1
10. The level of JOB SATISFACTION you get daily	6	5	4	3	2	1
11. The PRIDE you can take in your job	6	5	4	3	2	1
12. The degree of FREEDOM you have to make decisions	6	5	4	3	2	1
13. The TEAM you work with	6	5	4	3	2	1
14. RELATIONSHIPS with other departments	6	5	4	3	2	1
15. Telling people in the pub where you work/what you do	6	5	4	3	2	1

SECTION FOUR – YOUR MANAGEMENT

1. As LIKEABLE people	6	5	4	3	2	1
2. As worthy of RESPECT	6	5	4	3	2	1
3. For LEADERSHIP qualities	6	5	4	3	2	1
4. As DECISION MAKERS	6	5	4	3	2	1
5. As MOTIVATORS	6	5	4	3	2	1
6. As DELEGATORS	6	5	4	3	2	1
7. As COACHES and COUNSELLORS	6	5	4	3	2	1
8. For CONDUCTING BUSINESSLIKE MEETINGS	6	5	4	3	2	1
9. For FAIRNESS	6	5	4	3	2	1
10. As a source of HELP when needed	6	5	4	3	2	1
11. As TRAINERS	6	5	4	3	2	1
12. As reliable SOURCES OF INFORMATION	6	5	4	3	2	1
13. For SHOWING INTEREST in your ideas	6	5	4	3	2	1
14. For giving deserved PRAISE and REBUKES	6	5	4	3	2	1
15. As competent PROFESSIONALS	6	5	4	3	2	1

Figure 9.1 Employee opinion survey designed for the sales team but which could be easily adapted for other departments

The importance of knowing

The survey will provide a great deal of essential information. There are many other things, however, which every sales manager must know. I believe that the most important of these is each individual salesperson's **closing rate**.

If you know that Jim closes one sale in three, Jill is successful in writing an order in one out of every four customer contacts and John closes one in six you can manage all members of your team to maximise their individual contribution.

On our admittedly limited information Jim has little difficulty in closing the sale. All that you need to do as a manager is ensure that Jim comes face to face with a few more customers to generate more sales volume. Perhaps it would be appropriate to encourage and train him to prospect more effectively, or to pass him more 'house sales' to handle. Be careful not to overload him. It may be that his success is dependent on the time which he gives to individual customers.

Jill doesn't quite match up to Jim when it comes to closing the sale. It may be that she would benefit from some help or training in respect of one or other of the principle steps to the sale. By observing her at work it should be possible to establish whether she needs to:

- spend more time with customers;
- evaluate needs in more detail;
- present her product or service more closely in line with customer need;
- demonstrate the ability of her offering to satisfy the customer needs more effectively;
- handle objections with more sensitivity, empathy, skill or assertiveness;
- close the sale naturally and effectively.

Once you have identified Jill's problem area you can easily, and economically help to the solution. By identifying a specific problem the astute and creative sales manager can save a fortune on sheep dip sales training programmes.

Of course there may be other reasons for the difference in Jill and Jim's performance. Jill may simply be happy with her current level of sales success and may seek nothing more. Or she may be battling against a high level of unreasoning sexual bias among her customers. If you want to help Jill to reach her full potential training is not necessarily the only, or even an appropriate answer.

John's problem may be any of those which have been identified as possibilities for Jill. The difference is that you have potentially even more to gain by helping John to improve performance.

Having raised John and Jill's sales to the level of Jim's the astute manager realises that John and Jill now would do well to have more opportunities to come face to face with customers. And that isn't the end of the story. Jim's performance almost certainly falls far below the optimum. A combination of biological and psychological research suggests that we can win them all – or at least we can, given human proneness to error, win very nearly every time. Models in this chapter skim the surface of well-validated techniques. But this is an area where training really does come into its own, and since the approach requires the flexible and sensitive application of a range of models the normal three or five day injection of concepts won't do.

SALES SKILLS FOR A NEW BUSINESS AGE

I have made the point before that leadership skills will need to evolve to take account of the different needs of an information society. With quality and excellence increasingly recognised and demanded as the ultimate determinants of competitive advantage and the need to compete globally even on your own doorstep, the same is true of selling techniques.

Salespeople will need to focus beyond the immediate sale and concentrate as I have suggested above on the building of relationships. In the early 1930's an organisation was formed in the United States to analyse successful sales presentations and to develop a process which would facilitate the customer's unforced movement toward the decision to buy. Academia took a hand with the effect that a cognitive map of the sequence of customer thought was developed. That map (Fig. 9.2) has proved its value in more than sixty years of tough practical experience and experiment. If the customer reaches satisfactory answers, that is affirmative answers, to each of the questions implied, the mind moves smoothly to a positive decision. If not, you may or may not get there in the end, but the path will be long and weary. What is worse, success on one occasion will not justify the prediction of a similar outcome in the future.

This approach plays a small but important part as the foundation of my NFS programme. The rest of the programme would fill a book at least as long as this one, but if what follows is used alone, it will lead to a substantial increase in immediate sales volume and substantially improved customer relationships.

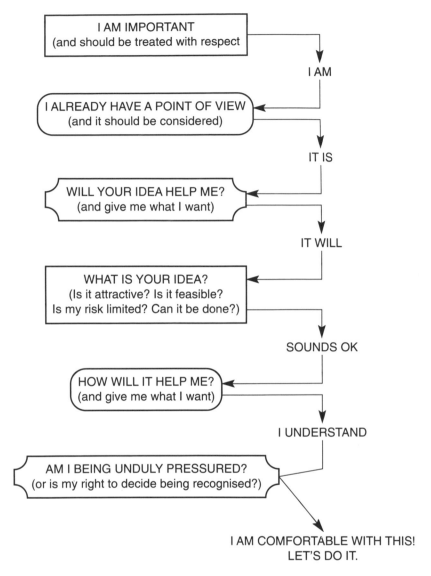

Figure 9.2 The path to customer assent based on understanding the customer's thoughts

The simplified sales plan

1. Plan your presentation from the buyer's point of view

- Make your customer feel important by basing your discussion firmly on his key objective.

- Test your understanding of the most important issues or problems your listener faces: from his viewpoint *not yours.*
- Remember that his present point of view is based on his past success and makes absolute sense to him. To change it will require compelling reasons.
- Match your mood and manner to that of your customer.

2. Create for the customer an awareness of the need to act now

- Demonstrate that conditions beyond the control of either of you are changing.
- Show how the changes taking place *could* cause your listener problems in the future.
- Indicate that you have the means to change potential threats to opportunities.

3. Maintain and build your customer's interest

- Mention one or two benefits which the customer will gain from using your services, products or ideas before indicating what you will do.
- Make sure he regards them as benefits and appreciate their worth.

4. Tell your customer *all* that he needs to know about your service, product or idea in sufficient detail.

- What you offer.
- When you can supply it.
- Who else will be involved.
- What special skills and knowledge you uniquely offer.
- Key features which give assurance that the promised benefits will materialise.
- Who else, that he respects, has already successfully used your services or products.
- What they say about the experience (if you have their permission to quote them).

5. Explain the benefits of your services

- Link the benefits logically to prove that if one is achieved the others follow as a consequence.

- Show that the final benefit in your chain of logic is the listener's key objective.

6. If you lose your customer's favourable attention during the discussion.

- Stop talking.
- Wait for your customer to speak.
- Listen actively.
- Show that you have listened by repeating a key idea or feeling in your own words.
- Diffuse the emotion by showing that you understand the right of the customer to react in any way that feels right to him.
- Deal with his problem.
- Continue when you are convinced that he is satisfied and ready to listen, not before.

7. Ask for the Order

- No tricks or 'Closing Techniques' – *just ask*.
- Look for 'buying signals'
  - Nods of agreement or approval.
  - Building on your ideas.
  - Willingness to give you supportive information or data.

8. Having asked – stop talking and remain silent until you have a reply.

The technique called SARAH when things start to go wrong

No matter how careful you are, regardless of the sensitivity which you show toward others' needs and feelings, there will be times when suddenly and for no obvious reason, your customer shows signs of disagreement and even anger. By word or gesture he will indicate that you have done or said something which triggers a negative response. It will seldom be clear to you where you went off track. Almost by definition you are choosing your words for the best possible effect so you can hardly help but be taken by surprise.

Many salespeople seeing the signs, break simultaneously into a sweat and a gallop. They feel that if only they can finish what they are saying all will be well. After all, they have an unanswerable logical case which they have thought through with great care. If only, we think, we can get all our logic expressed for the customer's consideration the misunderstanding, whatever it may be, will be resolved and the customer will be happy once more and the order assured.

Unfortunately trying to deal with emotions with logic does not work. Think about those times when *you* get upset with little reason. If someone tries to change your mood with logic do you listen to them? If you are anything like me you do not. What I do is to ignore what is being said or use it selectively to help me to think of all the convincing reasons why I am right to feel as I do. The more others try to make me feel better with their appeals to logic the worse I feel, and the worse I feel, the more aggressive I become. It seems that they have no interest in what I feel or what I am thinking and that makes me mad. They can gabble on all they please, but I am not listening. I nurse my grievance and wait until they pause for breath and then I let them have it. Meanwhile nothing that they say enters my consciousness unless it adds fuel to my fire of indignation.

When things start to go off the rails and signs of roused emotions appear think of the acronym SARAH.

Stop talking. Do not talk faster, in fact do not talk at all! Give your customer the opportunity to express their feelings. No matter how painful the silence seems to you, there is absolutely nothing you can usefully say. If there was, your buyer would not listen to it anyway. Hold your tongue and within seconds (it will feel like minutes) your listener will break the silence. When he does ...

Active listening. Listen as if your life depends on understanding how your customer feels and what they think. Make no attempts to second guess, always accept what is said as if it were true. Most of all, do not listen as some salesmen listen to customer objections with the intention of hearing some small error which enables them to think, 'Got you, you bastard!' followed by an attempt to devastate the listener with their lucidity and grasp of facts.

Feelings are facts, too; and in this situation it is your customer's feelings which are the most salient of all facts. So when he has stopped talking ...

Reflect content or feeling. Paraphrase a key statement your customer has made to demonstrate that you really have been listening. Say it musingly to show that you are carefully considering what is being said and not doing parrot-like imitations. If nothing coherent enough has been said then reflect what is clear to you about what the client is feeling. 'You are very upset,' or 'You feel that it is unfair?'

If you reflect feeling, wait for a response. The listener will almost certainly now expand on what the problem is and, if you have remained concerned but calm, you will find that the client becomes a little calmer too as he realises that there is no need to try to convince you of the validity of the arguments that he has been rehearsing internally to justify the mood swing. When he is ready ...

Act with empathy. Show him that you accept that others have an absolute right to feel any way they please. They may be wrong in fact. They may have completely misunderstood. You may have inadvertently triggered a prejudice of which any right-minded person would be ashamed. Nonetheless, they have an absolute right as individuals to deal with their own problems their own way. But be sure you can tell the difference between empathy and sympathy and take care that you never express sympathy: 'You are absolutely right to feel as you do', when you intend to convey empathy: 'You have an absolute right to feel as you do'. The difference allows you, after expressing empathy, to correct their thinking and consequently change their feeling. Once you have shown sympathy you are locked in to their feeling no matter how injurious it is to your case. 'Yes, the behaviour of our company toward its customer's is disgraceful!' will not help you to win a sale, or respect.

Neither will: 'That's nonsense, and I can prove it.' Empathy is shown in expressions like: 'I can understand you feeling that way, many people do.'

Handle objections. When your calm, sensitive handling of the situation has made it easy for your client to listen to reason again, deal with any objections raised. Always deal with what your client says. Never try to second guess 'what he *really* means'. You will almost certainly get it wrong. Even if you get it right, you will destroy the belief that you have been listening carefully and with empathy and understanding.

> *'Chi disprezza compra' (Who criticises buys)*
> Italian proverb

Objections and obstacles

Research over the last sixty years shows that objections can be classified and the most appropriate tactics for handling each type has been suggested.

The following are some of those which most frequently occur.

Price

Something appears to cost too much when it seems to offer insufficient benefit for the price to be paid in money or effort.

Use more benefits to demonstrate that your product offers exceptional value. Your product will deliver many benefits which will not fit into the logical flow towards the achievement of your customer's key goals. You will not therefore be using them as the main argument for the sale. Use them when the price obstacle arises to convince your listener that you are providing exceptional added value.

Habit

'We've always done it this way, and it works' is not an invitation for you to focus on why the old way is stupid and your idea is infinitely better. It does give you the opportunity, however, to recognise that you have not shown sufficiently clearly how the changes in the environment in which your customer operates are such that major problems may result in the future if steps are not taken now. You will of course need to convince him that the product or service which you are advocating will be effective in today's conditions.

Competition

'We have always been happy with our present supplier' is asking you to expand on what is unique about your offer. Your customer is asking you to give more detail about your product or service. Concentrate on what it is that you offer that gives the competitive edge. Any feature of your service which is unique should be explained in detail from the customer's point of view. Make it absolutely clear that additional benefits will result from giving the business to you and get the customer's agreement that it is worth his while to consider the change before you move on.

Products versus services

Customer attitudes, beliefs and therefore behaviours are different when buying services as opposed to products. It is an old adage that people love to buy, but they hate being sold to. The techniques outlined above help the potential customer to become a buyer by avoiding putting any barriers across the road to the sale. But it is arguable that although we may love to buy products where we can twiddle the knobs, admire the shiny newness of our purchase or otherwise entertain ourselves, most of us dislike buying services. A service may well solve a problem, or ineptly carried out it may cause the situation to worsen. There is nothing solid on which we may hang our expectations. Those who sell services or ideas are well advised to consider the disadvantage under which they operate and make special efforts to allow customers to buy, rather than sell.

Some research by George and Myers clarifies the differences:

Consumer's purchase perceptions:

- Services are less consistent in quality than goods;
- Any service purchase is a high risk purchase;
- Service purchasing is a less enjoyable activity than buying products (You cannot 'twiddle the knobs of a consultant');
- Services need to be bought with greater consideration of the seller's reputation.

Consumer's purchase behaviour:

- Consumers make fewer price comparisons when buying services;
- They place heavy reliance on the supplier's reputation and their own and others' experience;
- They are less influenced by advertising, and more by personal recommendations.

Personal selling of services:

- Customers seek greater personal involvement in the service activity;
- Long term satisfaction is greatly influenced by the salesperson's attitude and personality;
- Salespeople may need to spend more time reducing anxiety about the purchase.

THE PSYCHOLOGY OF BUYER MOTIVATION

During the 1930s psychology was still struggling to overcome a reputation for vagueness, and for being 'unscientific'. An interesting situation when you think that its lack of clarity and dependence on probability was exactly similar to the 'hard' science of sub-atomic and relativistic physics. As a result two movements began to dominate psychological thinking. One was Behaviourism, and the other was Psychometrics.

Behaviourism which made the mistake of thinking that it had the whole answer when, like every other school, it only had a partial, but significant contribution to make, has fallen into exaggerated and undeserved neglect.

Psychometrics, driven in part by business's lack of confidence in its own ability to make judgements is still riding high and unfortunately in many areas of business, it is largely misused by those who oversimplify its complex findings.

Two psychologists working in the field of psychometrics, Kaiser and Koffey developed a model which can be practically useful to the persuader in handling unacceptable and unpleasant buyer behaviour.

Psychometrics seeks to measure behaviour or personality traits. It often does so by taking simple measurements which place individuals on a straight line continuum. For example:

HOSTILE _____ x _____ WARM

suggests that the subject 'x' is somewhat more warm than hostile, but is close enough to the middle position to be verging on neutral. The problem with this one dimensional form of measurement is that many very different individuals would score the same on the single continuum and so with only one measurement:

- Information is limited;

- Difference can appear to be the same;

- Similarity also appears to be the same and there is no obvious way of identifying which is which.

Kaiser and Koffeys' solution was to take two measurements and put the scales at right angles to each other. That way instead of a straight line with a limited number of points we have a plane with each individual assigned to a unique position among an infinity of points. (Figure 9.3) As it happens Kaiser and Koffey chose to use two scales:

DOMINANCE to SUBMISSIVENESS

HOSTILITY to WARMTH

which are of particular value when considering the behaviour of 'difficult' people.

What makes a person behave badly is not some genetic predisposition to be a jerk. It is almost always a chosen tactic which from their current perception seems to offer the best chance of fulfilling a need. Even very self-destructive behaviours result from the individual either having found them to work in the past, (like somebody who 'childishly' carries forward the tantrums which worked so well in the nursery into adult life), or they are used because the individual knows of nothing better and there is no such thing as a behavioural vacuum.

DOMINANCE	
Aggressive and argumentative	Appropriately friendly
Makes dogmatic, generalised claims	Listens carefully and critically
May display negative emotion	Disagrees frankly giving cogent reasons
Overstates own achievements and status	Seeks full discussion of ideas and
Assumes no personal responsibility for	concepts
problems or mistakes	Accepts rational criticism of self or
Blames others or systems for errors	systems
Stubborn, resistant	Avoids alibis or rationalisations
Where not openly aggressive, aloof and	Insists on respect and fair hearing
sometimes patronising	Gives respect and a fair hearing
Does not listen	Businesslike, always seeking a better
Hears what he wants to hear	way of doing things
Rejects others' ideas as unworkable:	Welcomes ideas from any source
"We tried that years ago–it will never	Gets involved
work".	Probing and analytical
Blusters or patronises	Reacts strongly to time-wasting or
Initiates conflict	waffle.
Challenges to win	Exudes quiet self confidence
Will use fact, fantasy or sabotage to win	Uses 'working conflict' to create quality
an argument	outcomes
Adept at 'warring conflict'	Challenges to explore best alternatives

HOSTILITY	WARMTH
Withdrawn and apathetic	Over-friendly and eager to please
Over-protective of own thoughts and	Unquestioning agreement with the last
feelings	thing said
Seems afraid to express views	Vague when pressed, but eager to
Passively accepts what is said or demands	confirm if idea is paraphrased more
proof or justification	strongly
Cautious and non-commital	Avoids open disagreement unless values
Avoids promoting discussion or asking	about people are strongly confronted
questions other than those relating to	Goes off at tangents, rambles
guarantees or risk reduction	enthusiastically
Rarely openly disagrees, but only agrees	Generalises optimistically about outcomes
unwillingly under pressure	Makes easy promises
Procrastinates	Seldom delivers on promises made
Remote, uncommunicative	Genial
Sulks if relative status allows	Procrastinates if relations with others
Avoids conflict by withdrawal	might be threatened
	Appears to be good-natured
	Speaks well of others, but may strongly
	agree if you attack them
	Avoids conflict by denial

SUBMISSION	

Figure 9.3 Extreme behaviours by quartile, useful in assessing personality traits quantitatively and qualitatively. Characteristics in the top right quartile offer the best chances of closing a sale

The great advantage of Kaiser and Koffeys' approach is that it enables us to:

- Describe and recognise typical behaviours (Fig. 9.3);
- Accurately assign motivators to the overt behaviours we see and experience;
- Develop specific and detailed strategies to satisfy the motive and remove the need for the behaviour;
- Change the behaviour to one which is constructive and acceptable;
- Use our skills to communicate effectively with one whose behaviour is now favourable and positive.

Win them all?

Figure 9.3 shows some general behaviours which are typical of the segment shown. These behaviours are of course only examples, the balance between details can be very different as you will be shown. The important thing is that:

- Those in the top left segment tend to aggressiveness and unpleasantness;
- Those in the bottom left to demonstrate mistrust and avoidance of commitment;
- Those in the bottom right tend to a level of agreeableness which can mask a deep insecurity and a total inability to fulfill commitments;
- Those at the top right show assertiveness and sometimes a somewhat authoritarian pursuit of quality, but they are also open to new ideas, actively seeking them as a means of improving both processes and results.

In summary the characteristics of the person described by the top right hand segment are those which offer the best chance of a sale of an idea, product or service. They are tough minded, but open minded – convince such an individual that what you have to offer makes sense in the face of their need and you have more than a customer, you have an advocate.

The notes which follow take two typical, but essentially different behaviour patterns from each segment, identify the strongest motivators for each and provide specific step-by-step tactics to manage and change the behaviour, creating favourable attention to you and your ideas. By the specifics of your handling of difficult personalities you can remove any need for obnoxious behaviour and move each type towards and into the behaviour style of the upper right quadrant.

Using traits to advantage

In each descriptive heading the first word used is the controlling or major trait. So that someone categorised as 'HOSTILE – DOMINANT' is drawn from the top left segment and is more hostile (appearing more to the left than any other part of the segment), while 'DOMINANT – HOSTILE' comes from the same general cluster, but for this individual dominance is the more important trait. In short if you do not frustrate this person's desire to be dominant they may not experience any need to be aggressive, but the first example gets his kicks from aggression and allowing him to assume dominance which tends to encourage greater aggression.

It will quickly become clearer as we move on!

HOSTILE – DOMINANT

Key motivation: Desire for security

Motivation satisfaction strategy: Attack is the best form of defence

Typical behaviours:

- Brags incessantly
- Drops impressive names and relies on 'authorities'
- Interupts impatiently and often
- Shows impatience – finger drumming, etc.
- Unreasonably stubborn
- Argumentative without cause
- Makes broad generalisations and sweeping statements in argument
- Is dogmatic and opinionated and ignores or attacks contrary facts
- Makes frequent mutually inconsistent statements
- Reacts negatively without hearing the whole story
- Makes sarcastic comments
- Tries to belittle the product, the salesperson and the company
- Frequently personally abusive
- Looks for any opportunity to start a fight or take offence.
- Claims to have all the answers himself and never makes mistakes
- When things go wrong always looks for others to blame
- Must win the argument and will lie, invent or exaggerate to do so.

Management or salesperson strategies: More than anything else this individual seeks to remain in charge as a defensive mechanism. He will bully, lie and insult to try to throw you off track. If he can get you to lose control either by losing your temper or by driving you to despair, he will see that as a victory. He needs victims to allow him to bolster what is, somewhat surprisingly, a very low self-image. Having created victims he is able to reject them and their ideas together. That way he feels a little more important and a little more secure. You cannot afford to allow him the victory he craves so you need to *keep your cool – whatever he throws at you* and:

- Be courteous, but firm and assertive.

- Remember that you have nothing to lose. This person cannot operate in a vacuum. They must buy from someone and if you let them win, they will certainly not buy from you.

- Ask closed questions frequently to establish and keep control. (Closed questions can be answered with a single word usually 'yes' or 'no'.)

- Avoid justifying yourself or your product.

- Test every gross assertion and broad generalisation or wild exaggeration politely but firmly.

- 'Are you really saying that *all*...?' should be the question which is constantly on your lips. If that is answered with a further exaggeration continue to challenge it. 'Are you really saying that there are *no* exceptions?'

- Expect to meet resistance to closing the sale and expect exaggerated objections.

- *This is one situation where you simply cannot afford to allow the other to satisfy his needs – you must meet apparent strength with real strength. Use your communication skills to demonstrate that you cannot be bullied. If you can win this person's grudging respect you have won.*

DOMINANT – HOSTILE

Key motivation: Need for status and autonomy

Motivation satisfaction strategy: Precision and outward indicators of power

Typical behaviours:

- Is cold and detached
- If angered remains cool but biting
- Is angered if he believes that his status is being underestimated or ignored

- Stubborn in his precise demand for proper attention in keeping with his importance
- Makes very precise and accurate statements, particularly when making a complaint
- Is easily offended
- Holds tenaciously to his evaluation of his own worth
- Reacts negatively at what he perceives as a personal slight or failure to take his complaint seriously
- Avoids sarcasm, chooses instead to be cutting with accurate complaints which others might consider trivial, but which are important to him.
- Avoids argument by telling you accurately and in detail where you are wrong
- Demands efficiency and respect
- Responds badly to the opinions or experiences of others unless they are seen by him to be of equal or higher status than himself

Management or salesperson strategies: This person has, or believes he should have, high status. He believes that recognition of that status is a right and he insists on his rights at all times. In general the more that you can build a relationship of *mutual* respect with this person the more likely it is that you will influence him. It is not appropriate to demean yourself; he only respects those he perceives as being of similar standing. So you should:

- Stress benefits which offer prestige, autonomy, recognition, control and freedom of action.
- Expect an early response of: 'I don't need you' and be prepared to live with temporary rejection until you prove yourself and your idea.
- Show conviction and strength, but avoid being, or appearing to be, cocky, aggressive, argumentative or over-confident.
- Be courteous always. Remember that courtesy is not mere politeness, but implies a genuine respect for others.
- Precede all questions with a benefit. This type of person expects to ask questions, not answer them and you must sell by giving the information you need up front.
- Only ask for information which you really need.
- Never use leading questions with this person. He recognises and rejects what he sees as attempts to railroad him into a decision.

- Never allow this type to lose face. If he is wrong try to avoid mentioning it or make it clear how and why his information may be inaccurate without indicating fault on his part.

- Credit the customer with good ideas even if they are yours, but do it with sensitivity. Remember that it is his business that you want rather than his admiration if it comes to a choice. If possible, of course, have both.

HOSTILE – SUBMISSIVE

Key motivation: Security expressed through abnormal demands for protection.

Motivation satisfaction strategy: Excessively detailed 'what if' concerns

Typical behaviours:

- Expresses doubt about any statement made
- Thinks up and expresses the most unlikely scenarios in which things could go wrong
- Demands totally unreasonable guarantees
- Insists on discussing hypothetical and very unlikely potential problems
- Niggles and complains
- Doubts the validity of any new idea
- Incessantly asks questions, many of which are clearly impossible to answer
- Gives little, if any, information in return
- If asked even the most innocuous of questions is likely to demand to know 'why you want to know'
- Is aggressive in physical demeanour and body language
- Avoids committing himself to any agreement
- Is generally pessimistic
- Frequently asserts that he has been badly treated by the many who have betrayed his trust in the past, but avoids giving any examples
- Accuses others of lying, not explicitly, but by implication

Management or salesperson strategies: This type tends to treat the whole world with excessive mistrust and being more inclined toward hostility than defensiveness, knows his rights and seeks to have them through unreasonable and unrealistic guarantees and warranted outcomes. He treats the whole world this way and there is nothing personal in any hostility shown towards any individual. If his basic insecurity can be mitigated his behaviour will become more reasonable and more acceptable. It is important in trying to manage this behaviour that personal conflict is not allowed to develop. So you should:

- Remain consistently patient in the face of repeated disbelief.

- Assure and reassure and use convincing examples to illustrate the safe application of your ideas.

- Give guarantees in writing where possible and avoid ambiguities or small print – if you cannot give an absolute guarantee, it is better to say so than to build his mistrust through promises which cannot be honoured. You should always be seeking the long term relationship and if someone like this believes that they can trust you they are unlikely to risk going to someone else.

- Stress benefits which provide stability, low risk, assured outcomes, proven value, permanence and durability.

- Show genuine concern for the customer's needs

- Spend time exploring the buyer's key objective and don't expect him to tell you without a lot of arduous digging for information.

- Ask safe closed questions until he begins to open up, ask more open questions only when you are sure that he is at ease with you.

- Quote prestige users of your products, services or ideas.

- Be prepared to give this person a great deal of your time.

- Be sure that the investment of so much time is justified by the potential outcome. Once you start with this person you are committed to win, or be added to the long list of those who 'let him down' and if he blackguards you there will always be some to believe it and pass it on.

SUBMISSIVE – HOSTILE

Key motivation: Fear of becoming committed or involved

Motivation satisfaction strategy: Avoidance, withdrawal

Typical behaviours:

- Maintains maximum possible physical distance from others.

- Will actually seek to move away from salespeople or those perceived to be in authority.

- Volunteers no information and tends to become extremely tight-lipped if questioned.

- Says nothing unless sensitively probed.

- When he does speak says as little as possible.

- Prefers grunts and mumbles to audible expression of views and feelings. If forced to say something picks words with care.

- Avoids commitment by any possible means including physical withdrawal when other avoidance strategies are unavailable.

- Feigns illness to avoid involvement.

- Reluctant to take even minimal risk.

- Appears tense and ill-at-ease when in company.

- Refuses new ideas without listening to arguments if he has the power.

- More inclined to accept well-tried and safe products and ideas. If forced to a choice will invariably choose the low risk option.

- Preferred behaviour is avoidance and procrastination, but if forced to a decision prefers 'no'.

- Clings to habits, routine, rules and procedures.

- Uses rules and procedures, precedence or policy to avoid decision or justify rejection.

- Takes no personal responsibility for own actions blaming problems on others or things.

- Shies away from any discussion of a 'personal' nature.

Management strategies: This personality type's need for security extends even to the false perception of those who seek to help him/her as threats. Always try to avoid pressure with one exception: if you have reached the stage where closing is appropriate, be totally assertive as well as supportive. Assure and reassure until this person is confident that this time it will be alright. Where you can, identify where possible achievements from this type's past which were successful and apparently painless and compare the new strategy detail by detail with the old. So you should:

- Approach slowly without unnecessary *bonhommie* or unbridled enthusiasm.

- Predetermine an acceptable reason for approach if this person shies away.

- Offer specific help where appropriate as opportunity to get into conversation without perceived threat.

- Ask safe closed questions at first to initiate conversation. Safe questions are those to which this person can mumble a mono-syllabic reply which is either noncommittal or socially so acceptable as to offer no threat.

- Keep well away from personal questions until the personal relationship is well established.
- Stress benefits which minimise or obviate risk.
- Link benefits logically to product/service features so that there is no room for doubt that benefits will be enjoyed quickly and without risk.
- Present ideas slowly, a little information at a time and ensure that each is fully accepted before moving on.
- Avoid any sense of pressure.
- Be unusually patient.
- Expect long periods of silence. Wait for responses regardless of how long it takes.
- Reward with body language and encouraging words any signs of opening up from this person.
- Exhibit genuine concern for his fears. Be careful not to underestimate the importance of them to him.
- Build trust slowly. When he is prepared to talk listen carefully and demonstrate empathy.
- Guide firmly, but very gently.
- Accept all fears as real to him.
- Never joke about anything which he appears to take seriously.
- Bolster the individual's self respect and self image.
- If you choose to use leading questions at any point, be sure that they are non-threatening.

SUBMISSIVE – WARM

Key motivation: Above all things and regardless of the realities of the situation wants to be loved. Affiliation at the extreme, desire to be liked gone mad.

Motivation satisfaction strategy: Tries to be all things to all men at all times.

Typical behaviours:

- Becomes immediately and often falsely enthusiastic about any idea or product.

- Rambles incessantly and frequently talks at length and with enthusiasm of unrelated subjects.

- Responds quickly and positively to any and all suggestions.

- Eager to please and causes confusion by adopting any role or level of authority which is attributed to him however false.

- Avoids raising objections and denies them even where they patently exist.

- Is readily convinced, but closing the sale is time-consuming because of irrelevant gossip and red herrings.

- Seems to have all the time in the world.

- Promises anything asked of him and rarely keeps promises.

- After long discussion in which he has given absolute assurance that he is the decision maker, changes at the point of closing the sale to: 'Well I will put it to my boss. He has to make the final decision. Don't worry he always takes my my advice.'

- If you ask to meet boss he fobs you off with: 'He never sees ... (salespeople, other departmental managers, etc.) He leaves this entirely to me...'

- If he signs an order he cancels through a third party, or you find your invoice is rejected because he lacked budget or authority and didn't like to say.

- Often totally scathing of your competition ...and equally scathing about you to them.

Management strategies: If you have the feeling that of all the obnoxious people that this section has been about I dislike this individual the most, well done, you have read between the lines successfully. People like this are the biggest time-wasters in business. They make conflicting promises to everyone and are able to keep only those which are made to those with the greatest organisational power in their own company. What is worse, when they are found out they become vindictive and having become adept at doing harm to others in secret they can be dangerous. They are weak, but what they lack in strength they more than make up in cunning and are ace survivors in a bureaucratic environment. Sadly, the large numbers of bureaucratic companies in British and American business, and the tendency for DOMINANT – HOSTILE individuals to run them provides a fertile breeding ground for this type as does the political system. If you want models of this type to consider you probably need to think no further than your nearest bureaucratic organisation. So you should:

- Use closed questions to restrain garrulousness and excessive feigned enthusiasm.

- Be outgoing and friendly, but don't be sucked into irrelevances which cause you to lose control of the discussion.

- Stress benefits which provide personal acceptance, popularity and a chance to be seen as doing something for others.

- Focus on business, but give him some room to gossip.

- Personalise the discussion. He will ask you to use his first name on very short acquaintance. Do so – often.

- Guide his behaviour very firmly, but make it feel supportive.

- Try to create a feeling that the pair of you are operating as a team.

- Probe for hidden objections and avoid being taken-in by easy promises.

- If you get his signature on the order follow it up to ensure that he follows through.

WARM – SUBMISSIVE

The WARM – SUBMISSIVE person unlike the SUBMISSIVE – WARM is probably a very nice, kind and nurturing person who has a real concern for others. If he or she lets that concern dominate behaviour the WARM – SUBMISSIVE becomes almost as difficult to move to taking action as the previous type. The difference in motivation makes little difference to the outcome. Whether you are primarily motivated by a desire to be liked at all costs in order to mitigate your own sense of insecurity, or you are immobilised by your genuine concern for others into taking no action which might conceivably damage anyone, there is a problem. Since the SUBMISSIVE –WARM personality type is in a way also trying to present themselves as concerned and caring, the differences in behaviour are subtle and often difficult to discern.

Key motivation: Genuine sense of affiliation. A desire to do the maximum possible good for the maximum possible number.

Motivation satisfaction strategy: Seeks ways of actively pursuing the welfare of others.

Typical behaviours:

- Intent on being pleasant

- Responds supportively to most suggestions which do not threaten the wellbeing of others

- Responds more negatively to suggestions which might damage others, but tries to avoid conflict unless values and concern for others is seriously threatened in which case can become highly emotional.

- Tries to pick out the benefits of neutral ideas.

- Will procrastinate rather than reject ideas which are repugnant.

- Often gives the impression that agreement has been reached when strong reservations exist.

- Avoids raising objections unless the well-being of others is clearly threatened.

- Sometimes take on more than they can fulfill.

- Sometimes neglects important but impersonal work assignments in favour of helping someone out.

- At the forefront of socially valuable activities, charity collections, etc.

Management strategies: If this type of individual can be presented with ideas which genuinely offer the maximum good to the maximum number they will implement them with enthusiasm. The difficulty comes when hard decisions must be made. Unlike the SUBMISSIVE – WARM who only wants to be liked as a defense to their own sense of insecurity, the WARM – SUBMISSIVE genuinely seeks to do good for others and will fight for what they believe is right if they must. A simple example: assume that headcount restrictions have been imposed at a level which creates a number of compulsory redundancies. The SUBMISSIVE – WARM, with the sobs and sighs of Lewis Carroll's Walrus will pick out those who have threatened or rejected them and try to pervert whatever system is in place to lose these 'ungrateful' people their jobs. The WARM – SUBMISSIVE will, in contrast, try to find ways by which the loss of jobs can be avoided altogether – and if not avoided, delayed for as long as possible. In spite of the difference in their motivation both can be difficult to move toward action. So you should:

- Try to present ideas so that the benefits to people rather than institutions are emphasised.

- Where this is impossible do not assume that a lack of overt opposition means agreement or commitment.

- Try to create a role which maximises opportunities for personal interaction.

- Monitor and supervise implementation not only of tough decisions but also of anything which is impersonal and important.

WARM – DOMINANT and DOMINANT – WARM

This quartile and the people which it represents was seen by Lefton and Buzotta as being the ideal. The purpose of the tactics for each of the problem behavioural types is to move their behaviour from the difficult toward this perceived epitome of managerial conduct. Human nature is never quite that simple. Just as it is easier in general to demotivate than it is to motivate others, so it is perfectly possible to inadvertently move people from this open and accessible mode of behaviour toward or into one of the more difficult segments. That is another reason why it is essential for the manager or the salesperson to learn and practise techniques which are known to build rapport and long term individual relationships rather than indulge in short term approaches which get an immediate response yet build a barrier of defensiveness for the future.

Positive behavioural traits:

- Expresses views clearly and frankly
- Cuts short anything which he perceives as 'bull'
- Rejects political solutions and questions the motives of those who suggest a politically acceptable approach
- Asks pertinent and searching questions
- Probes tirelessly for the fullest answer
- Admits own lack of understanding or lack of knowledge
- Concentrates attention on what can be achieved
- Places high demands on others' values and principles as well as his own
- Demands high levels of achievement but keeps his demands within the confines of the individual's (stretched) abilities
- Comments frequently on the beauty of nature when appropriate and seems to see, in the commonplace, unusual worth with a little more clarity than most
- Acts naturally and appears comfortable with his role
- Expresses himself in simple straight-forward words
- Makes no attempt to impress others
- Avoids blaming others
- Seeks out problems for the joy of finding novel and attractive solutions
- Is comfortable to own a problem

- Is clear about his goals and objectives
- Holds strong views on what is right and acceptable and rejects any idea that what is ethically wrong can be defended just because it is 'practical'
- Is comfortable when solitary or in company and shows no concern about either condition
- In times of worry still manages to sleep well, have an undisturbed appetite and treat his situation with genuine humour
- Is loyal to the group, but expresses loyalty in terms of challenge to the group to reach ever higher standards
- Avoids change for its own sake
- Actively seeks opportunities for self-development
- Is open to new ideas even when the established way still appears to work
- Challenges ideas to ensure that they are ecologically sound. That is that they harm no-one and nothing
- Expresses and lives up to a passionate belief in the potential goodwill of people
- Shows an exceptional degree of understanding for the feelings of others
- Treats feelings as facts in any situation
- Uses delegation to encourage the personal and professional growth of others
- Selects for close colleagues an elite based on character, capacity and talent
- Seeks long term relationships rather than easy acquaintance and may seem somewhat distant until respect and liking are earned
- Is truly courteous rather than merely polite in that he shows respect for the integrity and value of others
- Has a gentle sense of humour and any butt of jokes is likely to be generalised or focused only on himself/herself
- Is creative and builds easily on ideas
- Acknowledges ideas from others and builds on them without taking them over

SELLING TO THE IDEAL CLIENT

You are assured of a careful though possibly challenging hearing. They will decide very much on the basis of fact and their own opportunity to build-in added value. Provide them with the full facts as concisely as possible with emphasis on how your idea can solve their problem or improve their process. The structured approach outlined earlier is ideal because it enables a comprehensive and logical case to be put concisely.

In *all* situations involving selling, influence and persuasion, make sure that you are talking to the MAN (acronym). That is the person who has:

The MONEY, AUTHORITY and NEED.

If you have any doubts check them out with others in the organisation.

Trends in sales techniques

The situation which is emerging in business is one in which skills will need to be directed increasingly to building long term relationships and less to the quick result approach to persuasion. The techniques outlined in this chapter are straight-forward, proven in research and experience, ethical and no more difficult to use than any of the old approaches. Use them; you can only benefit from their application.

PITFALLS OF SALES MANAGEMENT

- Assuming that because you reached the position of sales manager (as a result of being the top gun in sales) the new job is merely more selling with greater resources.
- Spending too much time on 'social' visits to important customers.
- Spending too little time visiting customers.
- Encouraging the sales team not to look beyond the immediate sales opportunity.
- Allowing individual salespeople to avoid the less pleasant or glamourous tasks such as prospecting.
- Not knowing each individual's closing rate.

PITFALLS OF SELLING

- Failing to understand and focus exclusively on the customer need.
- Assuming that sales techniques will compensate for a failure to understand buyer behaviour.

- Believing that everyone buys ultimately on the basis of price.
- Handling objections as if they were the basis of conflict – and part of a battle which the salesperson is determined to win.
- Attempting to use smart closing techniques which the buyer has probably known since the day after puberty.

10 CULTURE CHANGE IN THE POST-INDUSTRIAL WORLD

During the period of recession changes have be made which have affected the culture of the organisation. They have often been the result of something akin to panic, mixed liberally in some cases with vindictiveness, and like most panicky and vindictive actions, they have not been very bright. Some have been applauded by maverick economists as means of injecting more flexibility into the ailing business economy, but they, secure in their tenure, do not appear to concern themselves with whether their ideas work in practice. The effects have now been evaluated by business, mainly in the United States, and business does not like what it sees.

DEGENERATE POLICIES AND THE RISKS

It is not possible to put back the clock or to pretend that what has happened is some form of myth which will slowly subside into the mists of time. Actions such as unmerited downsizing of organisations, the replacement of experienced full time employees with unskilled part-timers (disposable workers) and the development of an artificially high turnover of staff by making people redundant just prior to two years service to deprive them of rights which they would have had at two years, has happened. It has been admitted to as part of company policy, and it has had its effect.

The recession has also been a reason, or an excuse, to cut back on salaries of the lower paid while, with a bizarre lack of logic, raising by huge percentages the already excessively high incomes of the top earners. The accentuation of an 'us and them' culture by all of the above means has been widespread. Without concern for any ethical considerations let me say that these policies are stupid. They are stupid because with the coming of recovery 'they' will once again be in the driving seat, and many of 'them' will neither forget nor forgive.

It is also stupid because it has deskilled businesses in which there has been insufficient investment in technology to survive deskilling. They are stupid because the development of a transient disposable workforce can attack the very foundations of the loyalty which ensures that when the need is there employees and management act as a cohesive team. A sense of loyalty which ensures that each individual is prepared to give the extra which is essential to success.

They are stupid because the history of western capitalism shows that sustained commercial advantage goes to companies and countries which are, on the micro and the macro scale, high wage, high added value economies. They are stupid because, in those countries which have paid insufficient attention to high quality, relevant training and development, skills are in short supply and with the return of opportunity, those that have exceptional skills and knowledge are uncommonly mobile.

THE NEED FOR CHANGE

It may be that your company has not been guilty of any of the crass behaviour outlined above. You may have been one of those few managers who, throughout recession has invested in people by maintaining the buying power of salaries and wages while top management showed restraint. You may, as IBM did long ago in Tom Watson's day, have built your business plan around the single over-riding objective of keeping good people in good jobs. You may have continued to develop your people, their skills and knowledge and loyalty throughout the difficult times which we have experienced. Does that mean that you have a culture the strength of which will enable you to fully exploit the opportunities to come?

Frankly I doubt it. Strong though your culture may have been through the days of adversity, it will serve now only as a firm basis for change as the days of opportunity come to fruition. In a changing world few things can afford to stand still. In the past, cultures have been able to emerge naturally and slowly without design or hurry. In today's restless world the luxury of slow evolution is denied. Add to the revolutionary nature of change today the idiocies of the recent past and planned and speedy culture change is inevitable.

Where your organisation is today is only a limited indicator of the urgency of change: in the medium term change is inevitable.

Do people really resist change?

It is often argued that people blindly and mindlessly resist change. How much truth is there in this assertion?

There can be little doubt that change makes most of us feel uncomfortable. Even desired change which we have carefully planned gives some cause for concern. What bride or bridegroom has not been assailed by some doubts, however fleeting, as the happy day approaches? How many budding entrepreneurs, having decided to leave behind a safe job in order to make it on their own, do so without at least some pangs of anxiety?

Probably very few. The risk of making any kind of change is always immediate, the rewards are at some point in the future. At the moment of making a change we are all entitled to feel that we are exposed. For a time at least we are potentially on a hiding to nothing.

But we still initiate changes in our lives. We get married, change careers, withdraw from the rat-race, have children. Our attitude to change is balanced. Rightly we fear adverse consequences, but equally rightly we feel the fear and do it anyway when we believe that the change is ultimately in our interest. We know that change is often desirable, always unavoidable and so we tend to seek the best available changes which are consistent with the world as we see it.

Changing our personal behaviour can be particularly difficult. Many of our most common behaviours have been reinforced by desirable results at some time in the past. In a very direct way it is my past behaviour which has often made me what I am today, what I have achieved in life is in a very real sense due in part to my entrenched behaviours. Is it any wonder therefore that I resist efforts to have me change the way I do things?

Many years ago I was conducting a workshop for the Board of an international company. One director, an elderly and very old-fashioned man had disagreed strongly and emotionally with most of my suggestions about the way in which the world was going and how change was, even then, inevitable. I was young, brash and something of a know-it-all and I had all the arguments and most of the group on my side so I was, in the usual spirit of a young knowall, rather enjoying disposing of his concerns with a barrage of facts, figures and academic theories. Finally his desperation became overwhelming.

'Are you trying to tell me,' he said, 'that I've been doing it wrong for the last forty years?'

'Probably' was my smug answer, and with that piece of gross insensitivity I finally lost the possibility of ever reaching him.

What was even more unforgiveable my crassness had lost me the support and interest of the rest of the group who had until that moment been firmly on my side. They recognised even if I failed to, that he wanted only a good reason to change. He wanted people to understand that his past behaviour had been right because at the time it had worked. If I had used my brain and my supposed high level of professional knowledge I would have won him over by recognising that his behaviour had been relevant to the situation of the past, but that the situation was now changing and to find a strategy to deal with the new world that was emerging made excellent sense. He would have had no difficulty with that. He had done it, as we all have, many times. But I preferred then to be a smartarse.

Organisational culture

EXCELLENT Our culture reflects simultaneously the needs of the market in which we operate and the aspirations of all our stakeholders. We regard as stakeholders in our enterprise our customers, our employees including our senior management team and directors, our shareholders and the communities in which we operate. The business is driven by shared beliefs and values which ensure the commitment of all involved in everything that we do. Those beliefs and values are internally and externally consistent and are communicated to our distributors and suppliers.

AVERAGE Our culture has emerged as a result of the continuance of the best traditions of the firm as interpreted by our most dominant and influential leaders. We communicate the key values of our culture to all and expect people to respect them. Our culture has some effect on our choice of suppliers, distributors and other commercial partners, but we do not feel justified in imposing our culture on others outside the firm. Our culture has contributed to the brand values which support our position in the market.

UNACCEPTABLE We do not consider culture as an important part of the business. What there is has evolved and there are contradictions between what is said and what is done. People's values and beliefs are their concern. Our concern, as a business, is simply to ensure that employees do as they are told and stick to policies and procedures which are laid down.

WHAT IS CULTURE?

The best and most succinct definition of culture is very simple; it is *the way things are done around here*. That uncomplicated approach to culture denies it the mystique which otherwise acts as a barrier to practical managers when they choose to consider culture.

If the way things are done around here ensures that you continually optimise your market opportunities, meet the aspirations of the workforce and the management team, are seen by the community in which you operate as a good neighbour and satisfy the expectations of your shareholders, you have the culture that you need – for now. If any needs or aspirations change, you may need to change your culture to continue to satisfy them.

If you choose to enter new markets with new products you must reconsider the present culture in the light of the new markets. Culture, like marketing plans is not infinitely transferable.

Where does culture come from?

David Drennan indicates twelve key causal factors which shape the company culture.

Influence of dominant leaders. Most companies begin their existence as entrepreneurial enterprises under the strong leadership of a more or less charismatic individual. Alternatively the period of greatest growth and consolidation is under such leadership. So the Ford Motor Company has its Henry Ford Senior and IBM has its Tom Watson

It is characteristic of such leaders that others create a mythology around them which, like national mythologies in a different context, exercises a great influence on the organisation long after the leaders themselves have moved on. Through this mechanism of myth the departed leaders can remain role models and their shadows can perpetuate a culture long after its usefulness is past

Company history and tradition. The international growth of General Motors in the two decades preceding the second world war was phenomenal. In view of the state of global trade for much of that period it verged on the miraculous. Such growth, in such conditions is unlikely to be without cost however. The cost to GM in the late twenties and early thirties was a loss of control and a strain on considerable but finite resources. As a result the financial management of the corporation was tightened and a treasury-driven bureaucracy was developed which still drove the organisation forty years later.

Technology, products and services. A major change to technology, products and services can have a devastating effect on an industry. Companies can change, almost overnight, from labour-intensive with a strong cultural emphasis on people and their skills, to technology-driven in which the ex-craftsman becomes a (hi-tech) button pusher. Such changes have an immense and too often unplanned effect on the evolving company culture.

Customers. The influence of dominant customers can be a powerful determinant of company culture. Where companies are unable to develop a wide customer base the effect which the one or two major customers can have on the way things are done is enormous and not always positive. Some companies which have been developed specifically to meet the needs of a major government department can find it almost impossible to diversify into other markets so marked and specific is the effect of the present key customer on their approach to business.

Company expectations. I have touched on the dangers of the volatile pursuit of the fad of the moment which too many companies are inclined to indulge in without adequate preparation. If the expectation of the firm is, or has recently been that people will do as they are told without question the expectations as they are expressed in actions will prove more powerful than will exhortations. Thus the firm which has recently disciplined those who have 'taken a chance' and bent the rules to satisfy customers in an emergency is unlikely to be quickly successful in introducing a culture of empowerment however sincere their intent.

Information and control systems. Whatever the intention, jobs are transformed by the introduction of new information and control systems. The change may, of course be for the good of employees as much as for the company, but the effect, for good or ill, is powerful and the cultural effects ought to be carefully considered.

Legislation and environment. The most benign, consistent and congruent of cultures will be interpreted locally according to local law and local culture. For the global conglomerate it is arguable that there is less of a corporate culture than a multitude of local cultures. The firm which operates purely domestically however, is subject not only to the effects of legislation, but also to the local culture. If a company has two factories in the same country, one in an area of full employment and the other in a development area the difference in culture may be marked – and the difference is often not what you would predict.

Reward systems. As with individuals, so with organisations. It is not uncommon to find that what is said to be required in terms of creativity, initiative, risk-taking is punished in practice. Many a company which describes itself as being innovative is, in fact hag-ridden by rules imposed by professional 'nay-sayers'.

Organisation and resources. Clearly the structural and organisational design of a corporation serves no other purpose than to provide a framework for the way things are done. And if the structure creates the constraints of the internal environment, the resources to a great extent dictate the means and therefore the process.

Goals, values and beliefs. The degree to which all those involved understand and share the goals, values and beliefs of the organisation is critical to the culture which emerges. If there is conflict between what I am told and what I experience as the 'true' goals and values of the organisation, my experience will drive my behaviour.

Cultural analysis

Long before one considers whether the culture which one has is appropriate to today's needs and certainly long before one seeks to change it there is real value in analysing what you have at present.

Cultural analysis is complex and a range of questions must be considered both in isolation and in their relationship to each other. For that reason I provide a specific instrument in addition to Fig. 10.1. The emphasis is critically different in each, and both may be used to provide a tool which meets the specific needs of your company today.

The cultural analysis of your company can be assessed with the use of a cultural audit with provides *thirty questions for internal change agents.*

CREATING A CULTURAL CHANGE

Cultural change is designed and created at the highest levels of the organisation. It is communicated from the highest levels clearly and unambiguously to those who have to make it work. It is not, however the sole responsibility of the top team.

The creation of a new culture is one area of business where there is no decision to be made concerning the participation of employees at every level. If there is not total involvement there may well be a change of culture, but it is likely to be a change from confidence and certainty to perplexity and chaos.

Figure 10.2 takes you step-by-step through the process of developing a major cultural change. In order to be able to move away from generalities and into the real world of culture change I have used as an example a change which many companies are considering or are engaged with – that of introducing **Total Quality Management.** TQM does not merely effect the culture of the organisation. It becomes the culture. On the other hand there is nothing so specific in the process of introducing TQM that the model cannot be amended and used across the full range of culture change strategies. So we have a model of general applicability with its feet on the firm ground of reality.

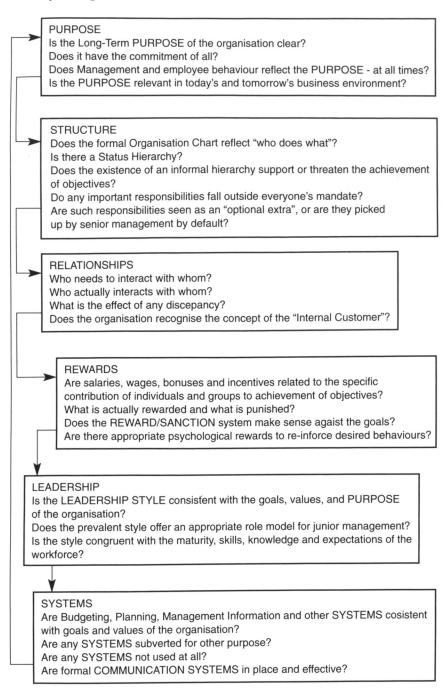

PURPOSE
Is the Long-Term PURPOSE of the organisation clear?
Does it have the commitment of all?
Does Management and employee behaviour reflect the PURPOSE - at all times?
Is the PURPOSE relevant in today's and tomorrow's business environment?

STRUCTURE
Does the formal Organisation Chart reflect "who does what"?
Is there a Status Hierarchy?
Does the existence of an informal hierarchy support or threaten the achievement
of objectives?
Do any important responsibilities fall outside everyone's mandate?
Are such responsibilities seen as an "optional extra", or are they picked
up by senior management by default?

RELATIONSHIPS
Who needs to interact with whom?
Who actually interacts with whom?
What is the effect of any discepancy?
Does the organisation recognise the concept of the "Internal Customer"?

REWARDS
Are salaries, wages, bonuses and incentives related to the specific
contribution of individuals and groups to achievement of objectives?
What is actually rewarded and what is punished?
Does the REWARD/SANCTION system make sense agaist the goals?
Are there appropriate psychological rewards to re-inforce desired behaviours?

LEADERSHIP
Is the LEADERSHIP STYLE consistent with the goals, values, and PURPOSE
of the organisation?
Does the prevalent style offer an appropriate role model for junior management?
Is the style congruent with the maturity, skills, knowledge and expectations of the
workforce?

SYSTEMS
Are Budgeting, Planning, Management Information and other SYSTEMS cosistent
with goals and values of the organisation?
Are any SYSTEMS subverted for other purpose?
Are any SYSTEMS not used at all?
Are formal COMMUNICATION SYSTEMS in place and effective?

Figure 10.1 Organisational diagnosis

CULTURAL AUDIT

1. *Does the organisation know where it wants to go?*

   Is its mission established?

   Are goals defined?

   Are mission, values and goals communicated to all?

2. *Are the goals meaningful in today's market/business environment?*

   Are key issues recognised?

   Opportunity analysis complete and current?

   Strengths related to customer/client need?

   Weaknesses prioritised in terms of barrier to quality of customer/client service?

   Are risks known, quantified and understood?

3. *What resources exist?*

   People?

   Finance?

   Materials?

   Plant?

   Equipment?

   Are the resources adequate for the changing needs of the business?

4. *What is the structure of the organisation?*

   Formal structure?

   Hierarchical?

   Matrix?

   Boundaryless?

   Is there an informal 'status hierarchy'?

   On what is it based?

   By whom is it valued?

   What specific effects does it have on the effectiveness of the organisation?

What is the evidence which separates fact and reality.

Are changes to the organisational structure indicated?

5. *What are the required interactions between people?*

   Who is required to communicate with whom?

   Who initiates work for whom?

   Are the present interactions appropriate to today's conditions?

6. *What are the actual interactions?*

   Who actually interacts with whom?

   What are the effects of the interactions?

7. *What is the reward and sanctions process?*

   What is actually rewarded?

   What is really punished?

   Is the existing economic and psychological environment appropriate to the desired outcome?

   What form do the rewards take?

   Are they recognised and valued by all employees?

   Do employees believe that they can achieve goals and enjoy the appropriate rewards?

   Is there enough challenge in the organisation for people to experience the appropriate psychological rewards for desired behaviours?

8. *How is the organisation driven?*

   By the hierarchy?

   By flexible use of the skill pool?

9. *Are flexible and appropriate problem solving strategies generally understood and applied?*

   Rational approaches (for deviations from norm)?

   Creative approaches (for attractive, feasible and novel solutions)?

   Morphological approaches (for developments from current or past success)?

10. *Are feedback systems timely, objective and accurate?*

Is feedback driven by problem solving?

By blame fixing?

Is the past treated as unchangeable?

11. *How bureaucratic is the organisation?*

Do goals take precedence over rules?

12. *What is the general psychological climate?*

Is the organisation people oriented?

product oriented?

market driven?

Is the orientation appropriate to the desired outcome?

13. *What are the sources of power within the organisation?*
Hierarchy?

Function?

Expertise?

Informal status?

Control of rewards?

Control of sanctions?

Do role models exist whose source of power is referrent – that is they influence people and events, because people seek to be like them and copy their behaviour?

Is their behaviour that which the company is seeking to foster?

Are the key role models appropriate to the present needs of the business?

14. *What is the limit of the power to act at various levels in the organisation?*

Is there a policy of empowerment?

Are employees at every level comfortable with their level of discretion?

15. *Do 'Champions for Change' exist?*

    Who are they?

    What is their level of organisational power?

    What is their degree of organisational influence?

16. *How is power wieded in the organisation?*

    Who wields power?

    On what is their power based?

17. *Who are the opinion leaders in the organisation?*

    On what is their influence based?

18. *How specifically is the organisation influenced toward change?*

    The influential people?

    The powerful people?

19. *How do we ensure that we achieve the required outcomes?*

    What lines of communication do we need?

20. *Do we have a leader, or leaders, whose personal style dominates the organisational leadership style?*

    Is the dominant style appropriate to the present needs of the business?

21. *How important is the company history and tradition in defining the culture?*

    What has changed?

    Do the changes indicate the need to reduce the perceived importance of tradition?

    How does the company tradition give us an advantage over our present competition?

22. *Does the technology that we employ have a major influence on the culture?*

    Are we sufficiently adaptable to change, or are we prisoners of our technology?

    Do we fully understand the relationship between technology, people, organisational structure and the job to be done?

23. *What determines our culture?*

   Is it unique?

   Is it at least distinctive?

   Are we unduly influenced by what the rest of the industry does?

24. *How do we see ourselves?*

   Do we see ourselves as winners?

   Do our customers see us as being arrogant?

25. *Do we consider ourselves to be losers?*

   Are we confident of recovery?

   Who do we blame for our failures?

26. *Do we respond effectively to the needs of our customers?*

   Are we really aware of our customers' needs and aspirations?

27. *Do we respond directly to the needs of our employees?*

   Are we absolutely clear about the behaviour which we expect from them?

   And which they expect from us?

28. *Do our systems support our goals fully?*

   If systems were to be changed, what effects would such a change have on our employees, the way they do things and the way that they perceived their contribution to the organisation to be valued?

29. *How does legislation inhibit change?*

   Does legislation limit our present power to act?

30. *What are the values which drive the company?*

   Are the values appropriate to our goals?

   Are they fully communicated to all employees?

   Are they shared by all employees?

   What's the evidence for your conclusion that values either are or are not shared?

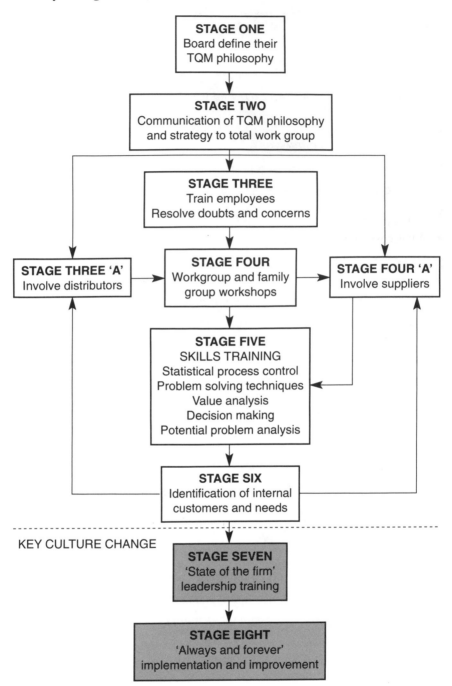

*Figure 10.2 Implementing cultural change through the principle of Total
Quality Management*

TQM stage one

Before anything else can be usefully undertaken the top team need to establish a shared view of what total quality means to them. If they are wise they will define TQM in words which are relevant to the business and the people it employs. They will at all cost avoid 'business school speak' and will describe TQM in simple, everyday language.

They will be specific in their understanding of how total quality fits into the business plan to the extent of predicting:

- What customers that they have now will be retained directly as a result of implementing TQM;
- What desirable potential business will be drawn to the company;
- What cost savings can be reasonably assumed to follow from reductions in customer complaints and improvements to processes;
- The cost to the firm of introduction and the probable payback period.

Only when they are convinced that the introduction of a new culture will support the achievement of the business plan, pay for itself in a reasonable time and be communicated to all who will make it work in simple and unambiguous terms which will build commitment, should they then proceed. If it takes longer to reach this condition than is at first anticipated, the additional time will be time well spent. It is essential that the top team should be perceived to be clearly singing from a single song sheet with every member living their intention.

I strongly suggest that this process of decision take the form of a facilitated, and preferably off-site workshop rather than be part of a regular board meeting. An external expert pushing without concern for their own position to ensure that a real consensus exists can be of great value. The facilitator should be a subject expert on TQM and group and individual behaviour, and, to ensure objectivity it might well demand an external consultant.

TQM stage two

The philosophy and strategy is communicated to the workgroup in simple terms. As far as is humanly possible the communication should be simultaneous and absolutely consistent.

TQM stage three

This may involve training employees in the basics of the new philosophy prior to conducting workshops. In any case an early opportunity should be taken to identify any immediate concerns and make an early attempt to resolve them.

If distributors are a key to the successful implementation of the new culture at the customer interface, they should be actively involved at the earliest possible stage.

TQM stage four

Workshops to develop tactical plans for implementation may be held on a workgroup, or cross-specialism family group basis. In TQM in particular where the concept of the internal customer is so important, the sooner people find themselves working with others outside their narrow functional teams the better. Distributors and suppliers can play a useful part in these workshops as well as benefiting from the opportunity to develop their role.

TQM stage five

Training needs will have been analysed and should have been confirmed by the workshops of stage four. Essential training should be undertaken as quickly after workshops as resources and training design permit and the high probability that training will need to be of the sheepdip variety should not be allowed to dilute the standards of materials, concepts or presentation.

Top management should find ways to be totally familiar with what is being taught even if they will not be personally using some of the material. Either they should attend sessions or should have their own accelerated overviews of the training programmes.

TQM stage six

This stage is specific to TQM and should involve all those who initiate work for colleagues establishing the form in which their internal customers need their inputs. There should also be a very proactive search by all employees while processes and outputs are under consideration to establish possible cost savings which can be implemented without detriment to customer service. The constant quest for process improvements is primarily the responsibility of management, but they will need a rich input from all involved of ideas and concerns. This constant search for improvements and economies must be reinforced at an early stage or there will be a tendency to emphasise customer satisfaction at any cost to the detriment of the firm's competitive position.

TQM stage seven

A change of culture will dictate a new relationship between managers and managed. I believe that this requires that new thinking is applied to the concept of leadership. Unless all managers demonstrate a clear understanding of the need for leadership flexibility allied to the proven ability to act sensitively in all situations some training will be essential.

TQM stage eight

Stage eight is the new culture in action. In the case of TQM it is a workteam totally devoted to the consistent satisfaction of customer needs at lowest cost for all time and in all situations.

Need I add by now that all stages from two to eight should be monitored and measured for effectiveness.

The future

A change of culture is not a one-off thing. The top team and management of any organisation should always be alive to the need to change even the most successful, excellence-driven culture as circumstances change. The most economic and least painful approach to culture change is one of planned evolution. Figure 10.3 will help the manager to keep his eye on the ball and take timely action.

PITFALLS OF CREATING CULTURE CHANGE

- Changing in response to the seductive siren call of the latest fad or fantasy regardless of the business realities.

- Expecting quick-fix answers through superficial change.

- Failure to establish and communicate clear goals.

- Establishing too many or conflicting goals.

- Failing to involve all employees in the change process.

- Lack of constancy of purpose or constantly moving goal posts.

- Culture change ideological rather than business-driven.

- Creating change overload by attempting too much at once.

- Failure to communicate the values of the organisation to all involved.

- Lack of management commitment. Change is always seen as being to the benefit of some to the detriment of others. Any change which empowers

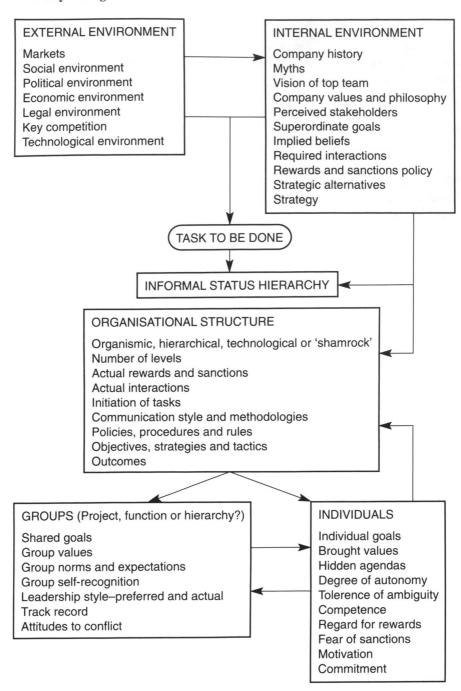

Figure 10.3 The business and its environment

employees is likely to be seen as leaving some members of management with less authority or responsibility or power. Management have feelings too and theirs are worthy of at least as much consideration as those of anyone else.

- Failure to monitor and adjust according to results.

- Looking for instant results. Look for instant results by all means, but if you find them regard them as a bonus. Don't expect them.

- Management behaviour which is inconsistent with the desired culture. Management response to crisis must be consistent with the declared approach, or employees will believe that games are being played and the bus stop syndrome will develop.

- Delegating beyond people's capacities. Push decision making down the organisation as far as the lowest level capable of making a quality decision, but never beyond that level until those below have been developed.

- Middle management or employee resistance. Explain the need for change, clarify people's roles and teach them how. Monitor and control until success is consistently demonstrated.

- Failure to change the structure to facilitate the new behaviours.

11 TRAINING AND DEVELOPMENT

Training is the consistent and effective transfer of appropriate behaviours which lead to the achievement of predetermined and specified outcomes.

'Communication is the transfer of meaning from one person to another'
American Dictionary definition.

'Be intelligent not intellectual'
Company handbook.

TRAINING IS A SERIOUS BUSINESS

Much is often made of the discrepancy which exists between the level of training which is enjoyed by British and Japanese managers. We are told, as I have indicated elsewhere, that we need more training to compete. Perhaps we do, but if we continue to have training of the standard which is common in this country, not merely from self-styled and badly trained consultants, but also from many internal trainers we are wasting time and money and accelerating our decline.

From Bruce Joyce's careful measurements at Columbia University it seems that, for the majority of training programmes, we may expect a niggardly 13 per cent transfer of knowledge from the conference room to the workplace. 13 per cent may be better than nothing, but is it worth the investment in money, time and lost output?

Rank Xerox carried out their own study in the mid-1980s which indicated that a full 87 per cent of whatever had been learned on a training course had been lost at the end of three months. Taken along with Joyce's findings it is highly likely that the average participant only learned about 10 per cent of the content of the programme which means that, at the end of three months, many managers have retained and used a little over one per cent of what was delivered.

What cannot be measured cannot be managed

I am frequently told by trainers that it is impossible to measure the value of training and education and that it is even more impossible, to measure its effect.

Training, if it is to play the role which only it can play in today's excellence – driven renaissance of western business must be:

- Based on effective and accurate needs analysis, subject to the precisely determined requirements of the Business Plan.

- Subject to objectives which are the expression of specific, quantifiable, observable and pre-determined outcomes.

- Designed to ensure full transfer, (i.e. better than 80 per cent by the least able), from the training situation to the workplace.

- Conducted by top class professionals in a manner which makes a significant contribution to developing a dedicated learning community throughout the workforce.

- Routinely measured, not once, but on an ongoing basis, to ensure that the knowledge is appropriately applied consistently at the workplace.

- Subject to the equitable availability of tangible or intangible rewards for consistent high performance.

- Able to demonstrate quantitively a significant contribution to the achievement of the Business Plan.

A tough requirement? Certainly, one is entitled to demand the highest standards from any profession. Impossible? Certainly not. Consider if you will Frizzell Financial Services Ltd.

THE TONY MILLER STORY

Tony Miller was recruited by Frizzell Financial Services for a very good reason. The CEO, Hamish MacKay, could have been content that his company was the market leader in its own field, but he was acutely and at times, painfully, conscious of the in-depth meaning of Tom Peter's teaching. Had he not been, the unprecedented growth from scratch by one now major competitor in six short years would have converted him. He knew that success could no longer be guaranteed to those who sat on their past triumphs and withdrew from the neverending search to find new and pertinent ways to offer ever higher standards of excellence to their customers.

His people were good. They were better than that, they had proved themselves historically, in a highly competitive business, to be the best. His problem was to ensure that they continued to develop as the market kept evolving. He sought an ally in the business of ensuring the ability of all of his team, at every level to, as they say in the States, 'think outside of the box'.

Tony Miller was his choice to make a key contribution to driving and supporting a new, even more customer-centred culture. Less than two busy years down the road they are happy through me to share with you some of their experience.

Intelligence not intellect

First it was clearly established that training was not to be seen as some sort of add-on which could exist in a tower, ivory or otherwise and go its own sweet way regardless of the realities of a rapidly changing market. The training plan could not deliver unless it was based firmly on a clear and far-sighted business plan. In an increasingly competitive and volatile market, the business plan necessitated the implementation of revolution by evolution. This meant that change had to be introduced at a speed which was in step with or preceding changing customer needs, but at a pace with which those who had the job of making it work could cope. That is a subtle balance to maintain. Failure to maintain that balance has wounded, sometimes mortally, previously excellent organisations.

And the business plan was and is ambitious. Details, of course have to remain confidential, but in the face of increased competitive pressure and rapidly evolving customer expectation, it required:

- A total re-engineering of the organisation and systems to raise the standards of customer service to levels of efficiency, effectiveness and excellence hitherto unknown in the industry.

- The development of a new culture which retained the best of past values while focusing attention on new ways of doing things, new relationships and new standards of service.

- Individual and organisational growth now and for all time was to become every employee's expectation and right.

- A continuance of the highest standards of customer service had to be sustained through the period of change regardless of any problems which might arise through novel systems or ideas.

- The development of a secure, self-reliant, confident, qualified and committed workforce genuinely empowered at every level through the organisation was deemed to be essential to the success of the scheme.

Change for the customer's sake

Early analysis of the situation as it existed prior to the project provided the usual mixture of results, some promising, much that was less so. There was a remarkable degree of similarity between the top management team and employees generally in the way in which they saw the organisation. Agreement was common on where the organisation stood at the outset and where it needed and was wanted to go.

So far so good, there is a consistency of view and that must make for cohesion. But cohesion is a two-edged weapon. Too little and teams cease to be teams. Too much and teams cease to be creative.

There was another problem. The discrepancy between the 'here and now' and the 'ideal future' was not merely significant, it was huge. Since it is unlikely that people started to think about the organisation for the first time when the external consultants did their analysis, (no internal bias was to be allowed to creep in), it is likely that many had desired change for some time, but lacked the skills, knowledge or perceived authority to bring it about.

Similarly most, if not all recognised the need to introduce a new level of creativity into the organisation, but personality and behaviour profiling showed a remarkable degree of similarity through the company. As Tony Miller put it: 'The people were all among the best at what they had been doing, but there was a cost. In growing professionally together they had all become to some extent the same person multiplied by sixteen hundred.'

Here was a team which recognised the need for change, but were prisoners in the granite of their own success to a remarkable degree. Training was expected to play a vital role in disimprisoning the people at every level. But the idealogically-driven 'set my people free' hand-waving training of the empowerment lobbyists was not going to be appropriate. With the best of good will, these people needed a framework in which to evolve, without threat, into the new world which they had glimpsed. They needed more than that.

They needed a reward structure which would ensure that the considerable effort required to quickly acquire, practise, apply and go on developing skills and knowledge would be worthwhile. Nobody underestimated the size of the challenge and from the beginning every consideration was given to ensuring the right psychological climate for success existed.

The rewards were to be threefold:

- Tangible in the form of payment for enhanced skills and the opportunity to link the acquisition of learning at work and externally to nationally recognised and valued qualifications.

- Intangible in the form of more interesting and varied work with a recognisable outcome in which the individual could take pride in achievement.

- Emotional in the strengthening of work teams and individual relationships through early and sustained shared success. All this taking place in an environment of major change in which the maintenance of the highest professional standards remained mandatory.

Systems and success factors

The secure framework is partly being provided through participation in the the systems and organisational change backed by timely and effective communication. But perhaps more important is the cultural framework which is a triangle forged from *Investors in People*, BS 5750, and, striding both like a colossus, Total Quality Management (TQM).

Investors in People is a national scheme to ensure, by external accreditation and monitoring, that individuals have the opportunity to participate actively in planning their own development. Everything that Frizzell is doing is dependent on people, and since they are in a very real sense entering the unknown together, this is an ideal nursery to grow the seedlings of participation and empowerment. People want to participate in what effects them most. The way their jobs are done and their own development. Once they get the taste for involvement they are ready to participate in the more obscure areas of the business, but not before. Frizzells were among the very first companies to be awarded the coveted *Investors in People* award.

BS 5750 or ISO 9000 is too well known to need lengthy comment or explanation. The key point is that it provides a specific framework in which to build quality. Of itself it does nothing to ensure more than consistency at any existing or emergent quality level, but used in an authentic learning and growing community it specifies, for those that need guidance, the whats', hows' and whens' of real customer care within and without the organisation.

Total Quality is the vehicle which above all others, enables the freed individual to make a growing personal contribution to delighting the customer, not just today, but for all time. And it carries its own rewards. The delighted customer provides repeat and referral business. It means business which is won and can be provided at lower cost. The constant improvement of processes means that costs are further reduced. Reduced costs mean more competitive prices and retained profits leading to more profitable business and that in turn makes jobs secure in an unsure world.

Thus the Total Quality philosophy of now and for all time meeting customer needs at minimum cost is in everyone's interest.

The background and preparatory work, much of which was a responsibility of the training department was, and remains, critical to the success of a near £20 million investment, but what about the training itself? What makes that worth studying, worth thinking deeply about and, perhaps, worth copying?

Training, the non-optional extra

The **training plan** is both systems-driven and individual. All employees have timely access to specific skills and knowledge workshops and seminars which provide them with the ability to serve all their customers – remember that the concept of the internal customer is well established in TQM – to the highest professional standards. Additionally each is involved in the building of an individual development programme with a time horizon of up to five years. Many of these programmes lead to, or include nationally recognised qualifications.

Frizzells trainers have been accredited to deliver courses for the National Examining Board for Supervisory Management, City and Guilds and the Institute of Management. All of these programmes lead to nationally recognised qualifications. Measurement of these courses is therefore both internal through the monitoring of consistent and effective application of skills and external through third party accreditation and certification of individuals.

Each module within each in-house programme and each individual training course is developed to meet specifically identified business and individual needs. Objectives are expressed as clear and unambiguous predetermined and identifiable outcomes. By constant improvement to programme design and delivery, the training intiatives contribute to profitability directly through measurable improved performance by individuals and teams, and indirectly through controlled and reducing training costs.

THE TRAINING AND DEVELOPMENT PROGRAMME

Cost savings are sought through constantly improved training processes, but the budget for training and development is significant. During 1993 no less than 10.2 per cent of the previous year's profits will be invested in training and development.

The development of training programmes in Frizzell Financial Services Ltd. follows and improves on the classic model as Fig 11.1 shows.

1. The training requirement is agreed with the appropiate manager(s).

2. The programme specification is completed and agreed both with the managers and with their directors to ensure support by the top team.

3. Programme objectives specifying participant behaviour after attending the programme are established and the course is designed to meet those objectives.

4. Training methods and materials consistent with the participant population and the objectives are selected.

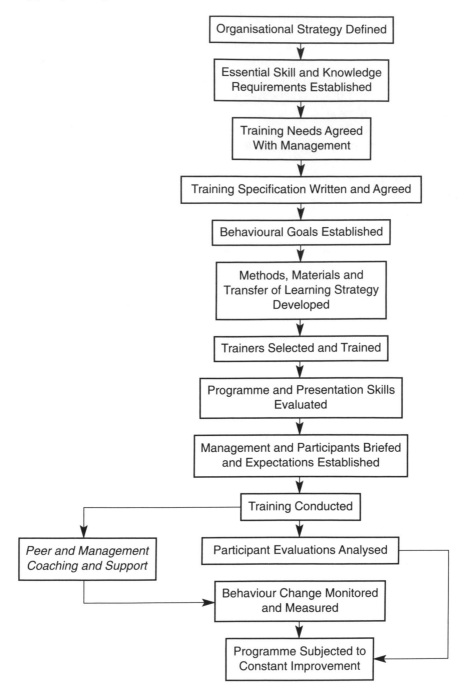

Figure 11.1 Training design and development

5. Trainers are selected and trained.

6. The effectiveness of the trainer training is evaluated and methods or manpower are adjusted as necessary.

7. The programme is tested, reviewed and, where necessary, improved.

8. Potential participants and their managers are positioned to ensure clear understanding of the purpose and outcomes of the training.

9. Participants are nominated and complete a pre-training questionnaire.

10. Training is completed.

11. Participant reactions to the programme are collected and analysed.

12. The training programme is subject to continuous improvement based on experience.

13. Longitudinal studies are completed and the consistency and effectiveness of participant's post-programme behaviour are monitored. The achievement of the objectives is quantified and recorded as are contributions to increased efficiency.

A little different, I trust you will accept, not only to the behaviour of the purveyors of canned programmes, but also perhaps a tentative model worthy of consideration by any professional trainer working within or outside organisations.

MANAGEMENT AS TRAINEES

Why this detail in a book devoted to management models? The answer is simple and yet deep. The success and survival of companies in the face of global competition will be dependent on the knowledge and actions of management. The relevance of that knowledge and the effectiveness of those actions will only be assured if management are given and choose to apply training of the highest quality.

Trainers have for too long hidden behind a ragbag of theory and mystique. They must be brought out into the marketplace alongside their clients. That means that managers at the proverbial sharp end must be given the information which will enable them, as the trainers' customers, to specify and insist on their needs. When needs are specified and outcomes measured the professionals will survive and prosper and management will actively use training as key results area of the business.

This business of pre-determined outcomes is one which is of vital importance. Unless the results of training can be, and are measured, the western world is unlikely to achieve the quality which it needs to prosper in a post-industrial society. Robert Mager gave guidance twenty years ago which still has validity today.

The right time for training

The first question which he addressed is 'when is training necessary?' For a simple, but far from simplistic answer consider the following.

An employee is performing below the required standard. If they lack the skill or knowledge which is necessary to perform, training will be required. But what if they have the necessary skill and knowledge and are simply not motivated to apply either or both? Will training help then? Almost certainly not. If anyone has the capability but chooses not to apply it, no amount of carefully designed training is likely to solve the problem. The problem simply does not lie in an area which training can address. The problem lies, almost certainly, in the psychological and physical environment in which the individual is struggling to perform. It may be that behaviours which are counterproductive are rewarded within the system.

For example, imagine two employees. One is conscientious, capable and willing, committed to the company and willingly makes any personal sacrifice when called upon. Given a tight deadline and a tough task nothing, not the needs of family, the pressures of peers nor declining health hinders the accomplishment of the task.

The other employee enjoys watching others perform and may even admire their dedication and industry, but there is little sign of emulation. Work is slapdash and invariably late and incomplete, a supervisor's nightmare employee who spends the greater part of the working day away from the workplace gossiping in other departments. To give such a person an important, difficult or time-sensitive job is to invite disaster.

So who gets all the tough and tricky jobs? Who is rewarded by the system? And will training help either of them? In the real world did not someone once announce that the greatest management principle is:

'What gets rewarded gets done.'

Consider if you will the employee subjected to vague and ambiguous, often incomplete instructions who never gets it right because no-one has ever indicated what right is. Will she change if trained?

Or consider the boss who constantly changes priorities. Who identifies any and all jobs as having the utmost importance and urgency, but always interrupts his team before they are able to complete anything, either with meaningless monitoring of progress, or replacement of the job being worked on by something of greater urgency. Whose catch phrase is: 'Leave that and start on this'. A catch phrase which is repeated to one or more employees all day every working day. Will his group benefit from going on a course?

Training is about skills, knowledge and behaviour. In the long term it is about attitude, motivation and commitment, but unless it can first ensure changes to skills, knowledge and behaviour, no other changes are likely. That is why Mager designed the manager's infallible system for evaluating training needs. As stated above, the Mager system requires one piece of equipment. A loaded gun.

To establish whether the individual needs training, or just managing differently the manager metaphorically takes the gun, places it firmly against the employee's temple and, after assuring the employee that it is loaded, snarls, 'This time, get it right or else!'

If, under these extreme circumstances, the employee gets it right, he or she needs no training. If they still cannot do it right – send them on a course. But be sure that you send them on a course which will:

- Teach, support and instill the required skills and knowledge.

- Identify and make transparent the appropriate behaviours.

- Enable threat-free practise of skills and behaviours in a learning environment as close as possible to the real world of the participant.

- Support the easy transfer of learning from the conference room to the workplace.

To be assured of this the course must have:

- Objectives which state specifically what the participant will do as a direct result of attendance. *Not, please note, what they will be able to do* – that's a cop out!

- A post-programme follow-up which is systematic, based on quantifiable information and relevant to the individual's world of work.

A TRAINING MODEL THAT REALLY WORKS

The transfer of learning from conference room to workplace can be increased to 92.5 per cent. The rest of this chapter explains a longitudinal study carried out over sixty organisations in the same sector, but of very different sizes, and covers a period from 1983 until the present. The study provides a detailed model of how to make good training stick.

In pre-recession days there was strong evidence that trainers could flourish by offering a range of interesting but mediocre programmes. Seminars and courses were filled to bursting point with fun activities. The training environment was perceived as being at least as important as the content of the programme. Participant feedback forms ('Happy Sheets') and unmonitored 'Implementation Plans' were the preferred and often only evaluation techniques in use. And everyone was happy. Trainers were happy because their activities brought pleasure to many hard-working executives, managers and work teams. Participants, if they learned nothing, enjoyed the break from routine. Senior management were happiest of all, they had fulfilled their responsibility to send people on courses, people returned satisfied and, better yet, nothing in the organisation changed.

So arose the myth which I have dwelt on at some length but which some trainers will die defending that the effects of training and education are beyond the ability of humankind to measure, but are nonetheless invariably good.

The longitudinal study which I referred to earlier (Gers and Seward – 1983 and continuing) sought to confirm Joyce's findings and overcome the major cost barrier to coaching implied in earlier studies.

An outline of the research

Gers and Seward showed that between the learning of a skill and the effective and consistent application of it on the job a period of discomfort intervenes. Key reasons for discomfort are:

1. New skills require greater effort, at least at first.

2. New skills make the individual feel awkward – normal activities may go less smoothly at first.

3. The more important the skill, the greater the discomfort as it displaces more valued behaviours.

Thus discomfort reduces the pleasure potential of practice and skill acquisition and leads to avoidance and rationalisation.

How do we reduce or eliminate this discomfort?

First, we establish and communicate comprehensive training objectives. Since trainers tend to a partiality for acronyms I will adapt an old favourite. Educational and training objectives should be **DOUBLE SMART**:

Specific in that they should define and demand observable behaviours.
Significant in that they make a valid contribution to the desired culture, vision, mission and goals of the organisation.

Measurable in that they are applied over time consistently and constantly in all appropriate situations.

Meaningful in that they are congruent with the values and proper expectations of the individuals who must make them work.

Achievable by the participants with effective training and other support.

Attainable within the organisational, economic, legislative and social climate as it exists.

Realistic in that adequate time is designed into the programme for sufficient threat-free practice by all.

Reward-driven within the existing or emergent culture so that desired behaviours will be reinforced in activity.

Timely so that they meet the credible present and future needs of the organisation.

Team-orientated* so that everyday support is seen as appropriate.

*Note: where the skills are to be applied uniquely and in isolation by particpants a somewhat different, but equally valid approach to implementation based on planned self-reward is required. This research addresses the more common situation where numbers of participants can and must exercise the same skills together.

After objectives, where next? The answer lies in the recognition that research shows that 'no training program supports itself...and unsupported learning invariably dies.' This is because the old learning with which the new training competes has, like a stool, three supports:

1. Force of habit;

2. The expectations of others;

3. Its past successes.

Add to the above the unavoidable learning dip which occurs at some point during implementation and the enemies of change are strong. The only economically viable answer is team-work, or to be more precise **peer coaching** and supervisor modelling.

During training peer coaching is set up and coaching skills are taught and practised. All participants are asked to identify a peer with whom they feel comfortable and the pairs attend training together. Partners agree on the detail of how they will work together to develop and implement skills. A predetermined coaching agreement is completed and the ground rules of giving 'technical feedback' are reviewed.

All participants are given a **Model Behaviours Checklist** which becomes an integral part of the coaching process within the classroom and into the real world of work.

The psychological effects of a signed coaching agreement should not be underestimated. (Cialdini *et al.* 1985) There are four key elements to such an agreement:

1. The desired performance level must be specified. We must know what the behaviours are and how well and with what frequency we must do them.

2. Feedback on target progress must be solicited and provided. We must know how well we are doing, but we must be told at a time when the information is acceptable and usable by us.

3. Appropriate progress must be reinforced by intrinsic and extrinsic rewards. (Pleasure, enhanced self-image, praise, encouragement, etc.)

In short, the process must be approached as an exercise in **behaviour modification.** In spite of the bad press received by behaviourists in recent years positive reinforcement remains the most effective and reliable way to direct behaviour.

Positive behavioural reinforcement

Three principles of positive reinforcement are relevant to peer coaching.

1. Immediate positive reinforcement principle. Rewards, tangible or intangible following immediately and consistently each correct performance.

2. Successive approximation principle. Rewarding behaviours which approximate to the desired end behaviour, with the approximations eliciting the rewards becoming necessarily closer to the behaviour over time. So that, in the end, only the perfect performance of the desired behaviour is rewarded.

3. Intermittent reinforcement principle. Rare, unpredictable, but highly valued rewards. The one-armed bandit principle. One-armed bandits and other slot machines appear to pay out randomly. In fact they are carefully designed to reward the gambler sufficiently frequently to keep him in play without the machine making a loss. By paying out substantial jackpots with precisely the right frequency the machine is able to exercise enough control over gambler behaviour to ensure that to all intents and purposes individuals become addicted to the process of putting money in the slot. We are not all necessarily prone to gambling addiction, but skilled exponents of intermittent reinforcement are able to manage the behaviour of most people. Another form of intermittent reinforcement was recently tragically brought to light through the Waco incident. Koresh, partly through the apparently erratic switching from rage to affection (punishment to reward) so increased the perceived value of the rewards that he exercised a degree of control which ultimately cost more than eighty people their lives.

Is it really economic?

Like effective training coaching takes time. Managers, supervisors and the team should work to accommodate it.

Gers and Seward found that a satisfactory and manageable schedule for the initial stages was 15 minutes of observation followed by one to two minutes feedback daily for each pair, a total of say 40 minutes per day for the first week, gradually reducing thereafter. This would be supported by management modelling the behaviours as appropriate and praising subordinates whenever progress is noticed as a result of day-to-day supervision of the team.

Tools to do the job

1. **Job Performance aids.** Where appropriate the training should provide aids such as a Model Behaviours Checklist in a form which participants can have on permanent display at their work station.

2. Supervisors and managers who do some of the same or similar tasks should be trained early and their skill development be supported so that they become consistent and effective **role models**.

3. **Group Action Plan.** Where complex sets of behaviours are in the process of change groups can agree to work on two or three sub-behaviours at a time to increase cohesion and fun.

4. **Learners as trainers.** With adequate support an effective way to sharpen a desired skill quickly is to enable the recent learner to become a trainer to others in the group. I repeat, with adequate support. Too many sheep dip programmes have been badly implemented in major organisations in the past through reliance on insufficiently trained and supported non-professionals to conduct them. (Often he or she who can most readily be spared.)

5. **Expect downturns.** Trainees should be reminded that the transfer of learning is, at times, challenging and difficult. It is reasonable to expect to experience phases when things go less smoothly than hoped. Such phases have to be accepted and used to accelerate learning in the longer run

6. Positive reinforcement including tangible **rewards** where appropriate.

7. Management rewards, encouragement and coaching including the **removal of threat** from the cultural environment.

The results

Seward and Gers have found a sustained 92.5 – 97 per cent transfer of learning from courses unchanged other than by introducing peer coaching and tightening-up on the establishing and communication of objectives. This change has been sustained over the period of nine years of research during which testing has been unannounced and infrequent. Behavioural change, which is reinforced as part of training, sticks.

Conclusion

Effective training is a joint responsibility of professional trainers and equally professional managers. The time spent in analysing needs strictly against the business plan, defining effective training and educational goals, comprehensive and participative training and peer coaching is not inconsiderable.
The costs are high.

The costs of not doing it are higher. The damage done to British and American organisations has not resulted from a lack of training. A lack of training, ironically as exists now – when training is most needed and budgets are most depleted – results from our inability to turn conference-style learning into goal-directed workplace action groups. How much longer can we accept a training effectiveness of less than 10 per cent, mask it by the avoidance of measurement and claim to be in the business of training? Unless virtually every established guru and futurist is wrong we are teetering on the verge of a new age, an age driven by knowledge and information. Trainers and educators are best placed to take the lead in that age. Will they respond to the opportunity and the challenge?

I look forward to a time when trainers display competence, commitment and courage as strongly as they have shown creativity in the past. How does your organisation measure up to the training strategy required for the future?

Training and development benchmark

EXCELLENT Training needs are initially determined, along with manpower needs, as part of the strategic planning process. Training professionals play a full part in that process, either as facilitators or team members. Subsequent needs analysis is firmly rooted in the business plan and measured progress toward the achievement of business goals. Objectives are written which specify readily identified behaviours, skills and knowledge and are agreed with senior management. Skills and knowledge levels of all selected participants are measured before training, and they are fully positioned by their own management so that they understand what is expected of them after training has taken place. Transfer of training from the conference room to the workplace is planned, and methods which are appropriate to support and ensure transfer are in place. Programmes are designed to provide optimal threat-free practice of required skills and behaviours and training methods are varied to facilitate learning by all. Skills and knowledge gains are measured at the end of each programme for each participant and follow-up is maintained to ensure that the consistent use of learning is supported and loss of skill and knowledge is minimised. A learning community, in which employees support each other in the development of relevant skills is encouraged and self-development is recognised and rewarded.

AVERAGE Needs analysis, based firmly on the business plan, precedes the design and development of each course. Objectives are established and pilot programmes are conducted to ensure that objectives are being met. Participants are briefed and de-briefed by their management before and after the programme, but the quality of briefing is known to be highly variable. Participants rate the programme through the use of 'happy sheets'.

UNACCEPTABLE Programmes are offered to management under a series of headings:

Problem Solving
Decision Making
Sales Training
Assertiveness
Customer Care
Product Knowledge

with little if any reference to the business plan. Objectives are expressed as wide 'Aims' and outcomes are not specified. Programmes are evaluated in terms of their popularity with participants and the slickness of their presentation. Top management programmes are perceived by all as an opportunity to break from the strains and stresses of daily operations and the location and facilities are often regarded as more important than the content.

PITFALLS OF TRAINING

- Inaccurate or incomplete needs identification.

- Failure to pre-determine outcomes relevant to the business needs of the organisation.

- Lack of Objectives, or objectives expressed as *'will be able to'* rather than *'will'*.

- Training seen by management and participants as having little or no relationship to real life.

- Excessive dependence by trainers on theory and chalk-and-talk training sessions.

- Trainers untrained or undertrained.

- Training programmes too short to enable deep learning to take place or skills to be practised.

- Use of inappropriate resources and training methods.

- Trainer self-indulgence leading to all sessions being fun sessions.

- Failure to pre-position the participants in terms of the company's expectation(s) of them after training.

- Failure to effectively de-brief participants after training.

- Dependence on dated and invalid research.

- Excessive use of 'good intentions' and 'flavour of the month training'.

- Training limited to lower levels of the organisation.

- Inability of top management team to walk like they talk.

- Use of training to meet social, ideological or political ends either of trainers or senior management.

- Failure to relate training directly to bottom line performance.

- Training design developed to accentuate enjoyable experiences and games rather than the transfer of learning to the workplace.

AFTERWORD

This book has been written with the intention of giving the busy manager a range of basic tools to use in a rapidly changing world. The tools are designed to be simple, but the concepts which lie behind them are complex. Management is a tough business: those who think otherwise are frankly in the wrong profession.

If there were a credo for management my choice would be:

It's seldom that simple.

The importance of models and other management tools is that they enable complexities to be thought through as simply as possible, one step at a time. Use this book and it will not make management easy, even if that were possible. Who would want to remove the challenge and spice of life?

It will however help to make management manageable. It will provide a framework in which the sophisticated business of management can be carried out with the least hassle and the optimum results. Times are changing and the new dawn in which the thinkers will finally triumph over the corporate bureaucrats will soon be with us!

Grasp the opportunity and the challenge!

Constantly ask 'What's it for?' and commit yourself to the idea that:

Nothing should be done in a business unless:

- **There is a good business reason for doing it;**

- **It will pay for itself in a reasonable time;**

- **It can be explained in simple language to those who will have to make it work**.

You will not need good luck, but you have my good wishes.

Tom Lambert
Greenfield

July 1993

BIBLIOGRAPHY

A bibliography can either be an arid list of references or, more usefully it can be offered as a recommended reading list. What follows falls into the latter category. Of necessity, therefore it is idiosyncratic in that it only includes those books which have significantly contributed recently to my thinking about management. (Since I admit to my idiosyncracies, let me go all the way and uncover a bias of which I am far from ashamed. If you haven't already done so, read everything that you can get your hands on by Charles Handy.)

ALLEN, David (1993) *Developing Successful New Products* Pitman.

BELBIN, R. Meredith (1991) *Management Teams, Why They Succeed or Fail* Butterworth-Heinemann

BLANCHARD, Kenneth, ZIGARMI, Patricia, ZIGARMI, Drea (1988) *Leadership and the One Minute Manager* Fontana.

BLANCHARD, Kenneth and JOHNSON, Spencer (1984) *One Minute Manager* Fontana.

BLANCHARD, Kenneth (1990) *The One Minute Manager Meets the Monkey* Collins.

BLANCHARD, Kenneth and PEALE, Norman Vincent (1991) *Power of Ethical Management* Mandarin.

BYHAM, William C. (1991) *ZAPP – The Lightning of Empowerment* Century Business.

CRAWLEY, John (1992) *Constructive Conflict Management* Nicholas Brealey.

D'ARCY, MASIUS, BENTON and BOWLES (1990) *Marketing – Communicating with the Customer* CBI Books.

DEMING, William Edwards (1988) *Out of the Crisis* Cambridge University Press.

DRENNAN, David (1992) *Transforming Company Culture* McGraw Hill.

DRUCKER, Peter (1992) *The Practice of Management* Heinemann Professional Publications.

DRUCKER, Peter (1992) *Post-Capitalist Society* Butterworth Heinemann.

FOSTER, Timothy R.V. (1991) *101 Ways to Generate Great Ideas* Kogan Page.

FURNHAM, Adrian (1992) *Personality at Work* Routledge.

HACKMAN, Richard and OLDHAM (1980) *Work Redesign* Addison Wesley.

HACKMAN, Richard (1990) *Groups That Work and Those That Don't – Creating Conditions for Effective Teamwork* Jossey-Bass.

HELLER, Robert (Ed) (1992) *Complete Guide to Modern Management* Mercury Pfeiffer.

HERSEY, Paul (1988) *Selling: A Behavioural Science Approach* Prentice Hall.

HERSEY, Paul (1984) *The Situational Leader book! The Other 59 Minutes* Centre for Leadership Studies.

HERSEY, Paul and BLANCHARD, Kenneth (1993) *Management of Organisational Behaviour* Prentice Hall.

HOFSTEDE, Geert (1991) *Cultures and Organisations* McGraw Hill.

HUNT, John W. (1992) *Managing People at Work* (3rd Ed.) McGraw Hill.

JAQUES, Elliot (1970) *Work, Creativity and Social Justice* Heinemann.

KAY, John (1993) *Foundations of Corporate Success* Oxford University Press.

KEPNER, Charles H. and TREGOE, Benjamin (1981) *The New Rational Manager* Kepner-Tregoe.

KINSMAN, Francis (1987) *The Telecommuters* Wiley.

LEAVITT, Harold J. (1978) *Managerial Psychology* University of Chicago Press.

MC CLELLAND, David (1980) 'Power is the great motivator', *The Structure of Competence* Teleometrics.

MC CLELLAND, David (1984) *Selected Papers: Motives, Personality and Socitety* Praegar.

MC CLELLAND, David (1988) *Human Motivation* Cambridge University Press.

MAGER, Robert F. and PIPE, Peter (1991) *Analysing Performance Problems* Kogan Page.

MAGER, Robert (1991) *Preparing Instructional Objectives* Kogan Page.

MANN, Nancy R. (1987) *The Keys to Excellence* Prestwick Books.

MANT, Alistair (1983) *Leaders We Deserve* Robertson.

MANT, Alistair (1977) *The Rise and Fall of the British Manager* MacMillan.

MOLE, John (1992) *Mind Your Manners* Nicholas Brealey.

MUNRO-FAURE, Lesley and Malcolm (1992) *Implementing TQM* Pitman Publishing.

OHMAE, Kenichi (1987) *Mind of the Strategist* Penguin.

P.A. Consulting Group (1990) *Information Technology – The Catalyst for Change* CBI Books.

PRICE, Frank (1990) *Right Every Time* Gower.

ROWE, Christopher (1990) *People and Chips* Blackwell Scientific.

TANNEN, Deborah (1992) *You Just Don't Understand* Virago.

THUROW, Lester (1993) *Head to Head* Nicholas Brealey.

TURNER, Charles Hampden (1990) *Charting the Corporate Mind from Dilemma to Strategy* Blackwell.

TURNER, Charles Hampden (1990) *Corporate Culture – From Vicious to Virtuous Circles* Business Books.

URY, William (1991) *Getting Past No* Business Books.

WILSON, Larry (1987) *Changing the Game* Simon and Schuster.

INDEX